American Literature Readings in the 21st Century

Series Editor
Linda Wagner-Martin
University of North Carolina
Chapel Hill, NC, USA

American Literature Readings in the Twenty-First Century publishes works by contemporary authors that help shape critical opinion regarding American literature of the eighteenth, nineteenth, twentieth, and twenty-first centuries. The books treat fiction, poetry, memoir, drama and criticism itself—ranging from William Dow's *Narrating Class in American Fiction* and Amy Strong's *Race and Identity in Hemingway's Fiction*, to Maisha L. Wester's *African American Gothic* and Guy Davidson's *Queer Commodities: Contemporary U. S. Fiction, Consumer Culture, and Lesbian Subcultures*.

Beginning in 2004, the series is now well established and continues to welcome new book proposals. Manuscripts run between 80,000 and 90,000 words, while the Pivot format accommodates shorter books of 25,000 to 50,000 words. This series also accepts essay collections; among our bestsellers have been collections on David Foster Wallace, Norman Mailer, Contemporary U.S. Latina/o Literary Criticism, Kurt Vonnegut, Kate Chopin, Carson McCullers, George Saunders, and Arthur Miller (written by members of the Miller Society).

All texts are designed to create valuable interactions globally as well as within English-speaking countries.

Editorial Board

Professor Derek Maus, SUNY Potsdam, USA
Professor Thomas Fahy, Long Island University, USA
Professor Deborah E. McDowell, University of Virginia and Director of the Carter G. Woodson Institute, USA
Professor Laura Rattray, University of Glasgow, UK

More information about this series at
http://www.palgrave.com/gp/series/14765

Alexandra Urakova

Dangerous Giving in Nineteenth-Century American Literature

palgrave
macmillan

Alexandra Urakova
University of Helsinki
Helsinki, Finland

ISSN 2634-579X   ISSN 2634-5803   (electronic)
American Literature Readings in the 21st Century
ISBN 978-3-030-93269-5   ISBN 978-3-030-93270-1   (eBook)
https://doi.org/10.1007/978-3-030-93270-1

© The Editor(s) (if applicable) and The Author(s), under exclusive licence to Springer Nature Switzerland AG 2022

This work is subject to copyright. All rights are solely and exclusively licensed by the Publisher, whether the whole or part of the material is concerned, specifically the rights of translation, reprinting, reuse of illustrations, recitation, broadcasting, reproduction on microfilms or in any other physical way, and transmission or information storage and retrieval, electronic adaptation, computer software, or by similar or dissimilar methodology now known or hereafter developed.

The use of general descriptive names, registered names, trademarks, service marks, etc. in this publication does not imply, even in the absence of a specific statement, that such names are exempt from the relevant protective laws and regulations and therefore free for general use.

The publisher, the authors and the editors are safe to assume that the advice and information in this book are believed to be true and accurate at the date of publication. Neither the publisher nor the authors or the editors give a warranty, expressed or implied, with respect to the material contained herein or for any errors or omissions that may have been made. The publisher remains neutral with regard to jurisdictional claims in published maps and institutional affiliations.

Cover illustration: INTERFOTO/ Alamy Stock Photo

This Palgrave Macmillan imprint is published by the registered company Springer Nature Switzerland AG.
The registered company address is: Gewerbestrasse 11, 6330 Cham, Switzerland

In the memory of my father

Acknowledgments

Gift-giving is the best aspect of the academic life. While writing the acknowledgments, I was surprised how many friends and colleagues I am to thank and how many gifts I am to return with gratitude and love.

Patricia García took the trouble to read the entire draft of my work and provided me with many insightful comments and suggestions; her faith in my work helped me survive the mid-book crisis and saved me from insanity. Another first reader of my book, Geoff Roberts has been remarkably patient with all my questions and concerns. His advice has always been unfailingly helpful and his support has been irreplaceable. I am much indebted to Werner Sollors whose generosity to me has been extraordinary. His faith in my project has been truly inspiring; his comments on my have been invaluable as have been our long conversations in Venice. Stephen Rachman figures in the background of this long-term project; his intellectual presence in my life has enriched this book in more ways that I can ever acknowledge. Leon Jackson has influenced my book in a significant way as is evident from references to his work, and my brief but meaningful collaboration with him helped me shape my work's direction. Tim Farrant has always been very supportive of all my projects including this one, while Sonya Isaak has given me a hand with many bits and pieces, to say nothing of emotional support and friendship. This book benefited greatly from my simultaneous engagement in a related research project on the dangers of gifts, together with Tudor Sala and Tracey Sowerby; Tracey has always been very generous in answering my arcane questions and has continuously set high scholarly standards in front of me.

The idea of this project originated many years ago when I was a Fulbright scholar at the University of Virginia. It would have not been possible to write this book without financial support from different foundations including John F. Kennedy Institute for North American Studies, Eccles Centre for American Studies, Institute for Advanced Study at the Central European University (IAS CEU), Helsinki Collegium for Advanced Studies (HCAS), Swedish Collegium for Advanced Study (SCAS), and Kone Foundation. There are always people standing behind institutions and I am especially grateful to Philip Davis, Nadia Al Bagdadi, Éva Gönczi, Olga Peredi, Agnes Forgo, Tuomas Forsberg, Hanne Appelqvist, Kaisa Kaakinen, Christina Garsten, Bjarne Graff, Klas Holm and many others for facilitating my research in many different ways. I am thankful to colleagues who were willing to help me with reference letters or institutional support. I want to thank Stephen Railton, Stefan Brandt, Rita Felski, Winfried Fluck, Andrey Kofman, Vadim Polonsky, and Mikko Saikku for their trust in my project at its insipient stages while Russell Belk's generous support has contributed to its completion. Susan Tane's travel grants allowed me to regularly attend Poe Studies Association conferences where I had many chances to discuss my work in progress.

My work has been inspired by existing scholarship and I owe much to my collaboration with scholars from different disciplines and schools that has taken various forms throughout my academic career. Margarida Vale de Gato, Helen Petrovsky, Sergey Fokine, Davide Torsello, Daniel Kane, and Magnus Ullén offered me fantastic opportunities to test and revise my ideas. The book has benefited greatly from discussions and criticism at conferences, seminars, and beyond. While it is impossible to acknowledge everyone, I want to thank especially Sergey Zenkin, Henning Trüper, Karsten Paerregaard, Jana Argensinger, **and** Mikhail Sverdlov for their generous advice.

I am grateful to the University of California Press for permission to reprint the portions of my work. One of them is Chap. 6 of this book based on my article "'I do not want her, I am sure' Commodities, Gifts, and Poisonous Gifts in *Uncle Tom's Cabin*" (*Nineteenth-Century Literature* 74 (4), 448–472, 2020); another one is a portion of the article "'The Purloined Letter' in the Gift Book: Reading Poe in a Contemporary Context" (*Nineteenth-Century Literature* 64 (3), 323–346, 2009) incorporated in Chap. 4. I am deeply indebted to Stephanie Palmer who was a Palgrave's reviewer of my book for her thoughtful reading and indispensable suggestions. I am grateful to everyone who assisted me with preparing this publication, from Palgrave editors to my copy-editor Míde Ní Shúilleabháin to my research assistants at the Helsinki Institute for Advanced Studies, especially the fantastic Shanna Constantinescu.

Finally, I would like to thank my friends and family, especially my mother who has always shown great support, interest, and care and my father whom I owe more than I was able to return; I dedicate this book to his memory.

Praise for *Dangerous Giving in Nineteenth-Century American Literature*

"Is the gift a cheery token of disinterested generosity or a Pandora's box? Inspired by theories of giving from Emerson and Mauss to Derrida and Lacan, Alexandra Urakova offers a fresh approach to 19th-century American writers whose work thematizes giving gifts or was published in the form of the "gift book." The hair locks and bracelets, bouquets and books that change hands in literature from Lydia Maria Child to Nathaniel Hawthorne and from Harriet Beecher Stowe to O. Henry here reveal their double-edged and deeply problematic dimensions."
—Werner Sollors, coeditor, with Greil Marcus, of *A New Literary History of America*

"Gifts are not always pleasant, and gift giving is not always disinterested. *Dangerous Giving in Nineteenth-Century American Literature* traces ambivalence about gifts and giving through a startling range of canonical and marginal literatures. Urakova deftly explains how this ambivalence relates to the country's belief in self-reliance and its vexed race and gender relations. By reading literature through an anthropological lens, Urakova offers fresh interpretations of sentimentality, the rise of commodity culture, and the canon."
—Stephanie Palmer, *Senior Lecturer in English, Nottingham Trent University, UK*

Contents

1	Introduction	1
2	"Hints" for a Gift Theory: The Ideology of Disinterested Giving and Its Discontents	23
3	Sentimental Potlatch and the Making of the Nation	47
4	Un-Gendering the Gift Book	71
5	Racial Identity and the Perils of Giving	99
6	The Poison of the Gift, the Race of the Gift	123
7	Pure Tokens and Venomous Bodies	143
8	The Gift/s of Death	169
9	"The Season of Gifts": Christmas and Melancholia	191
10	Conclusion	217
	Index	227

List of Figures

Fig. 4.1	"Affection's Gift." Philadelphia: Henry F. Anners, 1850. Library Company of Philadelphia	74
Fig. 4.2	"The Necklace." Engraved by William Humphrys from a painting by Charles Robert Leslie. Public domain in the United States	88
Fig. 5.1	*Am I Not a Man and a Brother?* Medallion by Josiah Wedgwood, 1787. Public domain	101
Fig. 5.2	Amy Matilda Cassey Album. Album page containing a drawing of a stem of forget-me-not and a poem about remembrance. By Margaretta or Mary Forten. Library Company of Philadelphia	118
Fig. 7.1	Illustration to the story. Paradise, Caroline Wilder Fellowes. "Brother Dunstan and the Crabs," *Godey's Lady's Book*, 1898, 136, p. 206. Public domain. (Courtesy of HathiTrust)	160
Fig. 9.1	Illustration to the story. Howells, William Dean. "Christmas Everyday." St. Nickolas; an illustrated Magazine for Young Folks (1873–1907); New York. (Jan. 1886). PDF Page 3. (Courtesy of ProQuest's *American Periodical Series*)	198

CHAPTER 1

Introduction

In 1838, Ralph Waldo Emerson wrote in his journal: "How painful to give a gift to any person of sensibility or of equality! It is next worse to receiving one. The new remembrance of either is a scorpion" (Emerson 1965: 489).[1] Six years later in his essay "Gifts," Emerson would express his distaste for gifts in a number of aphoristic statements: "It is not an office of a man to receive gifts... We do not quite forgive a giver. The hand that feeds us is in some danger of being bitten" (Emerson 1983: 536).

Emerson's negativity toward giving and receiving gifts did not prevent him from advising in the same essay what best to give for Christmas and New Year, while his correspondence demonstrates that he could on occasion make masterly use of the gallant language of the gift. "I send you two or three pieces, garnets for your 'Diadem'—if not too late," he wrote to his friend William Henry Furness (Concord, May 9, 1845) who edited a gift book called *Diadem*, marketed as a Christmas gift (Furness 1910: 39). While Emerson's eccentric attitude may be seen as exceptional rather than representative—after all, most people find giving gifts pleasing!—he was not the only nineteenth-century American author to reflect upon the dangers, either real or perceived, of giving. The gift appears as an ambivalent

---

[1] Leigh Eric Schmidt quotes this in his essay, but unfortunately he errs in abridging it. Cf.: "How painful to give a gift" instead of "How painful to give a gift to any person of sensibility or of equality!" (Schmidt 1997: 74).

© The Author(s), under exclusive license to Springer Nature Switzerland AG 2022
A. Urakova, *Dangerous Giving in Nineteenth-Century American Literature*, American Literature Readings in the 21st Century,
https://doi.org/10.1007/978-3-030-93270-1_1

and problematic locus in nineteenth-century American literature, whether conceptualized in early theoretical texts, represented at the level of narrative and plot, or suggested by rhetorical tropes.

Dangerous Giving investigates the complex and formative role of gift exchange in nineteenth-century literary texts by American authors, from the mid-1820s to the early 1900s. In contrast to previous research, this book focuses on the dark, unruly, toxic, or self-destructive side of this exchange, and explores the ambiguity of the gift in various social and cultural contexts, including those of race, sex, gender, religion, consumption, and literature.

The book is a contribution to gift theory, which has its origins in the tenets of classical anthropology but has since expanded into various disciplines including sociology, philosophy, history of ideas, theology, and, in the last couple of decades, literary studies.[2] Literature can offer us new insights into the nature of various social phenomena, including the gift, once we follow its own logic and rationale. A literary text is not a "window" into social history but rather an active agent in this history and while its matter may seem elusive and ephemeral, it is precisely due to this elusiveness, ambiguity, and polysemy that it enriches the ongoing dialogue between anthropology, material culture history, and intellectual history.

While such a universal and ubiquitous topic as gift-giving may be studied across centuries and nations, a number of factors make nineteenth-century American literature both a representative and a unique case. These factors include interaction with indigenous societies and awareness of pre-capitalist gift economies as part of colonial history; racial controversies and the phenomenon of slavery; the unprecedented expansion of market relations and of a liberal ideology that prompted an increase in domestic giving (Carrier 1990, 1995; Litwicki 2015), best exemplified, perhaps, by the "invention" of modern Christmas with its rituals of reciprocal gift exchange. Of relevance too is the Calvinist heritage that, despite the religious pluralism of the nineteenth century, had a lasting effect on American culture. Since Calvinism would not allow a believer to reciprocate God's gifts (Hénaff 2003: 313), there emerged a general resentment and suspicious attitude toward secular gifts, as alien to the spirit of self-reliance, independence, and enterprise traditionally attributed to American national self-awareness.

---

[2] Among these last are Blumberg (2005); Simpson (2005); Mahowald (2010); Rappoport (2011); Zionkowsky (2011); Pyyhtinen (2014); Colesworthy (2018). On American literature: Urakova (2009); Bullen (2011); Manheim (2011); Hoeller (2012); Tigchelaar J. (2014); Luck (2014: 138–187); Urakova (2016, 2020). Of interest is the section "The Gift and Artistic Commerce" that explores the gift in the literary texts from Catullus to H.D. (Osteen 2002b: 147–226).

That Americans were leery of gift-giving—the Puritan attitudes to Christmas were evidence of this—is encountered in, for example, the pages of *Domestic Manners of Americans* by English author and traveler Frances Milton Trollope: "It is not in the temper of [American] people either to give or to receive" (Trollope 1832: 108). Trollope describes how she helped a poor family in Cincinnati: they accepted help only on the condition of this being understood as a borrowing but ultimately never repaid anything. Rather than being simply unthankful, as Trollope insists, one might conclude that this nineteenth-century American family wished to remain on the "safer" territory of contractual relations instead of accepting Trollope's favors as an act of unrepayable benevolence.

Another crucial factor in prompting nineteenth-century Americans to change their attitude to gifts was the prominent role of sentimental tradition—especially in the antebellum period and reaching its peak in mid-century—which actively promoted gift-giving as a moral act and a true Christian virtue. American sentimentalism was called on to mitigate the rigidity of Calvinist ideology and to "mediate the complex and delicate transitions between premarket and market mentalities" (Fichtelberg 2003: 7). Crucially for the development of modern sensibility, sentimentalism fostered a new culture of sympathy, memory, reciprocity, and attachment via the circulation of souvenirs, mementos, and tokens of affection. Tangible tokens or keepsakes counterpoised to the "increasingly mediated and abstract" market exchange (Stewart 1993: 133) are "incarnated signs," to use Arjun Appadurai's term (Appadurai 1986: 38). Semiotic in character and rhetorical in use, the tokens contributed to the development of a language of sentiment that for a long time rendered sentimentality compelling despite its manipulative aspects. The publishing industry in inventing the holiday annual or gift book—a sentimental collection of poetry, prose, and engravings usually sold in the Christmas season—was an important actor in circulating and popularizing new values associated with gift exchange and charity; in this regard, it is especially important to consider the embeddedness of gift-related rhetoric in material and print culture.

It is this ambivalence at the heart of nineteenth-century American culture that my study of dangerous giving seeks to explore. Both terms in the book title require specification. The term "dangerous" suggests a "variety of implications ... from 'bad' (as opposed to 'good' or 'benign') and imperfect (as opposed to 'perfect') to harmful, threatening, poisonous, misconceived, and onerous" (Sowerby and Urakova 2022, forthcoming).

While the looseness of the term might be considered an obstacle, it also allows me to examine various facets of this complex phenomenon; dangerous giving can be repressive but, as this book will show, can also be challenging and redeeming. Dangerous giving may be understood as dangerous either for the receiver and the giver or, in case of reciprocal exchange, for both parties.

For nineteenth-century Americans, the word "giving" was loaded with symbolic meaning. Writing about antebellum Americans, Penne L. Restad observes that "giving joined two potent elements of the domestic ideal, those of family and religion, together." Thus, "in the context of religion, a gift symbolized God's gift of Jesus to Man, and the emphasis rested on giving rather than receiving. In a social context, the custom signified a bond between giver and receiver, and again stressed giving over receiving presents" (Restad 1996: 12). For the most part, I find the term "giving" more inclusive than "gift," the latter being often, albeit wrongly, confined to a material, tangible object. "Giving" also avoids association with the literary gift, in its meaning of talent or divine endowment and thus reduces the risk of confusion when dealing with gifts in literature. Finally, dangerous giving resonates nicely with the ideology of disinterested giving, a term used by Jonathan Parry that I discuss in more detail below.

Dangerous Giving considers a range of very different gifts, including material objects, slaves as gifts, acts of benevolence, the gift of love or freedom, death as a gift. This combination of material and immaterial gifts is far from whimsical. Rather, it is a feature of the modern (in the broad sense) gift, rooted in the Christian assumption that "everything we have is a gift of God, and what comes in as a gift has some claim to go out as a gift" (Davis 2000: 17). An examination of the usage of the word 'gift' in nineteenth-century texts highlights a wide range of literal and metaphorical implications. A word search in volumes of *Godey's Lady's Book* from 1830 to 1845 reveals meanings of gift that vary from a token to the gift of money or estate. Both a child and a beloved are referred to as gifts, as are abstract notions from faith to love, from high birth to nature; there is even the "gift of a broken and a contrite heart" offered by a female character at the altar of God (Davenant 1843: 161). While in each example discussed in this book there is an element of giving or exchange that limits and structures the choice of material, that there is a broad scope and array of meanings is taken into consideration.

One form of giving that this study does not address specifically is charity, even though benevolence and alms are discussed in Chap. 5. First, the history of nineteenth-century American philanthropy and its influence on literature is well-researched (Ginzberg 1990; Ryan 2003; Bergman and Bernardi, eds., 2005; Sawaya 2014, to mention just a few important studies). Second, I agree with Lee Anne Fennell that gratuitous transfers such as donations to charity present "somewhat different sets of motivations and characteristics" to social or personal gifts (Fennell 2002: 99). The same applies to "transfers of assets upon or in anticipation of death" (99), although here I make an exception in Chap. 8 when discussing *The Wings of the Dove*, considering that the rhetoric of the gift is crucial for the understanding of that particular bequest, especially in the light of Jean-Luc Marion's concept of pure "givenness" (Marion 2002).

In what follows, I will first situate the gift as a subject of critical inquiry in its relation to modern history, and to the nineteenth century in particular, before briefly reflecting upon the concept of dangerous gifts within gift theory. I then introduce my own interpretation of this theme in the context of the material I examine.

There is a long-standing tradition of beginning any study of the gift with a discussion of Marcel Mauss's pioneering work *The Gift* (1925). By contrast, I will start with references to recent scholarship, while keeping Mauss within view. This will allow me to outline the current state of arts and to build my argument by challenging three assumptions: (1) the nineteenth century is a blank page in the intellectual history of the gift; (2) the idea of disinterested, pure giving is universal; (3) the gift as an antipode of commodity is essentially benign.

Reconstructing the Western European intellectual history of the gift, Harry Liebersohn observes "a striking poverty of systematic reflection on the gift in the century preceding Mauss's essay" (Liebersohn 2011: 3). A few thinkers such as Emerson and Simmel "noticed it, but not in a revaluation sustained enough to leave an impact on their contemporaries." As a result, "no systematic or extended discussion of the gift" (Liebersohn 2011: 3) emerged from the nineteenth century. This argument is accurate only if we confine the discussion to the field of philosophy and political economy and to the writings of major (male) "European thinkers" (Liebersohn 2011: 4). While Liebersohn claims that nineteenth-century philosophical and economic thought failed to find an adequate language to express gift exchange, this study argues that nineteenth-century literature was at the forefront of developing and simultaneously revising this language as well as promoting and contesting a particular ideology of the gift. My premise is that literature, as a form of reflective thinking, had an important share in the intellectual discussion of the gift and the related issues of reciprocity, generosity, obligation, debt, and gratuity. For example, *Dangerous Giving* will demonstrate how some literary texts were forerunners of twentieth-century gift theory and will examine a few dazzling attempts at theorizing the gift—those by Emerson, Caroline Kirkland, Mark Twain (Chap. 2), and Frederick Douglass (Chap. 5). Fragmentary, brief, and sporadic, these attempts nevertheless suggest that the question of the gift in the nineteenth century was intellectually vibrant rather than dead or "near-silent" (Liebersohn 2011: 3). According to Liebersohn, it was primarily a reciprocal gift that "disappeared from theoretical thought" in the nineteenth century, being replaced by a conventional notion of the gift as "a voluntary offering that does not anticipate a return" (6). Following Francesca Sawaya, I would say that American nineteenth-century literature demonstrates instead that reciprocal practices of gift-giving were "very much on the minds of intellectuals" (Sawaya 2014: 192). The question of reciprocity comes to the fore precisely in discussions of the voluntary or disinterested gift, predominantly in late nineteenth-century texts (e.g., in Twain and James) though with Emerson as a notable earlier exception.

A study in literature rather than in intellectual history, *Dangerous Giving* contributes to what Rebecca Colesworthy neatly calls "a literary counter-genealogy of writing about gift" (Colesworthy 2018: 7). Colesworthy examines this counter-genealogy within the tradition of Anglo-American modernism, placing an emphasis on female modernist authors. Paying tribute to the earlier, pre-modernist period, she claims that "in literature, as in the social sciences, the question of the gift did not suddenly emerge ex nihilo following World War I" (15). At the same time, her own study gives the impression that pre-modernist "writing about gift" consists of a handful of male authors only (15) and that the relevant female tradition cannot be traced prior to modernism. By contrast, *Dangerous Giving* will demonstrate that nineteenth-century female writers, including such renowned authors as Lydia Maria Child, Catharine Maria Sedgwick, Harriet Beecher Stowe, Caroline Kirkland, and Mary Wilkins Freeman, offered original insights into the nature and the function of the gift even when using what were by modernist standards conventional narrative and rhetorical patterns.

In attempting to fill a significant gap in nineteenth-century studies of the gift, my book is not the first to address this subject in the context of American literature. Two important works by Mary Louise Kete (2000) and Leon Jackson (2008: 89–141) explore certain aspects and forms of gift-giving in nineteenth-century American literature, related to the culture of mourning (Kete) and authorial economies (Jackson), respectively. Hildegard Hoeller's (2012) is the only book-length study devoted exclusively to the gift in nineteenth-century American fiction and has the great merit of bringing our attention to female and Black narratives of the gift and covering a vast body of literature from Hannah Foster to Frank Norris—a "blind spot" in previous scholarship (Hoeller 2012: 12). However, Hoeller's study, largely "a Derridean inflected application of gift theory to American literature" (Sawaya 2014: 193), has serious limitations in its approach and method that I will address in various contexts below.

"The reality of the gift—the net of obligations it creates—has *always* coexisted with the wish for it to be pure and disinterested—outside of any economy. In that sense, the gift has remained desirable, confounding, and (im)possible to reckon with" (Hoeller 2012: 12; italics mine.—*A.U.*). The word "always" in this otherwise nicely written passage from Hoeller's abovementioned study is misleading. To make one rather obvious counter-argument, it is highly unlikely that this "wish" existed in "archaic" or indigenous societies, driven, as Mauss famously put it, by three obligations "to give, to receive, to reciprocate" (Mauss 2002: 50). As Jonathan Parry highlights in his seminal 1988 essay on gifts, Mauss considered indigenous gifts to be "the *combination* of interest and disinterest, of freedom and constraint" (Parry 1986: 456). The "ideology of disinterested giving" or "disinterested gift" (Parry 1986)—a term that will be used repeatedly in this study—is hardly universal.

Advocating for a distinction between the indigenous and the modern gift, Parry argues that the concept of disinterestedness is "most likely to arise in highly differentiated societies with an advanced division of labour" (467) and that "the ideology of a disinterested gift emerges in parallel with an ideology of a purely interested exchange" (458). In fact, economic self-interest and the disinterested gift are two sides of the same coin: both are "*our* invention" (458). Parry points out two important features of "disinterested giving," one of which is its imperative or prescriptive modality; Mauss, rather than "telling us how *in fact* the gift is never *free*," tells us instead "how we have acquired a *theory* that it should be" (458). The other is a universalistic character stemming from Christianity, "with its notion that all men are fashioned equally in the image of God" (468). This universalistic character of the concept may in fact be responsible for the universal fallacy described above.

While Parry himself does not outline a specific genealogy of this ideology, studies in the modern history of gift-giving tend to associate it primarily with the emergence of modern, market-oriented societies (see, e.g., Carrier 1995: 154–176). As Jackson puts it, while never ceasing being "economic—in the broad sense of the word," gift exchanges in the modern history cease to be "perceived as economic." And also: "[t]he ideology of the free gift legitimized the ruthless and disembedded world of commercial economics, that is to say, by holding out the promise that there remained one sphere of exchange that was wholly free of calculation or obligation, even though ... business and gift exchange had traditionally been mutually constitutive" (Jackson 2008: 141).[3]

Dangerous Giving will follow the intellectual tradition of historicizing the ideology of disinterested giving and will demonstrate that sentimentalism, whose own history coincided with the emergence of modernity, was one of its most important outposts. In sentimental tradition, disinterestedness is a guarantee of the moral goodness of the gift. James Carrier's observations on the modern Western present may well apply to how sentimental authors conceived of the good and the bad gift: "The good present is one that reflects or expresses the giver, and if it is good in that sense, the present is also morally good. Conversely, the present that is constrained and interested is repulsive, because constraint and interest conflict with the source of goodness, which is spontaneous expression" (Carrier 1995: 162). The "morally bad" gift is, after all, no gift at all since it betrays the very nature of disinterested giving in being too similar to the object of an interested exchange, a commodity; no surprise, then, that sentimental discourse of the gift endeavored to separate the wheat from the chaff. An essentialist attitude to the gift typical of sentimental discourse is guilty of another fallacy—the implied goodness of the gift.

The idea of gift-giving as something inherently, essentially good in contrast to mercenary transactions is so contagious that the risk of an idealistic or utopian attitude to the gift developing not only in popular culture but also in criticism is quite high. The most famous example is perhaps Lewis Hyde's study (Hyde 1983) that counterpoises free circulation of the gift, which best manifests itself in art and poetry, to consumerism and, at the same time and in the neoliberal spirit (Konstantinou 2016), allows for the

---

[3] Speaking more broadly and within a different intellectual tradition, scholars relate "the origins of humanitarianism" to the rise of capitalism, associating it with a change of modern sensibility (Haskell 1985, I: 342).

possibility of the free or pure gift under the conditions of capitalism. As Jackson observes, "for Hyde, there is no such thing as a bad gift, only gifts given or received badly" (Jackson 2008: 92).

Indebted to the theories of both Derrida and Hyde, notwithstanding the differences between these two theorists, Hoeller's abovementioned study on the gift in nineteenth-century American literature tacitly suggests that the gift, as opposed to a commodity, is inevitably good. Exploring nineteenth-century narratives of the gift, the book itself generates a metanarrative, as suggested by the title: *From Gift to Commodity*. Ending with a discussion of Frank Norris's late nineteenth-century anti-capitalist novel *McTeague*, Hoeller interprets the novel's "warning" in apocalyptic terms: "the end of the gift...might as well be the end of the world" (Hoeller 2012: 22).

While I agree that the gift provided late-nineteenth-century authors with a language that allowed them to "launch their critique of capitalism" (Hoeller 2012: 21), I find it hard to accept this metanarrative and its apocalyptic implications. Can we indeed describe the nineteenth century as a passage from presumably benign gifts to presumably evil commodities? Many turn-of-the-century texts—including such famous example as O. Henry's "The Gift of the Magi"—far from lamenting the impossibility and the loss of the perfect gift affirm its presence in the commodified world. The gap between domestic and market economies predictably widens toward the end of the century as the country enters the "Gilded Age" but this hardly signals the victory of "commodities" over "gifts," either in literature or in popular imagination.

The subtitle of Hoeller's study—*Capitalism and Sacrifice in Nineteenth Century American Fiction*—clearly indicates that it is concerned only with one specific type of the gift: *sacrifice* or rather *self-sacrifice* as opposed to self-interest. While self-sacrifice as a form of altruistic giving undoubtedly formed an important part of the ideology of disinterested giving, the gift was a broader and more inclusive category in nineteenth-century American literature, as this study hopes to demonstrate.

Finally, there is always a risk of taking declarations of nineteenth-century rhetoricians and advertisers at face value and, as result, of re-sentimentalizing the gift. In the introduction to his seminal collection, Mark Osteen calls for "sharper and more refined theory that steers clear of both the Scylla of sentimentality and the Charybdis of economism" (Osteen 2002a: 31). Without claiming that my study has achieved the desired balance, I do attempt to avoid these two dangers by (a) focusing on the language/languages of the gift and (b) tracing ideological patterns that mediated gift-giving and its representations. Following in the steps of scholars like David Cheal, who demonstrated that the gift versus commodity binary stemming from classical anthropology fails to explain the specificity of the modern gift (Cheal 1988: 9–12), *Dangerous Giving* relegates this binary to the field of language and ideology where it belongs and refuses to apply it as the sole explanatory model to describe the complex dynamics of the modern gift. The focus on the dangerous gift as the third, fluid, and contingent agent, in addition to the duo of gift/commodity—gift-giving may go well but may also go awry—allows us to avoid the aforementioned dualistic determinism.

My interest in dangerous giving has its roots in a tradition prominent in gift theory, including in classical anthropology. Mauss challenges the concept of the disinterested and morally good gift—the nineteenth-century intellectual heritage—not only by emphasizing that there is no such thing as a "free gift" but also by stressing how the gift's ambiguity is revealed in some European languages, the word "gift" meaning both "gift" and "poison" (Germanic languages but also Latin—*dosis*) (Mauss 2002: 81, 187).

Another Maussian challenge is his theory of *potlatch*, a North American ritual where two clans compete for social status and prestige by exchanging gifts, which potentially ruins the prosperity of each party. In his classification of different types of reciprocity, Marshall Sahlins identifies a so-called *negative reciprocity*, a gift exchange that borders on theft or barter in which one of the parties tries to get something for nothing—the direct opposite of altruistic giving (Sahlins 1997). Jonathan Parry describes how a particularly dangerous gift to an Indian priest could "poison" him with the sins and defilement of the giver (Parry 1986).

Philosophers such as Georges Bataille and Jacques Derrida were fascinated with the potentially redeeming character of dangerous giving; for Bataille (1988), it is the excess and "the suicidal impetus" in potlatch that "frees one from the dictatorship of property and ownership" (Sowerby and Urakova 2022, forthcoming). Derrida's *gift of death*, or to be more accurate, the giving of death ("donner la mort") imperils the feeling of stability and security induced by the Maussian gift economy (Derrida 1995). Pernicious transactions are of interest in sociology (for Pierre Bourdieu, rejection and lack of reciprocity are two risks associated with gift-giving; Bourdieu 1992: 98) and psychology (Barry Schwartz, from a psychological standpoint, analyzes the risks of the power relationship in gift-giving; Schwartz 1996). Gender theorists discuss the dangers associated with power relations that gift exchange inevitably entails, from women as objects of exchange—an indigenous practice that Claude Lévi-Strauss makes central to his own gift theory (Lévi-Strauss 1969)—to their subordinate position in courtship rituals and romantic or sexual relationships (Joy 2013; see also Belk 2022, forthcoming). Historians and literary scholars trace the specific dangers of gifts in national mythology, systems of beliefs, and the literary imagination of particular historical periods (Groebner 2002; Lyons 2012) or across times and cultures (Urakova, Sowerby, and Sala 2022, forthcoming).

Dangerous Giving is a study that attempts to be both history-oriented and theoretically informed in its approach: it follows the narrative logic and the language of the texts it examines while employing elements of social analysis as well as specific terminology developed within gift theory. Reading gift theory into nineteenth-century fiction undoubtedly risks retrolabeling and may be both far-fetched and misleading. As Osteen observes about literary studies of the gift, "too many critics are content to simply 'apply' mechanically the paradigms of Hyde, Derrida, Mauss or Bataille without acknowledging the limitations and blind spots in each..." (Osteen 2002a: 30). In his late work, Mark Twain repeatedly calls death a gift. Does this mean that Derrida's *donner la mort* is an explanatory model fit to describe Twain's ideas by default? No, though we can say that Twain's vision may have presaged certain twentieth-century tendencies in intellectual thought, including those represented by Derrida or Nancy, since Twain views death in its liminality and denies the religious idea of the gift of death as a gift of an afterlife.

At the same time, and as Jackson observes, sometimes we can gain a better understanding of nineteenth-century texts or textual objects "by viewing them through the lens of modern gift theory than through their own self-representations" (Jackson 2016). While it is tempting to agree with Groebner that a gift is "simply whatever contemporaries call a gift" (Groebner 2002: 1), this is not always the case. First, the rhetoric of the gift in the texts examined here may be deceptive or self-deceptive and blind to its own controversies. Shall we indeed take at face value the claim of the editors of gift books that those volumes were tokens of pure affection rather than commercial projects?

Second, there was no operative language to describe certain social and cultural phenomena. For example, its own controversial history notwithstanding, the anthropological term "potlatch" "does reveal something common to all gift exchanges" (Greenberg 1996: 154). Writing about dangerous gifts in Ancient Greek mythology and literature, Deborah Lyons claims that "although this kind of competition is not explicit in our sources, it is possible to read the unequal exchange of armor between Glaukos and Diomedes or the gifts offered by Agamemnon to Achilles in *Iliad* 9 in these terms" (Lyons 2012: 13). My own study will employ the term potlatch in the context of the frontier novel on the one hand and, after Lévi-Strauss, to describe the excesses of Christmas on the other: in both cases, this is a retrospective approach. The same is true for other terminology employed in the book, be it "givenness" (Marion 2002) or "munus" and "donum" (Esposito 2009) that, in my view, accurately capture certain literary and cultural phenomena that I explore. Finally, in the case of texts that have already been discussed within gift theory, such as Emerson's "Gifts" or O. Henry's "The Gift of the Magi," literary analysis can tease out disciplinary boundaries and engage itself in interdisciplinary dialogue.

With the exception of Chap. 2, which establishes a conceptual framework by analyzing the nineteenth-century ideology of disinterested giving in three theoretical texts by Ralph Waldo Emerson, Caroline Kirkland, and Mark Twain, the chapters are in chronological order, moving from the 1820s to the early 1900s (the latter considered as belonging culturally and ideologically to the nineteenth century as the upper bound of the so-called long nineteenth century). Chaps. 3, 4, 5, and 6 focus exclusively on the antebellum period seen as formative for the modern language and ideology of the gift. Chapter 3 demonstrates the ambivalence of the extreme form of disinterested giving—altruism and self-sacrifice on behalf of the "selfless savage"—in the context of colonial history, interracial relations, and nation building in Lydia Maria Child's *Hobomok*. Chapter 4 examines the gender aspects of the sentimental gift as epitomized by antebellum gift books, paying particular attention to the ways in which the mainstream heteronormative exchange of sweet tokens was contested and challenged in gift book stories by Catharine Maria Sedgwick, Nathaniel Hawthorne, and Edgar Allan Poe. Chapter 5 continues the discussion of gift books in the context of the anti-slavery movement, focusing on the concept of "the gift of freedom" and its racialist implications in *The Liberty Bell* on the one hand and on alternative attitudes to the gift, slavery, and race—including an attempt at building and maintaining a Black community via album writing (Cassey's album)—on the other.

Chapter 6 presses the question of the "race of the gift" still further by analyzing how the motif of a slave as a gift undermines the sentimental rhetoric of giving in Harriet Beecher Stowe's *Uncle Tom's Cabin*, with a special focus on the metaphorical language of poison that is associated with Black race and with the unwelcome human gift in the novel. Chapter 7 expands on the gender implications of the pure versus poisonous binary that was fundamental for nineteenth-century ethics of giving while also demonstrating its ambivalence in modern revisions of archetypal plots about poisoned gifts and poisonous bodies. By moving from Hawthorne to Oliver Wendell Holmes to the obscure late-nineteenth-century author Caroline Wilder Paradise, this chapter also serves as a link to the two last chapters, which deal predominantly with turn-of-the-century texts.

These last chapters demonstrate the persistence of the patterns of dangerous giving throughout the long nineteenth century but also reflect on cultural phenomena that become particularly marked toward the end of the era, including the secularization of intellectual and literary thought and the unprecedented commercialization of Christmas. Chapter 8 discusses how Mark Twain and Henry James revisited and modernized the sentimental ideology of disinterested giving by exploring an intimate connection between the perfect gift and death. Chapter 9 explores the melancholy side of Christmas giving and the anxieties associated with it in three Christmas stories by William Dean Howells, Mary E. Wilkins Freeman, and O. Henry, all written around the 1900s. The conclusion summarizes the patterns of dangerous gifts explored in this study and ends with an example of Native American writing of the gift in Zitkála-Ša's short story "The Coffee-Making," which I see as both consonant with and removed from that of most of the other texts discussed in this book.

While drawing from theoretical research in the field, *Dangerous Giving* is neither Derridean, nor Bataillesque, nor Maussian in its approach since it does not rely on any specific concept of the dangerous gift. Rather, it builds on the premise that "danger enters into the gift-giving process at multiple points. There is no one typology of dangerous gift or perilous exchange, and perhaps any straightforward typology would lead to unprofitable oversimplifications and conflations" (Sowerby and Urakova 2022, forthcoming). In what follows, I will highlight specific "areas where dangers could inhere" (Sowerby and Urakova 2022, forthcoming); these are gender, race, consumption, the religious or transcendental sphere, and literature.

There are several types of dangerous giving associated with gender in this study. The first is the transgression of gender norms and conventions, for example, those of a heterosexual romance which was often initiated in an exchange of tokens and signs of attention. The counter-practice often expresses itself through irony, humor, subversive critique, or meta-literary play. Where conventions and norms function as repressive cultural mechanisms, a dangerous gift may have a redeeming or liberating effect, as demonstrated in the example of antebellum gift books and three gift book stories in Chap. 3: Sedgwick's "Cacoethes Scribendi" (1829), Hawthorne's "The Minister's Black Veil" (1832), and Poe's "The Purloined Letter" (1844). A different type of danger relates to the perception of the giver's body, female or male, as polluted or contaminated (Chap. 7). Gifts in Hawthorne's "Rappaccini's Daughter" (1844), Holmes's *Elsie Venner* (1861), and in a late-nineteenth-century story "Father Dunstan and Crabs" (1898) by Wilder Paradise threaten or are perceived as threatening the bodily integrity of the receiver—for example, via contagion (poisonous touch) or digestion (crabs "poisoned" with the sins of the givers). Finally, there are risks associated with the feminization of gift-giving observed in modern Western societies (Cheal 1988; Godbout, Caillé 1998). Chapter 9 shows how Christmas shopping in O. Henry's "The Gift of the Magi" (1906) exposes a woman, the new type of female consumer, to the hazards of the big city. In extreme cases, the female burden of Christmas-time chores and the fatigue they induce may lead to the death of the giver (Twain believed, as briefly discussed in Chap. 8, that this happened to his daughter Jean).

Interracial gift exchanges are especially hazardous, being fraught with dominance and power. Using the example of Child's *Hobomok* (1824), Chap. 3 demonstrates how a bilateral interracial exchange of generosity and gentility may ruin one party and cause discontent to the other; the gift exchange of the story, placed at the origin of American nation, is suicidal, burdensome, and ultimately murderous. The gift relation appears to be even more problematic in the context of race and slavery. Chapter 5 explores different types of potentially dangerous interracial gift exchanges. Abolitionist writing in the pages of *The Liberty Bell*, an anti-slavery gift book, risks symbolically "enchaining" liberated slaves with the bonds of gratitude under the guise of the gift of liberty while, as Frederick Douglass argues in "The Bible for Slaves" (1848), the gift bestowed on an enslaved person is itself fundamentally wrong and impossible. In the short story "Dinah Rollins" by Edmund Quincy (1841), the subversion of this model when an independent Black woman becomes a donor to a white person bestows the former with a new identity but also puts her in subordinate position to the white recipient of her favors. Finally, the so-called Cassey's album (a friendship album owned by Amy Matilda Cassey) suggests an attempt to develop a community of givers among the free Black people of Philadelphia in the face of the dangers to which the fragility of their status exposed them. Another type of dangerous giving arises from a confusion between persons and things. While usually associated with the commercial transactions of slavery, this problem is equally relevant in the case of non-commercial transactions such as gift-giving. What happens when a slave is given as a gift? Would gift-giving in this case be distinct from commercial transactions such as buying or leasing or would it merge with the latter? Can a slave be an object of gift exchange and an object of benevolence? These and similar questions are addressed in the examination of Stowe's *Uncle Tom's Cabin* (1852) in Chap. 6.

The expansion of the market inevitably brings gift-giving and consumption together: to give a gift, one usually needs to buy it first. Excessive giving is the opposite of a balanced and rational commercial transaction yet it shares a passionate and irrational character with consumption, a progressing malady of the American middle class throughout the nineteenth century, as is briefly discussed in Chap. 9 with Freeman's Christmas story "The Last Gift" (1903). Christmas shopping risks becoming obsessive, burdensome, or financially ruinous, as demonstrated in the same chapter with the examples of Howell's "Christmas Every Day" (1892) and O. Henry's "The Gift of the Magi." This chapter explores a peculiar feeling of melancholia, nostalgia, and loss that goes hand in hand with the commercialization of Christmas, as is also present in Freeman's "The Reign of the Doll" (1904). American nineteenth-century authors considered different ways of mitigating or avoiding the danger of confusing gifts and commodities by, for example, advising giving handmade presents and keepsakes—for example, presents of low material but high spiritual or personal value, advocated by Kirkland (Chap. 2) among others. While it might seem counterintuitive, a dangerous gift can challenge commodification and consumption even more powerfully than can a perfect gift be removed from the commercial sphere. A worthless, wasteful, and harmful gift—for example, the gift of Topsy in *Uncle Tom's Cabin*, the purchase of whom is economically meaningless and excessive and who is compared to a repellent, dangerous spider—is one such example (Chap. 6). Another example is the "poison" of Beatrice Rappaccini's gift of love, which in "Rappaccini's Daughter" (Chap. 7) challenges her lover's consumerist longing to possess safely the object of his desire. On the transcendental level, the gift of death is, in Twain's interpretation (Chap. 8), a gift that brings to an end all trade, bargain, or exchange.

The history of religion is a history of dangerous gifts; in Christianity, God's prestations include death and calamities because everything that comes from God is considered a gift. At the same time, His benign gifts such as Eucharist may cause damage or even death to the unworthy recipient. Criticizing the initiative of giving bibles to slaves, Frederick Douglass provocatively argues that even Bible can become a harmful gift. However, this happens because the donor, not the receiver, is unworthy (Chap. 5). The gift of death bestowed by God on the devoted believer recurs in nineteenth-century spiritual novels, such as Susan Warner's *The Wide, Wide World* (1850) and Elizabeth Stuart Phelps's *The Gates Ajar* (1868) briefly discussed in Chap. 8. This same chapter demonstrates how modernity introduced a new kind of dangerous giving that stemmed but also stepped away from the religious sphere. Twain's transcendental agent—Philip Traum in *A Chronicle of Young Satan* (1897–1900)—takes on the role of God when he grants death as a gift but his gift is not intended to benefit the recipient with the afterlife bliss; its only merit is in putting an end to the bargain of life in which one pays with suffering for every happy moment. The seemingly transcendental Christmas gift—Milly Theale's bequest in James's *The Wings of the Dove* (1902)—is ultimately deeply ambivalent. Its dangerous nature, as I argue in Chap. 8, has to do not so much with any malice or revengeful intention on the part of the giver as with the transcendental effect of the gift itself, which imperils the recipient by generating a feeling of loss. Paradoxically, death becomes a condition of perfect giving while also casting a melancholy shadow on its perfection.

Given that the nineteenth-century American literary scene was competitive and often fraught with mutual enmity (Tomc 2019), it is not surprising that gift relations between authors were often tense and ambivalent (Jackson 2008, 2016). Twain was particularly disturbed to receive as a gift a book with a tacit request from the author to endorse it (Chap. 2). Chapter 3 suggests that the literary exchange between Child and James Fenimore Cooper—Child challenges Cooper by writing a historical frontier novel; Cooper allegedly borrows from Child's writing and then outstrips her in public recognition—may be described as a type of hazardous exchange akin to potlatch. In the first half of the nineteenth century especially, the poisonous or dangerous book was a common trope. Sedgwick's "Cacoethes Scribendi" compares gift books to Pandora's box; in the eyes of one of Stowe's Southern reviewers, *Uncle Tom's Cabin* was a poisonous offering to the reader. In his metafictional gift book stories, Hawthorne conceived of literary art as an ambivalent gift (Urakova 2016). His

"Rappaccini's Daughter," often read as an allegory of literature, may be seen as a "poisonous flower" in the bouquet gallantly presented to the reader (his own metaphor), the poison of the gift being associated with its sublimity and ambivalence (Chap. 7).

In addressing these and other questions, the book explores a wide range of texts and genres. However, it was not my intention to write a comprehensive history of dangerous gifts in nineteenth-century American literature and, as a result, the book has inevitable gaps and omissions.[4] There are certain principles underlying the selection of texts, one of which is diversity. I will consider authors as diverse as Poe and Sedgwick, Emerson and Kirkland, Hawthorne and Eliza Leslie, Howells and Wilkins Freeman, Mark Twain and Henry James; established classics alternate both with lesser-known, obscure, and anonymous authors and with popular authors like O. Henry, often not taken particularly seriously by literary scholars. Another, competing, principle is continuity, which in this book relates to the sentimental tradition. Acknowledging the protean nature of sentimental discourse (De Jong 2013: 5), *Dangerous Giving* follows those scholars who detect its elements across different traditions and styles in nineteenth-century texts.[5] A premise of this study is that in the nineteenth century sentimental language was an important reference point for any discussion or representation of the gift, even in the case of inversions, critiques, or parodies of this language. This allows me to examine literary texts in dialogue not only with each other but also with other print and written media, including such sentimental genres as gift books and friendship albums or Christmas editions of popular magazines.

Giving, with its usual connotations of generosity, devotion, self-sacrifice, and similarly positive values notwithstanding, is a practice hazardous in both its effects and counter-effects. Given the metaphorical affinity between writing and giving, the text and the gift, that our culture pursues and supports, writers and scholars are especially sensitive to these

---

[4] One such obvious omission is the work of Melville, especially "Bartleby the Scrivener," which has been read in the context of charity (Ryan 2003: 46–76). I decided to exclude this very important example of dangerous giving because charity is not a central focus of this book. *Dangerous Giving* for the most part focuses on prose not poetry which is another gap I would like to acknowledge.

[5] Chapman and Hendler (1999), for example, debunked the myth that American sentimentalism was exclusively female. Scholars have also found traces of sentimentality in male authors as diverse as Poe, Emerson, James, and Twain, to say nothing of more obvious cases (Hawthorne, Holmes). I will reference some of these studies throughout this book.

effects. My study, with this self-referential question as a backdrop, is ultimately seeking to inquire into the phenomenon of the gift and giving, departing from the premise that the focus on its dangerous side may reveal precisely what a widespread belief in the gift's good and benign nature otherwise obscures. The questions addressed by nineteenth-century American authors, either directly or indirectly and with the help of fictional forms and figurative language, are open-ended and have both relevance and resonance till today.

Works Cited

Appadurai, Arjun. 1986. Introduction: Commodities and the Politics of Value. In *The Social Life of Things: Commodities in Cultural Perspective*, ed. Arjun Appadurai, 3–63. Cambridge: Cambridge University Press.

Bataille, Georges. 1988. *The Accursed Share: An Essay on General Economy*. Vol. 1. Trans. Robert Hurley. New York: Zone Books.

Belk, Russell. 2022 (forthcoming). The Dual Dangers of the Gift. In *The Dangers of Gifts from Antiquity to the Digital Age*, ed. Alexandra Urakova, Tracey Sowerby, and Tudor Sala. New York and London: Routledge.

Bergman, Jill, and Debra Bernardi, eds. 2005. *Our Sisters' Keepers: Nineteenth-Century Benevolence Literature by American Women*. Tuscaloosa: University of Alabama Press.

Blumberg, Ilana. 2005. Collins' 'Moonstone': The Victorian Novel as Sacrifice, Theft, Gift, and Debt. *Studies in the Novel* 37 (2): 162–186.

Bourdieu, Pierre. 1992. *The Logic of Practice*. Trans. Richard Nice. Cambridge: Cambridge University Press.

Bullen, Ross. 2011. "The Alarming Generosity": White Elephants and the Logic of the Gift. *American Literature* 83 (4): 747–773.

Carrier, James G. 1990. Gifts in a World of Commodities: The Ideology of the Perfect Gift in American Society. *Social Analysis* 29: 19–37.

———. 1995. *Gifts and Commodities: Exchange and Western Capitalism Since 1700*. London: Routledge.

Chapman, Mary, and Glenn Hendler, eds. 1999. *Sentimental Men: Masculinity and the Politics of Affect in American Culture*. Berkeley: University of California Press.

Cheal, David. 1988. *The Gift Economy*. New York: Routledge.

Colesworthy, Rebecca. 2018. *Returning the Gift: Modernism and the Thought of Exchange*. Oxford: Oxford University Press.

Davenant, Mary. 1843. The Ideal and the Real. *Godey's Lady's Book* 27: 156–165.

Davis, Natalie Zemon. 2000. *The Gift in Sixteenth-Century France*. Madison: University of Wisconsin Press.

De Jong, Mary G. 2013. Introduction. In *Sentimentalism in Nineteenth-Century America: Literary and Cultural Practices*, ed. Mary G. De Jong. New Jersey: Fairleigh Dickinson University Press.
Derrida, Jacques. 1992. *Given Time: I. Counterfeit Money*. Trans. Peggy Kamuf. Chicago: University of Chicago Press.
———. 1995. *The Gift of Death*. Trans. David Wills. Chicago: University of Chicago Press.
Emerson, Ralph Waldo. 1965. *The Journals and Miscellaneous Notebooks of Ralph Waldo Emerson*, ed. Merton M. Sealts. Cambridge, MA: The Belknap Press of Harvard University Press.
———. 1983. Gifts. In *Essays and Lectures (Essays: First and Second, Representative Men, English Traits, and the Conduct of Life)*, 535–538. New York: Library of America.
Esposito, Roberto. 2009. *Communitas: The Origin and Destiny of Community*. Trans. Timothy Campbell. Stanford: Stanford University Press.
Fennell, Lee Anne. 2002. Unpacking the Gift: Illiquid Goods and Empathetic Dialogue. In *The Question of the Gift: Essays Across Disciplines*, ed. Mark Osteen, 85–102. London: Routledge.
Fichtelberg, Joseph. 2003. *Critical Fictions: Sentiment and the American Market, 1780–1870*. Athens: University of Georgia Press.
Furness, Horace Howard, ed. 1910. *Records of a Lifelong Friendship, 1807–1882: Ralph Waldo Emerson and William Henry Furness*. Boston: Houghton Mifflin.
Ginzberg, Lori D. 1990. *Women and the Work of Benevolence: Morality, Politics, and Class in the Nineteenth-Century United States*. New Haven: Yale University Press.
Godbout, Jacques; Caillé, Allen. 1998. *The World of the Gift*. Trans. D. Winkler. Montreal and Kingston: McGill-Queen's University Press.
Greenberg, Kenneth S. 1996. *Honor and Slavery: Lies, Duels, Noses. Masks, Dressing as a Woman, Gifts, Strangers, Humanitarianism, Death, Slave Rebellions, the Proslavery Argument, Baseball, Hunters, and Gambling in the Old South*. Princeton: Princeton University Press.
Groebner, Valentin. 2002. *Liquid Assets, Dangerous Gifts: Presents and Politics at the End of the Middle Ages*. Trans. Pamela E. Selwyn. Philadelphia: University of Pennsylvania Press.
Haskell, Thomas L. 1985. Capitalism and the Origins of the Humanitarian Sensitivity. Part I, II. *The American Historical Review* 90 (2, 3): 339–361; 547–566.
Hénaff, Marcel. 2003. Religious Ethics, Gift Exchange, and Capitalism. *European Journal of Sociology* 44 (3): 293–324.
Hoeller, Hildegard. 2012. *From Gift to Commodity. Capitalism and Sacrifice in Nineteenth-Century American Fiction*. Durham: University of New Hampshire Press.

Hyde, Lewis. 1983. *The Gift: Creativity and the Artist in the Modern World*. New York: Vintage.

Jackson, Leon. 2008. *The Business of Letters: Authorial Economies in Antebellum America*. Stanford: Stanford University Press.

———. 2016. The Gift, the Book, and the Gift Book: The Biography of an Antebellum Commodity. Presentation at the workshop "Gift Economy and the US Antebellum Market," Central European University, Budapest, Hungary, June 6.

Joy, Morny. 2013. Introduction. In *Women and The Gift: Beyond the Given and All-Giving*, ed. Joy Morny. Bloomington: Indiana University Press, 1–52.

Kete, Mary Louise. 2000. *Sentimental Collaborations: Mourning and Middle-Class Identity in Nineteenth-Century America*. Durham, NC: Duke University Press.

Konstantinou, Lee. 2016. Lewis Hyde's Double Economy. *ASAP* 1 (1): 123–149.

Lévi-Strauss, Claude. 1969. *The Elementary Structures of Kinship*. Trans. John Richard von Sturmer, James Harle Bell, and Rodney Needham. Boston, MA: Beacon Press.

Liebersohn, Harry. 2011. *The Return of the Gift: European History of a Global Idea*. Cambridge: Cambridge University Press.

Litwicki, Ellen. 2015. Defining the Gift: From Emerson to the Gift Registry. *Americana: E-Journal of American Studies in Hungary* XI (2). http://americanaejournal.hu/vol11no2/litwicki.

Luck, Chad. 2014. *The Body of Property: Antebellum American Fiction and the Phenomenology of Possession*. New York: Fordham University Press.

Lyons, Debora J. 2012. *Dangerous Gifts: Gender and Exchange in Ancient Greece*. Austin: University of Texas Press.

Mahowald, Kyle. 2010. 'It may nat be.' Chaucer, Derrida, and the Impossibility of the Gift. *Studies in the Age of Chaucer* 32: 129–150.

Manheim, D. 2011. "And row my blossoms o'er!" Gift-Giving and Emily Dickinson's Poetic Vocation. *The Emily Dickinson Journal* 20 (2): 1–32.

Marion, Jean-Luc. 2002. *Being Given: Toward a Phenomenology of Givenness*. Trans. Geoffrey L. Kosky. Stanford: Stanford University Press.

Mauss, Marcel. 2002. *The Gift: The Form and Reason for Exchange in Archaic Societies*. Trans. W.D. Halls. London; New York: Routledge.

Osteen, Mark. 2002a. Introduction: Questions of the Gift. In *The Question of the Gift: Essays Across Disciplines*, ed. Mark Osteen. London: Routledge.

———, ed. 2002b. *The Question of the Gift: Essays Across Disciplines*. London: Routledge.

Parry, Jonathan. 1986. The Gift, the Indian Gift, and the 'Indian Gift'. *Man* 21 (3): 453–473.

Pyyhtinen, Olli. 2014. *The Gift and Its Paradoxes: Beyond Mauss*. London: Routledge.

Rappoport, Jill. 2011. *Giving Women: Alliance and Exchange in Victorian Culture*. Oxford: Oxford University Press.

Restad, Penne L. 1996. *Christmas in America: A History*. Oxford: Oxford University Press.
Ryan, Susan M. 2003. *The Grammar of Good Intentions: Race and the Antebellum Culture of Benevolence*. Ithaca: Cornell University.
Sahlins, Marshall. 1997. The Spirit of the Gift. In *The Logic of the Gift: Towards an Ethic of Generosity*, ed. A.D. Schrift, 70–99. New York; London: Routledge.
Sawaya, Francesca. 2014. *The Difficult Art of Giving: Patronage, Philanthropy, and the American Literary Market*. University of Pennsylvania Press.
Schmidt, Leigh Eric. 1997. Practices of Exchange: From Market Culture to Gift Economy in the Interpretation of American Religion. In *Lived Religion in America: Toward a History of Practice*, ed. David D. Hall, 69–91. New Jersey: Princeton University Press.
Schwartz, Barry. 1996. The Social Psychology of the Gift. In *The Gift: An Interdisciplinary Perspective*, ed. Aafke Komter, 69–80. Amsterdam: Amsterdam University Press.
Simpson, Kathryn. 2005. Economies and Desire: Gift and the Market in "The Moments of Being: Slater's Pins Have No Points." *Journal of Modern Literature* 28 (2): 18–37.
Sowerby, Tracey, and Alexandra Urakova. 2022, forthcoming. Introduction: Unpacking Dangerous Gifts. In *The Dangers of Gifts from Antiquity to the Digital Age*, ed. Alexandra Urakova, Tracey Sowerby, and Tudor Sala. New York and London: Routledge.
Stewart, Susan. 1993. *On Longing: Narratives of the Miniature, the Gigantic, the Souvenir, the Collection*. Durham, NC: Duke University Press.
Tigchelaar, Jana. 2014. The Neighborly Christmas: Gifts, Community, and Regionalism in the Christmas Stories of Sarah Orne Jewett and Mary Wilkins Freeman. *Legacy: A Journal of American Women Writers* 31 (2): 236–257.
Tomc, Sandra. 2019. Edgar Allan Poe and His Enemies. In *Oxford Handbook of Edgar Allan Poe*, ed. Gerald J. Kennedy and Scott Peeples, 559–575. Oxford: Oxford University Press.
Trollope, Frances Milton. 1832. *Domestic Manners of the Americans*. London: Whittaker, Treacher and Co.
Urakova, Alexandra. 2009. "The Purloined Letter" in the Gift-Book: Reading Poe in a Contemporary Context. *Nineteenth-Century Literature* 64 (3): 323–346.
———. 2016. Hawthorne's Gifts: Re-Reading 'Alice Doane's Appeal' and 'The Great Carbuncle' in *The Token*. *New England Quarterly* 88 (4): 587–613.
———. 2020. 'The Ghost-Book' and the Gift Book: Editorial and Marketing Strategies in Eliza Leslie's *The Gift*. *American Periodicals: A Journal of History & Criticism* 30 (1): 43–59.
Urakova, Alexandra, Sowerby, Tracey, and Sala, Tudor. 2022, forthcoming. *The Dangers of Gifts from Antiquity to the Digital Age*. New York and London: Routledge.
Zionkowsky, Linda. 2011. Clarissa and the Hazards of the Gift. *Eighteenth Century Fiction* 23 (3): 707–721.

CHAPTER 2

"Hints" for a Gift Theory: The Ideology of Disinterested Giving and Its Discontents

2.1 Three Theoretical Nodes

It would be difficult to write about dangerous giving in the nineteenth-century context without addressing in more detail the subject of the wholesome, benign gift, conceived of as "disinterested," "pure," or "true," itself in constant danger of misconception and misinterpretation. Indeed, the emergent commodity culture heightened the risk of conflating gift and merchandise, not least because in the nineteenth century the gift was invented as a new type of commodity, from gift books to Christmas gifts and Valentine cards. Attempts to purify the gift from the taint of commerce and to dissociate it from the market were to prompt general discussions about exchange, reciprocity, self-interest, and disinterestedness; another source of heated debate was the subject of philanthropy, which inevitably raised questions of hierarchy, obligation, and power. As one might anticipate, the dark side of the gift—the shadow of the perfect gift—was actively present in these and similar discussions, as were pseudo-gifts and cases of misgiving.

One of the aims of this chapter is to demonstrate that the gift as a concept was not altogether absent from nineteenth-century intellectual thought. While more usually discussed in the specific context of advisory literature—for example, behavior books that sought to establish norms of good manners and etiquette—the gift was an object of theoretical speculation in a number of works by American authors. This chapter focuses on three texts with theoretical implications: Emerson's "Gifts" (1844),

© The Author(s), under exclusive license to Springer Nature
Switzerland AG 2022
A. Urakova, *Dangerous Giving in Nineteenth-Century American Literature*, American Literature Readings in the 21st Century,
https://doi.org/10.1007/978-3-030-93270-1_2

Caroline M. Kirkland's "About Presents" (1852), and Mark Twain's ["Reflections on a Letter and a Book"] (1903). All three authors—including Kirkland, whose essay is representative of the mainstream sentimental "philosophy of giving"—do not take the concept of the gift for granted but problematize it instead. Each of the three focuses on the question of the gift in the specific contexts of Christmas giving (Emerson), everyday gift-giving practices (Kirkland), and literary patronage (Twain), thus addressing three major spheres where the gift was relevant as a social phenomenon. Brief and somewhat insubstantial, these texts nonetheless approach the gift as an abstract category, asking: What is the gift? What is the free gift? What is the essence of giving? While Emerson and Twain use individual cases as a springboard for speculating about the nature of the gift, Kirkland offers a systematic analysis of different forms and aspects of giving based on exempla. This distinguishes the chosen texts from advisory literature they (Emerson and Kirkland in particular) borrow from.

Importantly for my general argument, these three theoretical nodes allow me to trace the arc of the ideology of a disinterested gift or disinterested giving (Parry 1986) over the course of the nineteenth century, from Emerson's "portion of thyself" through Kirkland's "sentiment of the thing," arriving ultimately at Twain's half-mocking, half-serious (re)vision of what he called the "absolutely free gift."[1] All three, including Twain's postbellum text, which is at a temporal remove from the others, thus give us insight into the mainstream gift-giving ideology of the nineteenth century while illuminating its inner controversies and shortfalls; all three use the negative image of the gift as a means to highlight the concept of the free, disinterested, or morally acceptable gift and ultimately, presage certain twentieth-century lines of thought. In what follows, I will read these texts as hinting at a nineteenth-century gift theory, paraphrasing the title

---

[1] By bringing Emerson and Kirkland together in one chapter, I follow in the steps of Eric Leigh Schmidt (Schmidt 1997) yet my analysis goes in a different direction. Schmidt considers Emerson's "Gifts" and Kirkland's "About Presents" as the two polar variations of what he calls the Romantic understanding of the gift. (The Romantic gift in Schmidt's interpretation encompasses both "the poison in the gift" and "the promise of the gift," e.g., the ambivalence associated with gift-giving and its idealization). He argues that, on the one hand, there is Emerson who is skeptical about gift-giving in both his essay and private correspondence and, on the other, Kirkland who, together with female contemporaries such as Sarah Josepha Hale, idealizes the free spirit of the gift and sees gift-exchange rituals in a positive light. In what follows, I intend to read these texts in terms of continuity rather than contrast while accounting for their fundamental ideological differences.

of an early printed version of Kirkland's "About Presents": "Hints for an Essay on Presents" (1845).

2.2 "Thou Must Bleed for Me": Emerson's Revisions of the Sentimental Language of the Gift

Of the three texts mentioned above, only Emerson's "Gifts" (1844) is a recognized theoretical contribution. While "largely ignored by Emerson critics"[2] (Gruzin 1988: 44) due to its brevity and "light" tone (Richardson 1995: 400), this text has over the last number of decades secured its place in the foreground of twentieth-century continental gift theory. It has been included in one of the major gift theory anthologies, alongside the works of Mauss, Benveniste, Bourdieu, Derrida, and others (Schrift 1997), and has been the subject of serious theoretical commentary (Osteen: 13; Shapiro 1997; LeCarner 2014).

There are at least two potential stumbling blocks for critical readers of "Gifts." First, the essay is controversial. Emerson begins with advice about what to give for Christmas and New Year, then suddenly shifts to writing about the inappropriateness of gift exchange as such before ending by praising love as "the genius and god of gifts" (538). Second, the essay's "simpering clichés" (Shapiro 1997: 279) and "commonplaces of manners and etiquette" (Shapiro 1999: 98) appear to be "more appropriate to Miss Manners or Amy Vanderbilt[3] than to the author of 'Self-Reliance'" (Gruzin 1988: 44). It seems that to appreciate Emerson as a theorist in this essay, one has to separate his thought from his style, content from form. "If Emerson can sound like Miss Manners when he writes that 'Flowers and fruits are always fit presents,' the insight takes on another cast when we read it, *as we should*, against the background of Kantian aesthetics" (Shapiro 1999: 98, emphasis mine.—A.U.). But should we? Or should we rather agree that both frameworks—conduct/didactical literature on the one hand and transcendentalist philosophy on the other—offer us equally legitimate tools for interpreting the essay, written by a philosopher who

---

[2] Since 1988, the text has received significantly more attention in American nineteenth-century studies; see Schmidt (1997); Kete (2000); Litwicki (2015). However, its place within Emerson studies continues to be marginal, especially when compared with canonical works such as "Nature" or "Self-Reliance."

[3] Both Amy Vanderbilt and Miss Manners (Judith Martin) were twentieth-century American authors writing on etiquette.

himself was more "edifying" than "systematic" (Rorty; qtd. in Cromphout 1999: 159)?

Following Richard Poirier, who claims that "the Emersonian individual exists ... in continuous struggle with the language by which it tries to get expressed" (Poirier 1992: 68), I argue that we should not underestimate the embeddedness of "Gifts" in mainstream antebellum gift-related rhetoric. Not only does Emerson largely borrow from this rhetoric, he also contributes to its development (Urakova 2016). His theoretical insights in this essay are the result of his rewriting and revising of the sentimental language of the gift, a process that may be traced "at the level of the sentence itself" (Deming 2007: 52). We can see how his original concept of the gift develops in the gaps and in the margins of the mainstream discourse within which he operates in this essay. As Emerson himself claimed, "[t]he very language we speak, thinks for us, by the subtle distinctions which are already marked for us by its words" (1904: 502).

In discussing what to bestow for Christmas and New Year, Emerson comes up with a list of appropriate presents for these occasions. Flowers are "always fit presents" "because they are a proud assertion that a ray of beauty outvalues all the utilities of the world [...] delicate flowers look like the frolic and interference of love and beauty" (Emerson 1983: 535). Further on in the same paragraph, he refers to flowers as "sweet hints" of nature: "Who am I to whom these sweet hints are addressed?" (525). Flowers, "breathing love in each tone" and speaking "a sweet language" (Osgood 1836: 233), were common motifs in poetry and fiction. Florilegia and flower albums were at the peak of their vogue in the 1840s, as were gift books, many of which had floral-inspired titles. The flower's ephemeral, transient character makes it a pure, almost verbal, sign or token, of affection. At the same time, one can keep and treasure the flower as a souvenir (a dried rose or a clover) or take care of it (a living plant).

Commenting on "Gifts," Gustav von Cropmhout states that "the essential role of flower is to embody beauty and since beauty eclipses utilitarian values, flowers are *essentially* useless" (Cromphout 101, emphasis in original). While this assertion reads as truly Kantian,[4] we frequently encounter similar statements in sentimental fiction. For example, in

---

[4] There is an apparent congruence between the Kantian and Emersonian visions if we consider the following statement from the *Critique of Judgment*: "Flowers, free designs, lines aimlessly intertwined and called foliage: these have no significance, depend on no determinate concept, and yet we like them" (qtd in Shapiro 1999: 103).

Harriet Beecher Stowe's short story "The Tea Rose" (1842), a female character, herself bearing a floral name—Florence—gives a "useless" gift of a beautiful tea rose to a seamstress instead of "something *useful*—a bushel of potatoes, a ham, and such things" (Stowe 1855a: 92, emphasis in original). "Why, certainly, potatoes and ham must be supplied; but, having ministered to the first and most craving wants, why not add any other little pleasures or gratifications we may have it in our power to bestow?" (92) As "sweet hints" or "little pleasures," flowers come as close as possible to the notion of the gratuitous, pure gift—being, unlike jewelry, a legitimate and innocent form of luxury.

In counterpoising flowers to jewels, those "apologies for gifts" (Emerson 1983: 536), Emerson succumbs to another rhetorical convention—a typically sentimental disjunction between "a simple flower" and "a cold jewel." Jewels are justifiable as sentimental gifts only in a figurative, metaphorical sense (a gem of a poem) or as tokens (a ring with an engraved forget-me-not or a locket containing a miniature portrait). The authors of behavior manuals usually list jewels among the presents they deem inappropriate, in this case, because of their cost: "To present a young lady with an article of jewelry ... ought to be regarded as an offence, rather than compliment" (Leslie 1853: 180–181). Jewels as gifts connote satiety and insincerity. In another piece by Stowe, "Christmas Story; or, The Good Fairy" (1850), a character is advised against buying her mamma a "hard, cold, glittering ring, that now cheers nobody, and means nothing, that you give because you must, and she takes because she must" (Stowe 1855b: 218). In similar terms, Emerson claims that it is "a cold, lifeless business when you go to the shops to buy me something, which does not represent your life and talent, but a goldsmith's" (Emerson 1983: 536). In the gifting of gems, he makes an exception for the goldsmith, the miner, and the sailor; the problem is not with the gems or jewels per se but in the commercial relations they incur.

The opposition of "commercial" versus "handmade" gift is another common binary in both conduct literature and sentimental fiction. The handmade present, like a flower or fruit cultivated in and picked from the garden, does not have the taint of the market upon it. It is more closely associated with the giver, expressing her personality as well as representing a personal contribution and effort; "the recognition of such associations was essential in a society still ostensibly wary of mass commercialization in commemorating personal relationships" (Dickinson 1996: 57).[5] In the second paragraph of "Gifts," Emerson aligns himself with this way of thinking: "we might convey to some person that which properly belonged to his character, and was easily associated with him in thought ... Therefore the poet brings his poem; the shepherd, his lamb; the farmer, corn; the miner, a gem; the sailor, coral and shells; the painter, his picture; the girl, a handkerchief of her own sewing" (Emerson 1983: 536).

There is a clear gender division in the cited passage: the girl alone is defined by her sex and not by her profession. The girl offers the gift of a handkerchief—the commonest handmade present—not because she is a seamstress but because sewing and embroidery was a common female occupation. This passage, which echoes the statement from Eliza Leslie's *Behaviour Book* (1834) that appropriate gifts are "things that derive their chief value from associations" (Leslie 1853: 181), was to further contribute to the context of gentility and good manners in gift-giving. For example, Samuel Roberts Wells, author of an antebellum behavior manual entitled *How to Behave: A Pocket Manual for Republican Etiquette, and Guide to Correct Personal Habits* (1856), not only extensively quotes ad verbatim from Emerson but also paraphrases him. While gentlemen are allowed to give commercial, albeit inexpensive, presents to ladies, gifts made by ladies to gentlemen "should be little articles not purchased but deriving a priceless value as being the offspring of their gentle skill: a little picture from their pencil or a trifle from their needle" (Wells 1872: 82). "A trifle from their needle" is a replica of Emerson's "handkerchief of her own sewing" presented by a girl. The example from Wells demonstrates that Emerson's essay was easily adapted to the needs of the advisory literature about the gift that was built upon gender conventions of the time.

In the same paragraph, Emerson formulates a pithy phrase that reads as an epitome of sentimental ethics: "The only gift is a portion of thyself. Thou must bleed for me" (Emerson 1983: 536). For Mary Louise Kete, this encapsulates the synecdochical nature of sentimental gifts: "such tokens of affection ... are actual vehicles or vessels of some essential quality of a person" (Kete 2000: 53). Kete also claims that "to give the self" is "possible only through the mediation of a synecdochically related subject

---

[5] Unless handmade gifts pursue self-interest or suggest a bargain. Eliza Leslie, for example, condemns young ladies knitting purses or working slippers for wealthy old gentlemen knowing that the "dear old man" would "reward them by a handsome present of some bijou of real value" (Leslie 1853: 181).

such as a tear, a lock of hair, or a verse remembrance" (54). In giving the gift of the essay and the gift of the poem that serves the essay's epigraph, Emerson is following his own advice.

"Thou must bleed for me" arrives as both the pinnacle of the sentimental discourse in Emerson's essay and as a rupture in its flow. Bleeding suggests the sentimentalist tendency toward transgression, liquid being a fundamental "affective principle of sympathy" (Elmer 1991: 109).[6] Yet the chosen verb "to bleed," evoking the image of self-sacrifice, seems dissonant with the placid discussion of Christmas and New Year presents that precedes it and marks the essay's turning point: the next paragraph brings in the theme of violence, antagonistic reciprocity, and "injurious patronage" (Mauss 2002: 83).

What follows comes indeed as a bolt out of the blue: "It is not an office of a man to receive gifts. How dare you give them? We wish to be self-sustained. We do not quite forgive a giver. The hand that feeds us is in some danger of being bitten" (Emerson 1983: 536). Emerson begins to read more like the "champion of self-reliance" (Osteen 2002: 13) than a partisan of sentimental tokens. In "Self-Reliance" (1841) he had expressed a deeply anti-sentimental vision of charity as that which "compromises one's identity as a self-reliant man" (Ryan 2003: 79). Here, expanding the scope from charity to gift-giving in the broad sense, Emerson's viewpoint comes across as even more radical: gift-giving is essentially violent. We are told that the debtor feels the urge to give his benefactor a slap and that the violence is reciprocal since giving is a usurpation that puts a debtor in eternal debt.[7] For Emerson, as for Mauss 80 years later, the gift *is* a debt, at least when hierarchy is involved.

---

[6] While "in the sentimental novel, what 'floweth' most of all are tears" (Elmer: 109), a bleeding heart was still its commonest cliché. In Richardson's (1986) *Clarissa*, a "bleeding heart" is mentioned ten times (390, 433, 958, 979, 994; 1101; 1220; 1337; 1339; 1372), in *Pamela* (2011), four (27, 117, 171, 229); in Brown's (1996) *The Power of Sympathy*, the first sentimental novel written in the United States, twice (41, 66).

[7] This idea would later be echoed in *Walden*, where Thoreau compares a benefactor with "that dry and parching wind of the African deserts called the simoom, which fills the mouth and nose and ears and eyes with dust till you are suffocated." He adds that he would run from such a person "for fear that I should get some of his good done to me—some of its virus mingled with my blood" (61). In Thoreau's (2008) interpretation of Emersonian ideas, benevolence is not only violent but also contagious.

Emerson makes an exception for the gift given between equals, which—like friendship—is the one true gift: "The gift, to be true, must be the flowing of the giver unto me, correspondent to my flowing unto him. When the waters are at level, then my goods pass to him, and his to me" (Emerson 1983: 537). He returns to the metaphor of fluidity when he describes the "true" or the pure gift exchange but only to dismiss such exchange as excessive: "All his are mine, all mine his. I say to him: How can you give me this pot of oil, or this flagon of wine, when all your oil and wine is mine, which belief of mine this gift seems to deny?" (537). Flowing unto someone that echoes the bleeding for someone in the previous formulation makes the very act of giving redundant and unnecessary; we are stuck with the choice between gift as an insult and gift as excess or surplus.

As Thomas LeCarner argues, "what Emerson has done here, effectively, is remove the entire concept of ownership from the gift exchange. If there is no ownership, there can be no exchange—there can be no giving of any 'thing' because the gift necessarily implies ownership and exchange of the thing given" (2014: 73). Removing ownership and exchange from the gift, Emerson pushes the idea of disinterested, selfless giving to its logical limit: if "all his are mine, all mine his," why give? A sentimental gift is a gift that is intended to be kept as the inalienable property of the receiver; the re-giving of a gift would be equal to its rejection. Emerson deliberately chooses examples of transient and "fluid" gifts (oil, wine) that merge the boundaries between the giver and the receiver, the two "flowing" their offerings into each other and thus annulling the "thingness" of the gift, without it ceasing to be material. Giving as conceived of as flowing or bleeding for someone may be seen as a process, an act of unity with the world, transcending the subject-object relationship limited by reciprocity. In "Love," while claiming that we "cannot approach [the] beauty" of roses and violets (Emerson 1983: 332), Emerson says that a lover "feels the blood of the violet, the clover, and the lily in his veins" (331).

In the last paragraph of "Gifts," Emerson suddenly returns to the rhetoric of sentiment and love:

> I fear to breathe any treason against the majesty of love, which is the genius and god of gifts, and to whom we must not affect to prescribe. Let him give kingdoms or flower-leaves indifferently. There are persons, from whom we

always expect fairy tokens; let us not cease to expect them. (Emerson 1983: 538)

Ironically, the essay's conclusion undermines the list of appropriate gifts presented earlier in the essay: if any gift is good enough as long as it is a "fairy token" of love, it does not really matter what is given—be it a flower-leaf or a kingdom. If love bestows gifts "indifferently," these gifts by default transcend the forced structure of exchange that, for Emerson, is rooted in self-interest and fraught with insult, violence, and debt. Yet the last paragraph also helps clarify why Emerson picks flowers as a model gift: just as oil or wine literalizes the metaphor of flowing, the flower, being a pure sign, has something about it that can be given but cannot be possessed. Likewise, in "Nature," he speaks of the land owned by Miller, Locke, and Manning: "But none of them owns the landscape" (Emerson 1983: 9).

Emerson's mistrust of gift-as-exchange aligns him with such twentieth-century theorists as Levinas or Derrida (Shapiro 1997, 1999; LeCarner 2014) while his interpretation of exchange in terms of power and violence anticipates Mauss (Osteen 2002). In revising sentimental formulas, Emerson eventually places the true gift beyond the relationship of possession and exchange and thus bridges a gap between the two centuries, providing modern intellectual thought with a missing link.

Emerson's theoretical insights in this essay are the result of the incoherent and controversial nature of his thinking, at odds with the fixed meanings and stylistic clichés that he, nevertheless, does not hesitate to use in exploring and expressing his thoughts. Caroline Kirkland's text, which I discuss below, is more coherent and is representative of what might be called the mainstream ideology of the gift. Its strength is in its systematization of gift exchanges and in its conceptualization of "the thing."

2.3 "The Sentiment of the Thing": Caroline Kirkland's "Philosophy of Giving"

The general tone of Caroline Kirkland's essay is, from the very beginning, more ambitious than Emerson's. Instead of advising what to give on any particular occasion, she seeks to understand "the essence of the presents" (Kirkland 1853: 91). There are two existing versions of the essay: "Hints for an Essay on Presents" (1845) as published in *Godey's Lady's Book* and

"About Presents," which was included in Kirkland's *A Book for a Home Circle* (1853). While both have been analyzed independently (Litwicki 2015; Schmidt 1997), they have not, to my knowledge, hitherto been brought together as I do here. I will focus on the second, revised and expanded, version but will refer to the first publication whenever necessary.

Caroline Kirkland is an antebellum author best known for her bestseller *A New Home: Who'll follow? Sketches of Western Life* (1839), which describes the household routine and experience of a woman living on the Michigan frontier. While this book received considerable critical attention (see, among others, Zagarell 1990; 1993: 153–155; Leverenz 1989, rpt 2019: 151–164; Floyd 2002: 124–140), with a particular focus on hospitality (Wood 2017) or consumption and material culture (Merish 1993; Maruo-Schröder 2016), Kirkland's shorter pieces are significantly less discussed. In these pieces, published in magazines and/or included in the author's collections, Kirkland touches upon subjects as diverse as fashion, hospitality, manners, reading, and writing. Kirkland was particularly good in the genre of small talk or intimate conversation that Sandra Zagarell and Janet Floyd describe using the term "gossip" (Zagarell 1990: 51; Floyd 2002: 131–132). What follows here is an attempt to restore Kirkland to her less-familiar role of "theorist," to use her own term (Kirkland 1853: 88).

At the beginning of "About Presents," Kirkland asks: "Cannot one give away the merest trifle, without suffering the insult of being *paid* for it by a 'present' ten times as valuable? And without the least disguise, too!" (Kirkland 1853: 88). She begins at the point that Emerson arrives at in the middle of his own essay: a pleasurable gift may very likely become its opposite, for example, an insult. The idea of the gift-insult as well as the erroneous contemporary understanding of what gift exchange means inspires Kirkland: she says that she "should have never have had half as many thoughts on the subject of presents, or half as clear an idea of it," had she not "been roused by this instance of mistake" (88).

Kirkland draws attention to the terminological obscurity of the word "present"[8]: "It is common to consider whatever is given, or appears to be given, as a present; but this is incorrect." The only way to understand the "true" meaning or essence of the present is to discredit its false semblances and "to bring good out of evil" (89). Kirkland's essay is a didactical text that relies on conduct literature to an even greater extent than does

---

[8] She prefers it to the term "gift" but, like Emerson, uses both terms interchangeably.

Emerson's "Gifts": a number of passages reproduce maxims on behavior and etiquette that were also circulating in antebellum guides. The "edifying" tone, however, does not prevent her essay from being simultaneously "systematic," to recall Rorty's epithets describing Emerson's work. The erroneous or misconceived, and therefore potentially harmful, instances of gift exchange that she describes fall into several distinct categories that I suggest classifying as follows: gifts bestowed with ill intentions; those with intentions incorrectly interpreted; those received in the wrong or improper way; and inappropriate objects of exchange.[9]

The biggest danger involved in gift-giving lies, for Kirkland, in confusing gifts with merchandise. Commodities mistaken for gifts become "a meaner sort of merchandise" (Kirkland 1853: 90)—meaner because they are disguised. In most cases, Kirkland refers to interested gift-giving, which includes: bribery; propitiatory gifts that "are offered with secret scorn, grudging and self-contempt … accepted, if at all, with still more debasing consciousness" (95); gifts offered as a bargain—"a dishonest form of traffic" when someone gives with the expectation to get an equivalent or a bigger present in return. Kirkland cites the example of a woman who bestows on her neighbor a turkey at Christmas and asks for a turkey in return the following year. The neighbor refuses because she believes that to offer one present in recompense for another is offensive to the giver of the initial gift. Among the errors that can be made in gift-giving is to pay back one gift with another. This return gift becomes "a cutting form of dismissal, as if one should say 'Now I am clear of you!'" (90).

Another type of interested gift is the one given with the intention of showing off, knowing that the gift will be exhibited and noticed. Kirkland disapproves of the vanity involved in birthday and New Year's presents, christening cups and spoons, and bridal gifts—*bijouterie* and *trousseau* (92)—the value of which is in their exposition. "Some gifts ought to be prefaced with, 'Know all men by these presents, that I, *A.B.*, am rich and magnificent,' if it were the fashion to be very candid" (92). Kirkland is hardly original in her critique of commercialized holiday rituals that encourage vanity. For example, Eliza Leslie in *Behaviour Book* disapproves of the fashion of "display[ing] all the wedding-gifts arranged in due forms on tables, and labeled with the names of the donors," which gives rise to the onerous "seeming necessity of giving something expensive, or at least

[9] Here I use the classification suggested in the introduction to a forthcoming volume on the dangers of gifts (Sowerby and Urakova 2022, forthcoming).

elegant" (Leslie 1853: 177). Sarah Josepha Hale makes a clear distinction between commodified and non-commodified gifts in her advice on how to decorate one's Christmas tree (qtd in Schmidt 1997: 78). What distinguishes Kirkland's essay is her underlying intention to clarify the term "present," which she does mostly through apophatic description, for example, by specifying what is *not* a true gift.

Another problem Kirkland highlights is that of misnaming and misinterpretation: not only do people wrongly identify as a present anything that is given as a present, they also make the opposite mistake. For example, Kirkland writes about "cynical people" who "sometimes sneer at birth-day and Christmas gifts in families where there is a common purse. 'As well,' say they, 'take money out of one pocket and put it in the other, and call it a gift.'" Kirkland calls such opinion "vulgar" (Kirkland 1853: 92). A mother unjustly scolds her daughter for giving a rose to papa because he could have plucked it himself. For Kirkland, the gift is justified not for its value as property (the girl's father already owns the garden with all its roses) but as a luxury (he would not have allowed himself to pluck the rose) and, most importantly, as a "pleasant memento" (93), a sign of love and care. Just as Emerson questions whether a gift exchange can take place if "all his are mine, all mine his," Kirkland asks whether one can be given a rose as a present if one already owns this rose. The answer is affirmative since the rose becomes a gift in the very act of giving, or rather the act of giving endows the rose with "giftness" (Pyyhtinen 2014: 59). This passage, which has the clear educational purpose of encouraging children to bestow spontaneous sentimental presents, anticipates the insights of those twentieth-century sociologists who were to examine the gift's unique status as a thing and an object of exchange as well as the relationships it builds or maintains (Kopytoff 1986; Pyyhtinen 2014).

For the same reason, Kirkland justifies expensive presents from rich people. Discussing the "art of reception" and maintaining that this is as important as "the philosophy of giving," she insists that even the costliest gift should be readily and freely accepted. "When we object to receiving [the present] *because* of its value, it is evident at once that the outer has outpowered the inner life of the gift, in our estimation" (Kirkland 1853: 100). Here she departs from the gendered ethics of conduct literature, which warned girls against accepting expensive presents from beaus and advised them to treat such offerings as an offense or insult. In Kirkland's interpretation, receiving becomes not only a question of good manners but also an altruistic act of acceptance, akin to free giving. Proper receiving excludes the sending of anything in return, as such reciprocity may "reflect suspicion of the mercenariness of the offering" (95).

While in this she is in agreement with Emerson, who does not deny "to the wealthy the highest pleasure of large possessions—the power of giving freely to those they love..." (98), Kirkland nonetheless describes occasions when such presents are inappropriate. The first of these is, as discussed above, when a present is an ornament designed to be exhibited and remarked upon, proclaiming the giver's wealth; the second is when an expensive gift is bestowed upon someone who already has plenty—in such a case, it becomes a superfluous, a sign of "disproportionate and capricious giving," inconsiderate of the receiver's needs. While agreeing that a gift should be useful, Kirkland is against giving something useful to the poor or inferior solely for practical or prosaic reasons: "O what a will-o'-the-wisp is that word 'useful' to conscientious people! Why must a calico gown or half-a-dozen stout pocket-handkerchiefs be alone useful to a poor girl? Has she no imagination—no taste—no heart—no pride—no affections?" Useful presents in such case become "unintentional insults" (99).

Finally, some presents masquerade as presents although they are not. "Vails" to servants should not be qualified as anything other than what they are, which is payment for a service. Gestures gifted in place of expected material help are harmful and misleading: the donor benefits from a feeling of "self-complacency, buoyed up, perhaps, by the sense of having 'given' something" (96). A philanthropist gives "a piece of advice" to a charity organization (96). A priest gives his blessing instead of alms, and the poor parishioner replies: "Thank you for nothing. I believe that if your blessing had been worth a half-penny, I should not have got it!" If such purely spiritual a gift as a blessing is given *instead* of alms, it becomes itself worth but a half-penny and may well be refused.

By contrast, the "true" present must be preserved from even the slightest suspicion or taint of commerce, of self-interest, or of self-complacency. The standpoint for Kirkland is one of benevolence, which she however does not address specifically. "Gifts of benevolence or duty" are the "most excellent" (except for the ill-conceived cases when a donor deploys the gift to exhibit her power over an inferior or expects gratitude in return). "They are offerings to God, and imply sacrifice and include utility." These three aspects: God as a third party, element of sacrifice involved, and utility—make charitable giving superior to horizontal exchanges.[10] In the first version of Kirkland's essay, gift exchanges come close to perfection when they are "altogether voluntary—pleasurable throughout—without alloy on each side" (Kirkland 1845: 29); in the second, they are "wholly pleasurable—voluntary—heartful—free—impulsive—without earthly alloy on either side" (Kirkland 1853: 99). Kirkland does not reject reciprocity but seeks a balance between giving and receiving (cf.: voluntary yet also pleasurable); these two acts must be free and independent. As sociologist Olli Pyyhtinen puts it, "as it establishes a relation, the gift also tries to free itself from all relations; while there is no gift that would not bind the donor and the donee, the gift also must be out of bounds" (Pyyhtinen 2014: 60). In a word, the logic of the gift is the logic of the paradox that Kirkland seems to have captured.

What would a perfect gift look like were we to think of it as an object of exchange or, in Kirkland's words, a "thing"? Early in the essay, she writes that "the essence of the present, properly so-called, consists in the sentiment of the thing" (91). Like the Maussian *hau*,[11] Kirkland's "sentiment" binds the giver and the thing given (it is the sentiment *of* the thing, e.g., the thing contains the giver's sentiment)[12] but instead of setting the gift in motion, this requires that the gift be kept as a memento. Kirkland's model gift, as she reveals toward the essay's end, is a keepsake: "The old term 'keepsake' is a most expressive term—genuine Saxon, and untranslatable. The French substitutes—*souvenir, gage*, etc. [in the first version: 'or whatever else has taken its place in modern days'; Kirkland 1845: 28]—are worth nothing in comparison" (97). In the first version of the essay, Kirkland gives the following examples of keepsakes: "the broken ring, the bent sixpence—the pocket-piece, of small intrinsic value—the book that has been used and marked—the ring that we have seen worn—these simple tokens often have a worth that no cost could give" (Kirkland 1845: 29). Revising this passage, she later omits the broken ring and adds "the precious curl or braid set in simple guise," the sentimental gift par excellence. The value of these items should be measured only "by the wealth of the soul" (97). In both versions, Kirkland retains the example of a spiritual

---

[10] Nonetheless, charitable giving and exchange often occurred together and shared common features: "both acts of giving acted as cathartic exercises in selflessness" (133).

[11] Hau (Maori term) is a force that binds the giver and the receiver.

[12] Schmidt draws more parallels between Kirkland and Mauss, for example, they both counterpoise the imperfect present and the idyllic pre-capitalist past where gifts were valued much more (Schmidt 1997: 79).

gift—the hymn-book bestowed on a bereaved mother with markings identifying particularly consolatory hymns—"received and treasured with a sensibility that showed how good a judge the giver was of a true nature of a 'present'" (97).

The keepsake is the perfect gift because in its very form and on its very surface it displays the "sentiment" it contains: "broken," "bent," "worn," "marked" are signs that the object previously belonged to the donor, that it was in use. Unlike the brand new commodity, the keepsake already has a history and a narrative; it speaks to the receiver. Not only does it retain the donor's touch, it also makes this touch physically visible. That which decreases its commercial value (as a worn or a broken thing) simultaneously increases its sentimental value. It is hard to imagine that anyone would give a keepsake as a bribe or out of vanity; an anti-commodity of a kind, it is likely to be bestowed only freely, with pure intentions. Another perfect thing to be given away is a living plant. Kirkland speaks of a superstition relating to a mimetic connection between a plant and its absent giver: "while the tree or flower lives and thrives, the absent giver and his friendship are in health and safety" (99). Advising against reading too much into this dangerous superstition—one cannot trust sun and shower—she does not altogether deny the connection: plants are "sweet parting presents" because of it (100).

Like Emerson, Kirkland believes in the importance of association: "Something so closely associated with a dear friend's individuality as to recall him inevitably, is a treasure during absence." And then: "What he gives is no more necessarily precious, unless it is something characteristic of him, and carrying a special significance" (99). However, for Emerson the true gift is associated with the giver's biography or occupation—give away what you produce not what you buy—while Kirkland's perfect present is related to the recipient's individuality and to her body, whether metonymically (keepsake) or metaphorically (plant). In other words, give what you own and what is dear to you. Emerson's recommended gifts are fragile (flower) and transient (fruit, wine, oil); Kirkland's keepsake or a plant is instead long lasting. While Emerson is satisfied with the gift serving as a pure sign of love, Kirkland wants the present to be kept, ideally forever, as the lasting presence of the absent giver. The concept of the keepsake explains her preference for the word "present." The present, this materialized "here and now," reminds us of the shared past and the giver's absence while simultaneously denying these. The sentiment becomes the essence of the present not only through the giver's disinterestedness and affection but also through the combined power of association, nostalgia, and longing on the part of the receiver.

Kirkland's essay systemizes sentimental ideas about gift-giving in a way that makes her own work a model study of the sentimental gift—a sentimental gift theory in utero. Not always original in her ideas, she takes a pioneering step toward the conceptualization of the present in breaking with mere didactical and instructional purposes. Her interest in the material side of the gift (the gift as an object or a thing) anticipates the work of those sociologists and cultural historians who were to predominantly work with specific, everyday "domestic" practices. Kirkland's essay demonstrates that the sentimental attitude to the gift is both idealistic and ambivalent as at its heart it tries to reconcile moral obligation and freedom, disinterestedness and ownership, thingness and spirituality.

2.4 Twain's "Absolutely Free Gift" and the Compromise of Patronage

Mark Twain's ["Reflections on a Letter and a Book"], an autobiographical sketch believed to have been written in 1903, is of interest in the context outlined thus far because it directly addresses the subject of free and disinterested giving in the postbellum and post-sentimental era. Twain was writing about gifts in a very different climate, in the Gilded Age (his own term) of the corporate capitalism, huge-scale investments, massive industrialization, urbanization, and commodification that were merely incipient in the antebellum years. "Both a sharp critic of capitalist excess and the virtual spokesman for a confused and contradictory middle class" (Lawson 2011: 365), by the 1900s[13] Twain had developed a particularly pessimistic view of what he called the "human race"; the all-pervading self-interest leaves little place for genuine affection or altruism.

The text by Twain that I discuss in this section is built upon a question: can a gift be free from the taint of trade that pervades all spheres of human life and, if so, how? For Twain, as for his antebellum predecessors, the gift, to be true, must be free and pure; in this sense, his autobiographical piece is a homage to the sentimental tradition he elsewhere mocked and satirized. (In Chap. 8, I consider in more detail Twain's ambiguous attitude

---

[13] Although his writing on "money and greed" ("central themes of Twain's critique of the Gilded Age") was a "lifelong project that commenced in his early journalism years" (Bush 2002: 60).

to and use of sentimentality.) Although addressing a theme of personal interest, and one that recurs in his other work written in the same period, Twain succeeds in simultaneously developing an ironic distance from this same theme.

The piece is written in the form of an unpretentious autobiographical anecdote: Twain describes how he received a letter from a stranger who had hoped to obtain an endorsement for a book that had he sent to Twain as a present. The recounting of this anecdote, however, leads Twain to theoretical speculation and to conclusions that I suggest can be seen as the radicalization of the sentimental ideal: there is no free giving when there is *any* exchange or reciprocity involved. Twain develops an asymmetrical ethics of the gift that echoes the Emersonian transcendentalist vision, although Twain approaches it from a different perspective.[14] If for Emerson the gift is by definition excessive and meaningless unless it is love's "fairy token" transcending the onerous structure of exchange, Twain sees gift-giving as a practice tainted and thwarted by human egotism.

The letter Twain receives is a seemingly innocent gift of a compliment; its forced humorous tone is "peculiarly depressing" because it does not cheer the receiver, who easily sees through to the intention behind it. The "depressing" gift recalls Kirkland's "most melancholy" propitiatory present that can never be accepted with due satisfaction (Kirkland 1853: 95). The Twainian example of the letter fits perfectly within Kirkland's "meaner sort of merchandise" subgroup. Unlike Kirkland, however, Twain believes that self-interest is a universal norm rather than temporary deviation: "we are all beggars. Each in his own way. One beggar is too proud to beg for pennies, but will beg a loan of dollars, knowing he can't repay; another will not beg a loan, but will beg for a postmastership" and so on (Twain 2010: 181–82). No human being is without mendicancy, Twain claims, and giving is a form of what is believed to be its very opposite—begging. Here Twain sounds almost Hobbesian: while for Hobbes, everyone is engaged in the universal warfare with everyone else (bellum omnium contra omnes), Twain claims that trade underlines every form of social activity—no one gives "something for nothing" (183).

---

[14] Twain's interest in selfless, disinterested giving in his late period is a counterpoint to his lifelong interest in business and speculation, which extended to the literary sphere as well. "More so even than most writers, Twain regarded his books as commodities to be marketed, and even his famous pseudonym registered as a trademark" (Sattelmeyer 2001: 89). At the same time, and despite his literary success, his attitude to money was "vexed" and "contradictory" (Wonham 2014: 1, 2).

In a similar vein, he compares a giver with a man who goes to the grindstone to grind his ax: the gift always comes with an ax. Even though the man's intention is to grind the ax, not to kill anyone, the ax is a telling metaphor, suggesting the forced, onerous nature of exchange: "He knows you framed your letter with deliberation, to a distinct end: to compel an answer. You have paid him homage: by all the laws of courtesy, he has got to pay for it." The receiver "cannot choose the way: he has to pay for it in thanks and return-compliments" (Twain 2010: 183). We are used to thinking about a compliment as something light and trifling that costs nothing and that is bestowed spontaneously and freely. Twain deliberately addresses this non-tangible or virtual form of the gift to prove otherwise. The gift does not have to be a costly item, such as a jewel, for trade to take place.

In most cases, a compliment is a calculated exchange, even though the giver may not be aware of calculation:

> When an audience applauds, it isn't aware that it is requiring pay for that compliment. But it is; and if the applause is not in some way thankfully acknowledged by the recipient of it,—by bow and smile, for instance—the audience will discover that it was expecting an equivalent. Also, it will withdraw its trade, there and then; it is not going to give something for nothing, not if it knows itself. (Twain 2010: 183)

Besides instances of public recognition (a letter to a writer, applause from the audience), Twain touches upon gallantry and courtship: "When a beautiful girl catches a compliment in our eye, she pays spot cash for it with a dear little blush" (183). Again, if she does not blush but shows "offended dignity," "she would get no more of our trade on those terms" (183). The market vocabulary that Twain uses profusely (e.g., pay, cash, trade) emphasizes that the seemingly innocent offerings we accept without question are in fact deeply corrupt.

In the same essay, Twain identifies one exception: a compliment given away with "no bill presented." He recollects that once, when he was 29 years old and was lecturing in London, he "received a most lovely letter, sparkling and glowing with cordial and felicitous praises—and there was no name signed, and no address!" A letter with no return address breaks with the pattern of begging-while-giving; it is an example of a rare disinterested gift: "I know it can occur as much as once in a century, for it has happened once to me, and I am not a century old, yet" (183). For Twain, the only way a gift can be free is for it to be given anonymously and unilaterally. Asymmetrical giving opens up the possibility of breaking with the symmetry of reciprocal obligations that can render gift-giving indistinguishable from trade: "It was all mine—all free—all gratis—no bill enclosed, nothing to pay, no possible *way* to pay—an absolutely free gift!" (183).

In developing the idea of disinterested giving (with due regard to Matthew's maxim on giving in secret; Matthew 6: 4), Twain affectionately returns to the memento of the anonymous compliment in his later *Autobiography*. Many years after the original gift of the letter, he repays his debt of courtesy to the anonymous giver by acknowledging the compliment publicly. We have no reasons to suspect that Twain is not serious in his sentiment; amid his skepticism, the letter offers tangible proof that giving freely is exceptional but possible. At the same time, there is little doubt that Twain is adopting an ironic or self-mocking tone. The use of sentence fragments, dashes, and exclamation marks makes the cited sentence resemble an advertisement or a sensational newspaper headline as shouted out by a newsboy. The use of synonyms is also telling. While for Kirkland "free" is synonymous with "voluntary," "heartful," and "impulsive," Twain equates it with "gratis," "no bill enclosed," and "nothing to pay" (183). He continues to speak ironically of the pure gift in economic and financial terms, placing it within the binary of "free" versus "paid" or "billed." The free gift is not free in the sublime sense, for example, untainted by "any earthly alloy" (Kirkland 1845: 99); it is simply something you get for free. The Twainian choice of words simultaneously desentimentalizes his own sentimental feeling about the gift of a letter.

Unlike the essays by Emerson and Kirkland, Twain's sketch does not draw from conduct literature; however, toward the end of the sketch, Twain adopts an edifying or advisory tone, claiming that "it is not right for a stranger to send me his book himself. Why not send it through B, and instruct B to say to me, 'Take no notice of this unless you are really moved to do it, for A is modest and sensitive, and he would be offended if he knew what I am doing'" (184). Ultimately, Twain advises the unfortunate author to camouflage his mercenary intentions so that the receiver feels less awkward and ashamed: "I have not earned this treatment, I have not done him any harm" (184). The latter will be more willing to find merits in the book in the absence of the weight of obligation held over him, and both parties will benefit from it. This is an example of Twain's awareness of the fact that "success in the modern literary market continued to be shaped by patronage and an emergent philanthropy" (Sawaya 2014: 102)—his homage to corporatism, as it were.

In a way, Twain's advice to the author is a step back but it is also an indication of his general pessimism. Twain also describes in detail how he dealt with the author of the letter begging for an endorsement. He replied by thanking the sender for the book, which had not yet arrived, that is, he sent his thanks rather than the expected endorsement. This set him free to read the book without putting himself under an "obligation of any sort" and though it was a "costly adventure" for him to read the book at the expense of other things he could be doing, he found himself unable to put it down until he had finished it. "It embarrassed me a little to write to the author and confess this fact, right on the heels of that courteously-discourteous letter which had preceded it, but I did it" (185). This way, Twain was able to give a "costly" gift (it cost him both time and embarrassment) of a compliment freely instead of reciprocating under the "ax" of obligation. Yet he immediately confesses that his gift was not free but bound with self-interest, being as it was a benevolent act of patronage: "Were you thinking I did it to give that author pleasure? I did—*at second hand*. We do no benevolences whose *first* benefit is not for ourselves" (185). Or rather, the free gift is not "absolutely free."

While Twain is trying to find a compromise between self-interest and altruism, freedom and coercion (let the other at least pretend that she gives away freely!), his ["Reflections on a Letter and a Book"] is a symptom of his growing skepticism concerning the purity of giving within a structure of exchange, even where the exchange is unilateral. Despite its seemingly insular, anecdotal character, the text has a broader theoretical appeal. Adopting an almost Socratic manner (a hallmark of his later essay "What is Man?"), Twain develops a fundamental hermeneutics of suspicion concerning the question of the gift, in what was to become a relevant tool in twentieth-century debates. From compliment to endorsement, the gift that is immaterial and therefore seemingly without cost makes us realize even more acutely that disinterestedness is an illusion. At the same time, Twain's critique of human duplicity—which he interprets in economic terms—is inseparable from a genuine quixotic quest for something "real," for example, absolute, non-commodifiable. As I will show later in the book, in this same period Twain was to discover a solution in the gift of death, the only true gift that breaks with the vicious circle of bargaining and commerce.

Fundamentally, the disinterested gift is an uncomfortable concept for a theorist. One of the biggest issues, especially for Emerson and Twain, is that exchange can be easily confused with barter, which entails self-interest and profit or incurs power relations. A related problem is that of ownership and value, and here we encounter a paradox of a sort. On the one hand, love (Emerson) or sentiment (Kirkland) is enough to sanctify a gift of any value; on the other, the pure gift is likely to be either handmade (Emerson) or used (Kirkland); this way its only value is sentimental, associated with the giver's biography or personality. For Twain, on the contrary, a free gift should be at least anonymous: any association with the giver would call for an acknowledgment that, in turn, would constitute reciprocity. However, even if the gift is non-reciprocal, it is still not free from self-interest; Twain's paradox of "the absolutely free gift" is one step removed from the Derridian idea of the perfect (impossible) gift as that which must not be "perceived or received as gift" (Derrida 1992: 16).

The idea of the disinterested gift, for all its utopianism, was to provide a strong theoretical impulse to intellectual thought, mapping out directions for future speculation and research. The texts discussed here demonstrate a complex or ambivalent response to this idea, which circulated in the form of an unambiguous cliché within the framework of sentimental culture and which the emergent consumerist culture was to employ for its own ends. We have also seen that whenever the authors discuss the perfect or the free gift, the image of its harmful or dangerous counterpart lurks. The language of dangerous giving—from Emerson's "slap" to Twain's "ax"—is especially meaningful. On the one hand, when you do not give freely, you are endangering either yourself or the recipient, or both. On the other hand, the idea of "absolutely" free and disinterested giving, once it becomes an object of reflection and speculation, itself borders on the impossible, with Emerson's flower, Kirkland's keepsake, or Twain's anonymous letter being examples of gifts approaching perfection. One of the ways to mitigate the dangers of improper, untrue, or unfortunate giving is pragmatic didacticism, which all the three texts exhibit and that, to a certain extent, serve to smooth over the inner contradictions. The chapters that follow will demonstrate how dangerous giving manifested itself in nineteenth-century fictional texts, keeping the sentimental theory of disinterested giving in view.

Works Cited

Brown, William Hill. 1996. *The Power of Sympathy*. In William Hill Brown, *The Power of Sympathy* and Hanna Webster Foster, *The Coquette*, 1–150. New York: Penguin Classics.

Bush, Harold K., Jr. 2002. 'Moralist in Disguise': Mark Twain and American Religion. In *A Historical Guide to Mark Twain*, ed. Shelley Fisher Fishkin, 55–94. New York: Oxford University Press, Inc.

Cromphout, Gustaaf van. 1999. *Emerson's Ethics*. Columbia: University of Missouri Press.

Deming, Richard. 2007. *Listening on All Sides: Towards an Emersonian Ethics of Reading*. Stanford: Stanford University Press.

Derrida, Jacques. 1992. *Given Time: I. Counterfeit Money*. Trans. Peggy Kamuf. Chicago: University of Chicago Press.

Dickinson, Cindy. 1996. Creating a World of Books, Friends, and Flowers: Gift Books and Inscriptions, 1825–60. *Winterthur Portfolio* 31 (1): 53–66.

Elmer, Jonathan. 1991. Terminate or Liquidate? Poe, Sensationalism, and the Sentimental Tradition. In *American Face of Edgar Allan Poe*, ed. Rosenheim Shawn and Stephen Rachman, 91–120. Baltimore: The Johns Hopkins University Press.

Emerson, Ralph Waldo. 1904. Address at Opening of Concord Free Library. In *The Complete Works of Ralph Waldo Emerson: vol. XI: Miscellanies*, 493–509. New York: Houghton Mifflin.

———. 1983. *Essays and Lectures (Essays: First and Second, Representative Men, English Traits, and the Conduct of Life)*. New York: Library of America.

Floyd, Janet. 2002. *Writing Pioneer Women*, 124–144. Columbia: University of Missouri Press.

Gruzin, Richard A. 1988. 'Put God in Your Debt': Emerson's Economy of Expenditure. *PMLA* 103: 35–44.

Kete, Mary Louise. 2000. *Sentimental Collaborations: Mourning and Middle-Class Identity in Nineteenth-Century America*. Durham, NC: Duke University Press.

Kirkland, Caroline Mathilda. 1853. About Presents. In *A Book for the Home Circle*, 88–102. New York: Charles Scribner.

———. 1845. Hints for an Essay on Presents. *Godey's Lady's Book* 31: 27–29.

Kopytoff, Igor. 1986. The Cultural Biography of Things: Commoditization as Process. In *The Social Life of Things: Commodities in Cultural Perspective*, ed. Arjun Appadurai, 64–91. Cambridge: Cambridge University Press.

Lawson, Andrew. 2011. *Mark Twain, Class, and the Gilded Age*. Cambridge: Cambridge University Press.

LeCarner, Thomas. 2014. A Portion of Thyself: Thoreau, Emerson, and Derrida on Giving. *Revue française d'études américaines* 3 (140): 65–77.

Leslie, [Eliza]. 1853. *Miss Leslie's Behaviour Book: A Guide and Manual for Ladies*. Philadelphia: Willis P. Hazard.

Leverenz, David. 2019. *Manhood and the American Renaissance*. Ithaca: Cornell University Press.
Litwicki, Ellen. 2015. Defining the Gift: From Emerson to the Gift Registry. *Americana: E-Journal of American Studies in Hungary* XI (2). http://americanaejournal.hu/vol11no2/litwicki.
Maruo-Schröder, Nicole. 2016. A(t) Home on the Frontier: Place, Narrative, and Material Culture in Caroline Kirkland and Eliza Farnham. *Zeitschrift für Anglistik und Amerikanistik* 64 (1). https://www.degruyter.com/view/journals/zaa/64/1/article-p43.xml?tab_body=abstract.
Mauss, Marcel. 2002. *The Gift: The Form and Reason for Exchange in Archaic Societies*. Trans. W.D. Halls. London, New York: Routledge.
Merish, Lori. 1993. 'The Hand of Refined Taste' in the Frontier Landscape: Caroline Kirkland's *A New Home, Who'll Follow?* and the Feminization of American Consumerism. *American Quarterly* 45 (4): 485–523.
Osgood, Fanny. 1836. The Language of Gems. *The Court Magazine and Belle Assemblee*, London. Vol. 8 (6), 233.
Osteen, Mark, ed. 2002. *The Question of the Gift: Essays Across Disciplines*. London: Routledge.
Parry, Jonathan. 1986. The Gift, the Indian Gift, and the 'Indian Gift'. *Man* 21 (3): 453–473.
Poirier, Richard. 1992. *Poetry and Pragmatism*. Cambridge, M.A.: Harvard University Press.
Pyyhtinen, Olli. 2014. *The Gift and Its Paradoxes: Beyond Mauss*. London: Routledge.
Richardson, Samuel. 1986. *Clarissa: Or the History of a Young Lady*. New York: Penguin Classics.
———. 2011. *Pamela, or, Virtue Rewarded*, ed. Thomas Keymer and Alice Wakely. Oxford: Oxford University Press.
Richardson, Robert D., Jr. 1995. *Emerson: The Mind on Fire*. Berkeley: University of California Press.
Ryan, Susan M. 2003. *The Grammar of Good Intentions: Race and the Antebellum Culture of Benevolence*. Ithaca: Cornell University.
Sattelmeyer, Robert. 2001. Steamboats, Cocaine, and Paper Money: Mark Twain Rewriting Himself. In *Constructing Mark Twain: New Directions in Scholarship*, ed. Laura E. Skandera Trombley and Michael J. Kiskis, 87–100. Columbia: University of Missouri Press.
Sawaya, Francesca. 2014. *The Difficult Art of Giving: Patronage, Philanthropy, and the American Literary Market*. Philadelphia: University of Pennsylvania Press.
Schmidt, Leigh Eric. 1997. Practices of Exchange: From Market Culture to Gift Economy in the Interpretation of American Religion. In *Lived Religion in America: Toward a History of Practice*, ed. David D. Hall, 69–91. Princeton, NJ: Princeton University Press.

Schrift, Alan D., ed. 1997. *The Logic of the Gift: Towards an Ethics of Generosity*. London: Routledge.
Shapiro, Gary. 1997. The Metaphysics of Presents: Nietzsche's Gift, the Debt to Emerson, Heidegger's Values. In *The Logic of the Gift: Towards an Ethic of Generosity*, ed. Alan D. Schrift, 274–292. London: Routledge.
———. 1999. 'Give Me a Break!' Emerson on Fruit and Flowers. *The Journal of Speculative Philosophy* 13 (2): 98–113.
Sowerby, Tracey, and Alexandra Urakova. 2022 (forthcoming). Introduction: Unpacking Dangerous Gifts. In *The Dangers of Gifts from Antiquity to the Digital Age*, ed. Alexandra Urakova, Tracey Sowerby, and Tudor Sala. New York and London: Routledge.
Stowe, Harriet Beecher. 1855a. The Tea Rose. In *The May Flower, and Miscellaneous Writings*, 89–98. Boston: Phillips, Sampson, and Company.
———. 1855b. Christmas Story; Or, The Good Fairy. In *The May Flower, and Miscellaneous Writings*, 212–223. Boston: Phillips, Sampson, and Company.
Thoreau, Henry David. 2008. *Walden, Civil Disobedience, and Other Writings* (Norton Critical Editions). New York: Norton.
Twain, Mark. 2010. Scraps for my Autobiography [Reflections on a Letter and a Book]. In Twain, Mark, *Autobiography*, ed. Harriet E. Smith, Benjamin Griffin, et al. Vol. 1, 181–185. Berkeley: University of California Press.
Urakova, Alexandra. 2016. 'Subtle Distinctions': Emerson's 'Gifts' and Sentimental Rhetoric of Gift-Giving. *Revista Anglo-Saxonica* 3 (12): 245–269.
Wells, Samuel Roberts. 1872. *How to Behave: A Pocket Manual for Republican Etiquette, and Guide to Correct Personal Habits…* New York: Wells.
Wonham, Henry B. 2014. Introduction: Mark Twain and Economy. *American Literary Realism* 47 (1): 1–3.
Wood, Michelle Gaffner. 2017. 'I was in a Fidget to know where we could possibly sleep': Antebellum Hospitality on the Margins of Nation in Caroline Kirkland's *A New Home. Who'll Follow?* and Eliza Farnham's *Life in Prairie Land*. In *Anglo-American Travelers and the Hotel Experience in Nineteenth-Century Literature: Nation, Hospitality, Travel Writing*, ed. Monika M. Elbert and Susanne Schmid. London and New York: Routledge.
Zagarell, Sandra A. 1990. Introduction. In *A New Home, Who'll Follow? Glimpses of Western Life by Mrs. Mary Clavers, An Actual Settler*. xi–xliv. New Brunswick, NJ: Rutgers University Press.
———. 1993. 'America' as Community in Three Antebellum Village Sketches. In *The (Other) American Traditions: Nineteenth-Century Women Writers*, ed. Joyce W. Warren, 143–163. New Brunswick, NJ: Rutgers University Press.

CHAPTER 3

Sentimental Potlatch and the Making of the Nation

3.1 POTLATCH AND SENTIMENTAL POTLATCH: DEFINING THE TERM

The history of thinking about gifts as free from reciprocity or payment is closely intertwined with fictional narratives of colonial history and of the interracial communication between colonists and the indigenous population. Authors of frontier novels inherited the Rousseauvian image of the noble savage[1] and promoted a highly poeticized and romanticized "cult of the Vanishing Indian," wedded with the idea of sublime, disinterested sacrifice.[2] At the same time, interracial relations were commonly represented as continuous warfare: violent exchange of blows as a form of antagonistic exchange.[3] The native either generously gives away his land

---

[1] Harry Liebersohn also demonstrates how the selfless savage was counterpoised to the European driven by self-interest in the late eighteenth and nineteenth-century theories of primitive communism; see Liebersohn 2011: 61-95.

[2] The literature on the subject is exhaustive. To name some classic studies only: Fiedler 1968; Slotkin 1973; Berkhofer Jr.1978.

[3] For example, Nina Baym writing about frontier fiction of the 1820s states that "the stories mainly saw Indians as unalterably hostile to whites, unwilling to coexist with or assimilate to white civilization" (Baym 1992: 67). Mark Niemeyer argues that "positive—and romanticized—images of Native Americans began to make their appearance in literary works of the United States" only "around the middle of the second decade of the nineteenth-century." Niemeyer 2015: 1.

© The Author(s), under exclusive license to Springer Nature Switzerland AG 2022
A. Urakova, *Dangerous Giving in Nineteenth-Century American Literature*, American Literature Readings in the 21st Century, https://doi.org/10.1007/978-3-030-93270-1_3

and his life[4] or forcefully takes lives, engaging the white antagonist in competitive and exhausting circle of reciprocal bloodshed. He is either a superior human being who acts disinterestedly, driven by the natural inclination to goodness, or a non-human creature described as a "beast," a "demon," an "incubus," or else a "thief" and an "Indian giver." [5] In a word, the polarized image of the Native American in frontier fiction conformed to two patterns of social behavior—altruism and generosity or mercilessness and villainy, each corresponding with a different type of exchange relationship described in gift theory: unilateral giving on the one hand and negative reciprocity on the other.

Lydia Maria Child's debut novel *Hobomok: A Tale of Early Times* (1824) places the heroic and noble self-sacrifice of the Native American character, Hobomok, at its center. No surprise that *Hobomok* has been traditionally read as a novel about a native who must vanish, "nobly sacrificing his life and progeny to the rightful claims of the white race" (Brown 2001: 138). In this chapter, I will argue instead that Child's novel exhibits a more complex relationship between selfless, altruistic giving and interracial antagonism. Sentimental discourse serves here as a form of sublimation as it redirects and also disguises violent confrontation. Although replicating and blending the racialized binaries that lie at the heart of the frontier fiction of the 1820s, *Hobomok* shows a deeper anthropological intuition or sensibility than is present in conventional historical romances written by Child's contemporaries. In the overall context of this study, *Hobomok* is relevant as a novel that weds the idea of dangerous giving with the foundation of the new nation.

In order to capture the ambivalence of giving in *Hobomok*, I propose an operational term: "sentimental potlatch." This term derives from the

---

[4] From the mid-1820s through the mid-1850s, not only novelists like Cooper or poets like Longfellow but also ethnographers (Henry Rowe Schoolcraft) and historians (Thomas McKenney) "dramatized American Indians as people ... destined to die out if they remained unable to accept acculturation in the new nation" and thus supported the official policy of removal. See Sundquist 2006: 70.

[5] Merriam-Webster Dictionary defined the Indian giver as someone who "gives something to another and then takes it back or expects an equivalent in return." Albeit first registered in John Russell Barlett's *Dictionary of Americanisms* in 1848, the concept of the Indian gift/giver that stood behind this offensive and racist term was known since at least late eighteenth century, as described in Thomas Hutchinson's 1765 *History of the Province of Massachusetts Bay* and later in Meriwether Lewis and William Clark's report of their 1804 expedition to the West. Just as the noble savage and the bloodthirsty Indian, the Indian giver and the self-sacrificial native occupy two opposite poles in the antebellum racialist imagination.

anthropological concept of potlatch, a hallmark of Maussian gift theory, which describes a competitive, agonistic, and self-destructive exchange between two tribes—a "struggle of wealth" (Mauss 2002: 47) that may lead to depletion of resources and ruin. Potlatch in anthropology is the polar opposite of the idea of the sentimental disinterested gift inasmuch as it is the opposite of the Western profit-seeking exchange: you compete instead of gratuitously giving; you reciprocate the gift because you are obliged to do it. Maussian potlatch debunks the myth of the selfless savage,[6] demonstrating how the obligations to give, receive, and reciprocate underlie the mechanism of indigenous gift exchange in its excessive or extreme form. Sentimental potlatch, instead, is a hybrid construct that blends seemingly incompatible patterns—selfless, nonreciprocal giving on the one hand and competition, rivalry, or antagonism on the other. It seems a contradiction in terms; however, if we accept the widespread anthropological understanding of potlatch as "sublimated warfare" (Sahlins 1997: 88), it is in fact a step further in the same direction. Rivals not only exchange gifts instead of blows; they also replace fight with gentility, blood with tears. The suggested term serves as a lens to examine Child's original interpretation of the early American history, thus revealing the controversies of the national past by displaying the dangerous proximity of self-sacrifice and murder, generosity and violence, sensitivity and cruelty.

[6] It is important to mention, however, that Mauss himself has been long criticized for the generalized and utopian interpretation of the meaning of this indigenous ritual known in North America and Canada. For his postcolonial critics, potlatch is a token of the "Western imperialism and racism" that characterizes "the whole problematic of the gift, such as [we] receive it from Mauss" (Lyotard 2004: 106); on the critique of the potlatch concept from the poststructuralist and postcolonial perspective, see in Bracken 1998. On Maussian "Occidentalism," see Carrier 1995.

A different opinion is expressed, for example, by Ghassan Hagge who argues against oversimplifying colonial aspects in Mauss (Hagge 2018: 128-129). Though it would be indeed oversimplifying to say that potlatch is an invention of European colonialism and imperialism, it is likewise hard to deny that the Maussian model is embedded in the long-standing Western tradition of juxtaposing "primitive" or "archaic" and "civilized" or "modern" cultures.

3.2 The Poetics of Gift Exchange in *Hobomok*: Typology

For decades marginalized in the national literary canon, *Hobomok* is now considered "central to American literature" as it introduces themes and stylistic devices adopted by frontier romances that followed (Bergland 2000: 67). The novel takes place in the seventeenth century and describes the life of the early American settlers. The main character, Mary Conant rebels against her Puritan father who objects to her marriage with her Episcopalian lover George Brown. Believing her fiancée to have drowned, she marries a native man Hobomok in a "moment of derangement" (Child 1824: 170) and gives birth to the mixed-race son. When George miraculously reappears in the colony safe and sound, Hobomok physically removes himself for the sake of Mary, giving her a chance to reunite with her long-lost English lover and build a new life on the new continent. Conant gladly accepts his new son-in-law seeing her daughter's marriage with an Episcopalian as lesser evil than miscegenation. Hobomok's son takes Brown's family name and forgets about his descent.

Telling the story of frontier conflict as a love story and focusing on the female character and her feelings, *Hobomok* belongs to the hybrid genre of "domestic frontier romance" (Tawil 1998: 99; 2006: 92-128). A woman-centered novel, it challenged and revised the masculinist ideology of the male frontier fiction; especially this concerns Mary's "erotic plasticity," given "the ease with which [she] transfers her affections from Charles Brown to Hobomok and back again" (Baym 1992: 71). However, as Tawil claims, frontier domestic romances, along with the frontier fiction written by male authors, contributed to producing racial ideology or, as he calls it, a racial sentiment. Neither Child's early novel was free from this sentiment despite the author being "rightly known as one of the period's boldest and most uncompromising Anglo-American advocates for Native-American and African-American rights" (Tawil 2006: 98).

The novel, a historical romance, allegorically describes the making of America that entails a temporary union with the native, the native's removal, and consolation of Episcopalian church with Calvinism under the aegis of shared race and nation. A "New England story" told by an "American," *Hobomok* overtly participates "in the patriotic work of establishing and affirming national origins, characters, and values" (Bergland 2000: 62). The politics of the gift complements the novel's "erotic politics of nationalism" (Bergland 2000: 62): the "ritual of consensus" that crowns the novel[7] becomes possible only because of Hobomok's sacrifice. In its turn, this sacrifice is embedded in the exchange of gifts that involves Brown and Mary. It is also part of "the web of gift exchanges that make up the very fabric of Child's entire novel" (Hoeller 2012: 50-51) or, broader, of the "world of contract, exchange, and fraternization" that we encounter in *Hobomok* (Shreve 2014: 657). Therefore, before turning to the climax scene, it is important to speak of other gift exchanges in the novel. In this paragraph, I am suggesting a tentative typology of gifts in *Hobomok*—ceremonial, sentimental, and hybrid—at the same time showing that they are all represented as (potentially) perilous; gift-exchange rituals border on danger and violence, or gifts themselves have unforeseen fatal consequences in the long run.

Ceremonial gift is a term suggested by the anthropologist Marcel Hénaff, to distinguish traditional rituals of public and reciprocal recognition with modern forms of gift economy in market-oriented societies (Hénaff 2010: 107-155). *Hobomok* pays tribute to the ethnographic description of native ceremonies. It is remarkable, however, that the ceremonial gift-giving ritual described in the novel at some length ends in deadly confrontation. Hobomok refuses to reciprocate the present of his bride and violates the rules. His antagonist Corbitant, a "bloodthirsty savage" type, takes the insult personally, because the bride is his kinswoman: "…Hobomok asked that the child of Pokanecket might be his squaw; but his beaver skins were not brought, and she cooked the dinner for Ninigret's son" (Child 1824: 40). In the footnote, Child explains: "In an Indian courtship the young man makes a present of beaver skins, and the intended bride returns venison of her own cooking" (40). The bride cooks venison as a return gift for the beavers that Hobomok is expected to bring but never does.

The failed gift exchange leads first to the verbal insult. Corbitant says: "Hobomok saves his tears for the whitefaced daughter of Conant, and his blood for the arrow of Corbitant, that his kinswoman may be avenged." Hobomok reacts by lifting his tomahawk "in wrath": "Who dares speak of groans and tears', said he, 'to him whose heart has been calm in the fight, and whose eye winked not at the glancing of arrows?" (40) Since shedding tears is unmanly for a warrior, Corbitant's words are "insulting" (40) and must be washed away with blood. But "the Great Spirit loves not the

---

[7] As Susanne Opfermann argues using the famous term of Sacvan Berkovitch. See Opfermann 1999: 32.

sacrifice of young blood, when it shed in quarrel," as the old chief Sagamore John says, offering the two enemies a pipe of peace and a gift of the stories about "the days that are gone by" (40). Refusing the stories would have been "contrary to all rules of Indian decorum" (40). We should not forget that Hobomok, a mediator between his people and the colonists, comes to the tribe with gifts; killing a gift-giver is another serious violation of the rules of hospitality and diplomatic conventions; no surprise Sagamore John steps in and solves the conflict.

Using "almost anthropological details" (Hoeller 2012: 50), Child pictures a traditional society tightly bound by rules and ceremonies and simultaneously demonstrates the fragility of the order based on mutual obligations and reciprocity. The boundary between gift exchange and bloodshed is easy to cross. The example of Hobomok's and Corbitant's lasting conflict shows that the peacemaking effect of Sagamore John's hospitable gesture is temporary: Corbitant will not forgive the insult because, according to a widespread racial stereotype, vengeance is an "Injin's gift," as Cooper's Natty Bumppo would nail it in *The Deeslayer* a decade later. Gift-related rituals and ceremonies practiced by Native Americans in Child's novel clearly illustrate "a continuity between hostile relations and the provision of reciprocal prestations" (Lévi-Strauss 1969: 67).

Sentimental tokens that the novel's white characters bestow on each other have a different nature, function, and route. Given spontaneously and unconditionally, they connect the Old World and the New World by overcoming distance and replacing the absent giver. Such gifts have a tinge of melancholy: Mary's mother receives a prayer book as "a token of love" and forgiveness from her English father whom she will never see again. Mary also gets a prayer book from her beloved George Brown together with his miniature portrait. "Mary gazed upon [the portrait] till her eyes seemed laughing and beaming, in all the brilliancy of life, then turned away and wept that the mockery of the pencil had such power to cheat the heart" (131). Brown's presents both partially substitute the giver and function as signs of his absence: "And to you my dear girle, I sende what I knowe will be more welcome than anything but myself" (130).

Brown's gift of a prayer book plays an important symbolic and narrative function in the novel. It is a model sentimental gift, beautiful from the outside and the inside and, above all, charged with feeling. "Bound in the utmost elegance of the time" (128), it becomes one of Mary's most precious treasures and relics. At the same time, the prayer book contains a political message that makes the transaction political inasmuch as it is sentimental. "It was ornamented with gold clasps, richly chased; the one representing the head of king Charles, the other the handsome features of his French queen; and the inside of both adorned with the arms of England" (128). The double coding endows the gift with ambiguity: it is at once a love token for Mary and an insult, albeit unintentional, to her anti-royalist Puritan father. The prayer book eventually brings discord and becomes fatal for Mary and her lover. When the grieving Mary hesitates about her hasty consent to become Hobomok's wife, her father angrily seizes the prayer book and attempts to throw it into fire. Mary rescues the gift from flames but immediately after, leaves the house and entrusts her life to Hobomok. "That single act decided the fluctuating fate of [Conant's] child" (152). Of course, her father could not have possibly foreseen the grave consequences of his violent and unwelcome gesture but neither Brown could have known that his gift would throw Mary into the arms of the "savage."

Child shows that sentimental transactions are as potentially dangerous as the ceremonial gift exchanges albeit in a different way. The prayer book standing for the absent Brown represents his royalist, Episcopalian self that Mary loves but her father rejects and abhors. The sentimental and the political aspects of Brown's identity come together as the golden claps of the prayer book. Conant's attempt to burn the sacred relic as an attempt to eradicate the memory of Brown becomes an impossible trial for the sensitive heart and leads Mary to what the novel describes as a mad and fatal decision; the trajectory of the gift takes an unforeseen turn.

By hybrid gift exchanges, I mean interracial exchanges that combine ceremonial and sentimental aspects. In his letter to Mary, Brown mentions a pipe he is sending to Hobomok: "...I thoughte it mighte please him to knowe that I remembered him in the big island across the water" (130). The pipe is a token of remembrance as well as of friendship and sympathy though with a taint of racial superiority; calling England "the big island across the water," Brown mockingly imitates the native way of speaking as a parent would imitate the child's babble. While the meaning of transaction is sentimental (e.g., a token of friendship), the purpose of the given object is ceremonial: Brown sends Hobomok a pipe of peace intended for sharing during indigenous ceremonies. Ironically, Hobomok wants to use Brown's gift at his own wedding but Mary recognizes the pipe, utters a piercing shriek, and cries, "Send it away, send it away" (157). For Hobomok, the pipe has no sentimental value; for Mary, it is a memorable keepsake reminding her of Brown. However, Hobomok immediately understands his bride's feelings and, after the ceremony, buries "Brown's beautiful present in the earth" (157). He performs this ceremony because he believes that the pipe contains the giver's spirit and considers this dangerous for his marriage. Mary believes in the same thing when she keeps Brown's presents as relics and begs Hobomok to send away the pipe, feeling the pangs of remorse.

Just as Protestant Spiritism and sentimental "religion of feeling" would resonate with "West African religious beliefs introduced into slave populations" in Stowe's *Uncle Tom's Cabin* (Wardley 1992: 171), Child brings together sentimental spirituality and traditional animism, crosscutting racial boundaries. In each instance, the question of the gift is inseparable from the question of the giver's self. When Hobomok refuses to bring the beaver's skins to his bride, he refuses to give himself as a husband to the bride and her kinsmen. When George Brown sends a "splendid" (131), richly ornamented prayer book with royalist symbols to the Puritan's daughter, his Episcopalian self comes as part of the sentimental "package." When Hobomok buries Brown's pipe, he hopes to get rid of the ghostly presence of his rival but never quite succeeds because Mary keeps Brown's tokens and honors his memory. Hobomok's ultimate gift to Mary and Brown, the deer killed in a hunt, symbolizes his own "conveniently dead body" (Samuels 2008: 71).

The gift exchanges described in Child's novel whether they take place between the natives (ceremonial), the whites (sentimental), or between races (hybrid) are not set far apart. Rather, they mingle and complement each other[8] anticipating the overlap of the unilateral and selfless sacrifice, on the one hand, and agonistic exchange and competition on the other in the novel's climax scene. The examples listed above also demonstrate that giving may become dangerous in the following cases: when the rules of social recognition are violated; when the gift has a double or ambivalent message that may affect the third party involved; when the gift is a "portion" of the absent giver whose memory may pose a danger to the current relationship. The ritual may go awry; the sentimental message risks being misinterpreted; the well-intended token may turn into a haunting memory. Child's novel shows the author's awareness of the fact that giving is essentially a hazardous act and its outcome may be far from what is originally designed or anticipated.

---

[8] This logic to a certain extent corresponds with religious or broader spiritual pluralism in the novel. See about it: Sederholm 2006, Shreve 2014: 655-683.

3.3 "I WILL BE GENEROUS TO YOU AS I HAVE BEEN": THE BURDEN OF THE GIFT

In her reading of *Hobomok*, Nancy Sweet argues that Hobomok "evolves into so much exemplar of Christian virtue that for Child's characters—and some readers—he no longer plausibly resembles a Native American." Sharing the widespread critical opinion that "Child essentially renders Hobomok as a white man," she speaks of his sacrifice in terms of "martyrdom." Eventually, we get a Christianized image of the noble savage who becomes even nobler and yet remains a "savage" representing "the wild and untamable in America" (Sweet 2005: 120-21). There is no doubt that Child intended to show how Mary's tender influence and cultivation make Hobomok an even "better" "Indian"—an "Indian" who becomes "almost like an Englishman" (172). His son, the second Hobomok, will fully accomplish this goal by becoming a "distinguished graduate at Cambridge" (187) and moving to England to continue his studies. Yet Child never makes Hobomok baptize into Christianity, unlike his historical prototype. While she certainly bears on clichés drawn from frontier fiction, the question remains: to what extent can we call Hobomok a conventional figure of a Christian(ized) martyr in the guise of a Wampanoag chief?

There has been a long tradition of idealizing Hobomok. For example, in her now classical study, Nina Baym claims: "With his good looks, his high ideals, his romantic love for Mary, his excellence as husband and father, Hobomok is a perfect fantasy lover—at once romantic, sexual, and domestic—who puts in question adequacies and pretensions of white men" (Baym 1992: 71). Such reading certainly finds support in Child's text with its focus on Mary and her romantic attitude. At the same time, we should not forget that, as Harry Brown reminds us, "the formerly heroic Indian lover" takes advantage of Mary whose "dreamlike 'insensibility' during her three-year marriage to Hobomok even casts the Indian as an incubus, preying on a woman who in her 'stupefied state' is unable to resist" (Brown 2001:139). In this sense, *Hobomok* intersects with popular captivity narratives; Mary is a voluntary "captive" but Child makes heavy emphasis on her temporary "insanity."[9] The circumstances of Mary's marriage cast a shadow upon the otherwise noble and ideal character of Hobomok; they signal

---

[9] For example, a very popular captivity narrative, *A Narrative of the Life of Mrs. Mary Jemison* was published the same year as *Hobomok*.

Child's ambivalent attitude to her "savage" who at once appears tame and dangerous, selfish and sacrificing, violent and pleasing.

Hobomok's sacrifice, however, seems to outbid the controversies of his personality and transcend him far above other characters. Read in the patriotic context of the historical romance, his is a nourishing sacrifice for the growing nation. "Without his 'services,' America could not have grown as it did, [Child] insists," according to Hoeller. Challenging Carolyn L. Karcher's disappointment with the novel's ending ("Child ultimately succumbs to the familiar white fantasy that the Indian will somehow disappear," Karcher 1994: 32), Hoeller insists that Child "envisions gift exchange as a more fruitful, responsible, and enlightened form of social interaction" even if fraught with dangers for the givers. She aligns Hobomok with female characters of the novel who daily sacrifice themselves, suffering from the hardships of their marriages in the New World. "For Child, gift giving and its potential as a model for better citizenship are exemplified in both Native American and female culture." The novel counterpoises this marginalized culture to the mainstream selfishness and self-interest of "white, male characters" (Hoeller 2012: 65-66).

I find Hoeller's interpretation of *Hobomok* objectionable. Aligning Hobomok with female characters, she develops Karcher's idea that "the dichotomy of nature versus culture... associates the Indian with women, traditionally consigned to the outskirts of culture" (Karcher 1994: 28). However, the novel also emphasizes Hobomok's "manly" beauty (46) and character that make it hard to imagine him as feminine. Child is certainly sympathetic to the female characters, such as Mary's mother and Lady Arabella, who die because they cannot bear the severe life in the colony. Yet as we have seen, she hardly idealizes indigenous gift exchanges represented in the novel as chains of onerous and precarious obligations. In the abovementioned interpretation, white male characters monopolize self-interest as opposed to female and Native American disinterestedness. But Child is far from demonizing her male characters; even Mary's fanatical and stubborn father is a controversial figure, capable of relenting to his daughter's desires and of sentimental attachment to his mixed-race grandson at the end. It would be equally unfair to say that only white male characters pursue their interests in the novel. So does Hobomok when he takes Mary as his wife despite her confusion and bewilderment; so does Mary herself when she chooses marriage and survival instead of dying of a broken heart as expected from a stereotypical heroine of romance. Child's novel is original precisely because it both adopts and challenges conventional images, familiar to the readers of romantic narratives and frontier fiction.

Finally, focusing mainly on the exchange between Mary and Hobomok, interpretation of the novel in a gender perspective does not take into account the third party—Charles Brown. This character usually remains in the shade and interests critics predominantly in the status of Mary's English lover or, later, her authoritarian husband who insists they never talk about Hobomok. However, as the analysis that follows will show, the part he plays in the scene of Hobomok's sacrificial act, is crucial for understanding the structure and the overall meaning of the scene. The negligence of Brown's character in criticism may be explained by the traditional focus on Mary's character and the tendency to see both Hobomok and Brown as projections of her erotic fantasies and anti-patriarchal rebellion. We find this tendency already in Karcher's canonical study where she suggests that Hobomok and Brown "actually function as doubles, rather than rivals" (30).

> [T[he novel consistently links the two men to each other, as well as to its female rebels against patriarchy and Puritanism. Brown's very surname associates him with the "tawny" Indian—an association reinforced by his "dark, eloquent eyes." To the Puritans, in any case, both Episcopalians and Indians are minions of the devil, "the Black Man." Thus, Roger Conant calls the Episcopalian a worshiper of Baal. (Karcher 1994: 28)

While these and other affinities between the characters are compelling, it would be erroneous to assume that doubles and rivals are exclusive categories. As Romantic tradition stricken with the homosexual panic and obsessed with male-male antagonism illustrates, rivals nearly always double each other. In Mary's imagination, Brown and Hobomok complement one another: she grieves over Brown when married to Hobomok and keeps memory of Hobomok's "devoted, romantic love" (188) as Brown's wife. At the same time, their rivalry exists independently of Mary's sentiments as revealed in the key scenes of the novel including the discussed episode with the pipe when Hobomok both rejects the gift and symbolically buries the giver. The antagonism between the characters manifests itself most fully during their encounter after Brown's unexpected return to the colony—the scene that is central to the present discussion.

Hobomok is terrified of Brown's apparition as he takes him for a ghost. Brown who immediately understands the source of terror briefly tells the story of his shipwreck survival followed by three-year captivity and concludes by saying: "You used to be my good friend, Hobomok, and many a piece of service have you done for me. I beseech you feel of my hand, that you may know I am flesh and blood even as yourself." For Hobomok, however, "the certainty that Brown was indeed alive" was more "dreadful than all the ghosts that could have summoned from another world" (173). Brown calls himself Hobomok's "old friend" but "a strange mixture of sorrow and fierceness" in the eyes of the native makes him lay his hand upon the rifle, "half fearful his intentions were evil" (173). Brown's fear reveals his racialist attitude: he instinctively does not trust a "savage" whom he meets in the middle of the woods, their former friendship notwithstanding. As for Hobomok, after disclosing the "distressing truth" to Brown, he "[gazes] upon his rival, as he [stands] leaning his aching head against a tree; and once and again he [indulges] in the design of taking his life" (173). The encounter of old friends goes awry: one lays his hand on the rifle, another thinks of taking his "rival's" life.

It is symptomatic that Hobomok's sacrifice springs from violent confrontation; the generous act of self-removal replaces a desire to kill: "'No', thought he, 'She was first his. Mary loves him better than she does me; for even now she prays for him in her sleep. The sacrifice must be made for her'" (174). In his inner dialogue, Hobomok abandons the figurative "Indian English." Now he speaks as an educated and sensitive young man, "almost" an Englishman. One may argue that this shift becomes possible because of his three-year-long "sentimental education" with a "superior" white spouse. Yet, more likely, Hobomok becomes a sentimental subject the moment he adopts the sentimental tongue. The language of the sentiment is necessary to bridge the gap between the savage fierceness and the sublime disinterestedness, between murder and symbolic suicide. This is reflected in the narrator's comment that follows: "It recks not now what was the mighty struggle in the mind of that dark man. He arose and touched Brown's arm..." (174). Calling Hobomok the "dark man," the narrator again refers to his murderous thoughts. Yet instead of the blow, there comes a touch. Touching Brown's arm, Hobomok speaks of his own feelings ("the Great Spirit only knows how much I have loved her"), Mary's feelings ("the heart of Mary is not with the Indian"), and his plans to go to the West where the "red men" will dig him a grave. The return to the "Indian" dialect albeit touched with melancholy and sentiment reconstitutes Hobomok as a noble savage, the polar opposite of the bloodthirsty "Indian" he almost becomes.

Brown's response to Hobomok that has hitherto received little critical attention introduces the structural pattern of equivalent exchange that challenges the Christian model of unilateral sacrifice:

> "No," answered his astonished companion. "She is your wife. Keep her and cherish her with tenderness. A moment ago, I expected your arrow would rid me of the life which has now become a burden. I will be as generous as you have been. I will return from whence I came, and bear my sorrows as I may. Let Mary never know that I am alive. Love her, and be happy. (174)

Not only does Brown refuse to accept Hobomok's sacrifice but offers him an equivalent. "I will be as generous as you have been," says Brown as he suggests physically removing himself and giving up his love to Mary. The rivals who a moment ago were ready to kill each other now compete in generosity. Hobomok refuses to accept Brown's refusal: "The purpose of an Indian is seldom changed" (174). Reaffirming his decision to leave Mary and his son, he also pops up the price of his sacrifice that Brown will be unable to outbid: "For Mary's sake I have borne the hatred of the Yengees, the scorn of my tribe, and the insults of my enemy" (175). He reminds Brown that he gave up much to be with Mary: now he is sacrificing everything he has sacrificed for her sake. He also describes his own doom in darker colors. If Brown says he will bear the burden of his life and its sorrows in his homeland, Hobomok stresses that he "will be buried among strangers, and none shall black their faces for the unknown chief" (175). Finally, he speaks of his tears: "You have seen first and last tears that Hobomok will ever shed" (175). Tears clearly mark the shift from violence to sentiment. Instead of shedding blood, the character sheds tears even though, as we already know from his earlier confrontation with Corbitant, he believes crying to be shameful for a man and a warrior.

The sentimental potlatch, a type of exchange in which Hobomok and Brown become involved, implies rivalry and competition (the more I sacrifice, the higher is the price of my gift) and suppresses violence that nearly broke out. At the same time, the characters become sentimental subjects once they enter the territory of sentimental discourse; both talk about their feelings, sorrows, or tears, and ready to commit a selfless act of generosity and altruism. The object of exchange is one's own happiness that each is willing to self-sacrifice for the sake of Mary's well-being but ironically, Mary herself becomes an object of exchange, a spoil that each party generously surrenders; the characters are making their decisions on her behalf without asking her consent. We encounter a typical situation of homosocial rivalry where a female acts as an object of desire; here, this object has exchange value, its "price" being a happy future of one of the lovers.

Hobomok wins the competition only because he runs away, giving Brown no opportunity to reply. The noble savage is always physically superior to his white counterpart. Brown "eagerly pursued him, with intention of restoring the happiness he had so nobly sacrificed. But there were few of the swiftest animals of the forest could outstrip the speed of Hobomok." By withdrawing himself from the competition with Brown, Hobomok burdens his rival with the gift that the former is unable to repay. The gift *is* a burden to Brown as his emotional state clearly testifies. While Hobomok throws himself upon the grass in despair, Brown sits on the rock and thinks about his wretched fate: "Existence must now be as sad as those clouds which are so fast gathering" (178). He has to marry a woman who became a wife of the savage and now nurses his son in the Indian wigwam. He must bring up a mixed-race child and as we learn later, he shall not return to his sweet England because of the little Hobomok. The gift that Hobomok bestows on him demands sacrifice on Brown's part that has all the risks to deprive him of happiness and peace.

Finally, Hobomok's gesture makes Brown feel inferior. In the conversation with old friends Colliers who are genuinely surprised that he met Hobomok alone and lives to tell thereof, Brown says: "I have a story to tell of that savage, which might make the best of us blush at our inferiority, Christians as we are; but I cannot tell it now" (181). However, Brown never tells the story of Hobomok in the novel, as he prefers not to speak about it. Silence and oblivion become his means of coping with the everlasting burden. When Mary attempts to speak of the father of her little Hobomok, he interrupts her by saying: "Let's talk no more concerning this subject... The sacrifice that has been made is no doubt painful to us both; more especially to you, who have so long known his goodness; but it cannot be remedied" (186). Immediately after, he offers Mary his hand and suggests giving her child his name.

Brown who lost in the competition with Hobomok starts a new contract with Mary offering her marriage and adoption of the child in exchange of silence: "Let's talk no more concerning this subject." A couple of hours before, he was ready to give away his own happiness putting it on the same scales with Hobomok's sacrifice. Now that the sacrifice has been made and the gift has been accepted, he needs to get rid of his generous rival—the same way Hobomok tried to rid of him in the past by burying the gift of the pipe. Mary says that she can only repay her "debt of gratitude" by loving her son and Brown altruistically joins in. But Brown's gratitude has a dark side: obliterating all the traces of little Hobomok's biological father is a symbolic destruction of the latter: "His father was seldom spoken of; and by degree his Indian appellation was suddenly omitted" (188). Brown eventually defuses the burden of Hobomok's gift by repaying it but in a way that also eradicates the memory of the donor.

The one who loses in the competition eventually becomes a winner taking possession of both the woman and the land and living happily ever after. Just as Hobomok, a noble savage, never quite becomes an "Englishman" even though he speaks and thinks like a sensitive young man of the eighteenth-century sentimental novel, Brown manages to restore his racial "superiority" after he engaged himself in the potlatch-like exchange with his rival on equal terms, lost it, and suffered from being inferior to the former.

Tawil speaks of Mary Conant's race in anthropological terms of "essential and *inalienable* property":

> *Hobomok* thus constitutes the heroine's race as what anthropologist Annette Weiner has called an 'inalienable possession.' In her white subjectivity, the sentimental heroine possessed something which could not be lost, no matter what she did. If [Mary] Jemison's captivity had demonstrated that whiteness could not be taken away, Mary Conant's out-marriage showed further that it could not even be given away. (Tawil 2006: 114)

Brown's case is even more complex than Mary's. He gives his racial identity to Hobomok's mixed-race son together with his name, calling the boy his "own." As a result, the "brave boy" (Child 1824: 185) grows into a white gentleman and a college graduate. In this sense, whiteness is something that can be passed on or given as a gift; the novel radically emphasizes, ahead of time, the conventional nature of racial differences. By passing on his race to Hobomok's son as if repaying "the debt of gratitude" to his father, Brown simultaneously becomes engaged in the paradox that Annette Weiner describes as "keeping-while-giving" (Weiner 1992). Race remains essentially "inalienable" property of the white man that allows him to preserve the racial integrity of his family and start a new life with a new contract leaving the potlatch in the past. Brown's ambivalent generosity is, ultimately, a form of survival or, to use Hoeller's term—preservation, that converts him from the Englishman to the future American, a severe colonist who seeks to survive at all costs. Preservation as the polar opposite of self-sacrifice allows Brown to finally step out of the self-destructive and burdensome exchange. However, in doing so in this particular way, he also abandons both his national and sentimental identity, as if clasped together—the one of a loyal British royalist and the other of a romantic lover ready to give himself away for the sake of the beloved. It comes as no surprise that Mary secretly rebels against Brown's patriarchal power by cherishing the memories of Hobomok's love and devotion.

Sentimental potlatch that takes place between Hobomok and Brown at once reveals Child's racial prejudices and a more complex vision of the national past that distinguished *Hobomok* from contemporary fiction. A competition of generosity between two rivals is a better alternative to the warfare but it is far from being innocent or idealistic. The outcome is destructive for one of the parties and burdensome for another; consensus comes at the price of the donor's symbolic murder as the gift exchange gives place to bargain. Sentimentality, in its turn, discloses its masochistic elements and suppressive mechanisms.[10] Child's sentimental potlatch is part of the essentially controversial attitude to the indigenous nation in the frontier fiction but the novel is by no means blind to these controversies. Due to the ambivalence of his gesture, at once sacrificial and competitive, Hobomok's character seems anthropologically more truthful than stock Indian figures of frontier fiction. The novel also refuses to show Brown's fatherhood as a white man's benevolence; rather it reveals a more intricate dynamics of gift and contract, victory and loss, sacrifice and survival looming behind it. On the national level, giving is an alternative to warfare but it is dangerous giving implying suppression of violence, competition, and exclusion.

3.4 "Even American Ground is Occupied": Child's Exchange with Fenimore Cooper

This last section is an afterword that seeks to demonstrate how gift exchanges within the fictional world of Child's novel may have reverberated with actual or presumed literary exchanges between Child and James

---

[10] As discussed, for example, by Noble 2000.

Fenimore Cooper. I will argue that since Child viewed her own position of a debutant in the field of historical romance as precarious, she was willing to take risks in order to outdo such maîtres as Scott or Cooper. When projected onto the field of literature, giving becomes fraught with dangers of misunderstanding and misrecognition while literary debts might never be acknowledged.

Preface to *Hobomok* stages a dialogue between (presumably male) narrator and his friend Frederic who shares with the former his design to write "a New England novel."

> "A novel!"—quoth I—"when Waverly is galloping over hill and dale, faster and more successful than Alexander's conquering sword? Even American ground is occupied. 'The Spy' is lurking in every closet,—the mind is every where supplied with 'Pioneers' on the land, and is soon likely to be with 'Pilots' on the deep." (Child 1824: 3)

Frederic expands the metaphor by modestly saying that his "wildest hopes" have not "placed" him "even within sight of the proud summit which has been gained either by Sir Walter Scott, or Mr. Cooper" (3). Yet he does not surrender no matter how "barren and uninteresting" (3) New England history may seem and hands in a manuscript a couple of weeks later that the narrator approves by signing "Send it to the Printer" (4). As Renée L. Bergland observes, "it is notable that Child chooses the metaphor of occupied ground to assert her relation to Cooper, since the occupying of American ground is one of the central concerns of the frontier romance, and since Child's work emphasizes the indeterminate and uncertain nature of ownership and occupation in the American borderland" (Bergland 2000: 66). While her character Hobomok gives away his native land, the novel *Hobomok* claims the right to have a place in the fictional ground of historical and frontier romance. Frederic's humility notwithstanding, the military metaphor ("occupied ground") frames the novel with the theme of rivalry and competitiveness. Rather than acknowledging her debt to Cooper, Child's alter ego challenges his full ownership of the American frontier.

It is also noteworthy that in the "Preface," Child says nothing of her real source of inspiration, the review of the poem entitled *Yamoyden, A Tale of the Wars of King Philip, in Six Cantos* by James Wallis Eastburn and Robert Sands (1820) in *North American Review*. The reviewer, John Gorham Palfrey, also refers to Scott as well as uses spatial metaphors calling *Yamoyden* a landmark in American literature and claiming that "[t]he wide field is ripe for the harvest, and scarce a sickle yet has touched it" (Palfrey 1821: 484–85). Child's "Preface" registers a shift from agricultural to military metaphors and bows to James Fenimore Cooper who starting with his 1821 novel *The Spy*, challenged Palfrey's quest "to lay his scene here." Palfrey invites authors to cultivate the new fictional field; a couple of years later, this field or the ground is already "occupied." Even if climbing to the "summit" is unthinkable, the field must be conquered. In her recollection of the decision to write *Hobomok* under the impression of the *Yamoyden* review, Child also uses the language of impulse and ambition:

> I had never dreamed of such a thing as turning author; but I seized [*sic*] a pen, and before the bell rang for the afternoon meeting I had written the first chapter, exactly as it now stands. When I showed it to my brother, my young ambition was flattered by the exclamation, "But Maria did you *really* write this? Do you *mean* what you say, that it is entirely your own?" (Qtd. in Karcher 1994: 20–21)

The words "seized" (accentuated by Karcher) and "ambition" capture the competitive spirit that enkindles the "Preface." Seizing a pen as Alexander's "conquering sword," Child, in the guise of a male author, paved her way into the antebellum literary market. Considering Child's metaphorical language, it is very tempting to speculate that she, perhaps subconsciously, was seeking to outbid Cooper's frontier fiction by the originality of the story. She borrowed the topic from *Yamoyden* but also radically revised a conventional elegiac love-and-death plot. Predictably, "the subversive possibilities Child's innovations portended did not escape contemporary reviewers, who hastened to spell out the guidelines American writers would have to follow" (Karcher 1994: 33). The plot was the main issue for contemporary reviewers who called it "unnatural," "revolting," or a sign of "very bad taste." Karcher is correct when she argues that not the interracial romance as such was scandalous but Mary's "sexual freedom," a freedom "to divorce, remarry, and retain custody of her child." Hence, the contrast between the reviewers' "reactions to the interracial love plots of Child's *Hobomok* and of Eastburn and Sands's *Yamoyden*, which had avoided censure by punishing its erring heroine with death" (Karcher 1994: 34).

Although *Hobomok* remained a novel with a "defect" in the eyes of critics even after Child had gained an established literary reputation (Anon 1837: 77), it twice attracted attention of the *North American Review*, in 1824 and 1825, respectively, which alone was a success for a debut literary work. The author of the 1825 anonymous review, for example, gives quite a favorable opinion:

> We think this book has suffered much from the general prejudice against the catastrophe of the story, and that its animated descriptions of scenes and persons, its agreeable style, and the acquaintance with the history and the spirit of the time it evinces, has not received credit due to them. But we doubt not that it will be one day regarded with greater favor, and it is by no means of the same ephemeral class, with some other of our American novels. It will stand the test of repeated readings, and it will obtain them. (Anon 1825: 94–95)

"The catastrophe of a story," as the reviewer calls it, both attracted interest to the novel and nearly became a literary suicide of the young author, as being too radical and too scandalous for the contemporary literary taste. Child was pleased when her authorship became known: "Praises and invitations have poured in upon me, beyond my utmost hopes" (Karcher 1994: 38). Afterward, she would sign some of the works as "the author of 'Hobomok.'" However, the fame of the novel in Child's lifetime and long time since was nothing compared to that of Cooper's *The Last of the Mohicans* published in 1827. Certainly, unlike Child, Cooper had already been famous by the time of publishing his most well-known work, but his novel was also considerably more adapted to the tastes and expectations of contemporary readers than Child's.

Starting with Karcher, critics have argued that *The Last of the Mohicans* was an indirect response to *Hobomok*:

> Although we are uncertain whether Child and Cooper ever met, it is most likely that Cooper had learned about *Hobomok* and its author, since gossip from the Boston literary circles usually spread to New York City, where Cooper lived at the time. Moreover, in her preface Child modestly bows to Cooper and acknowledges his mastery in the field. (Opfermann 1999: 29)

As I argued above, Child not only modestly bowed to Cooper as Susanne Opfermann put it, but also challenged his "ownership" of the literary field. Cooper, on his side, never acknowledged his debt to the novel of the obscure author as Child was at a time: the interracial love story introduced by her in the frontier novel constitutes one of the two major plotlines in *The Last of the Mohicans*. The story of Uncas and Cora perfectly fits in the romance conventions that Child challenged. As it has been many times highlighted, the racial gap between the Native Uncas and the mixed-race Cora is not as big as between Hobomok and Mary. Cooper's characters timely perish and even death keeps them apart. Symptomatically, Cooper both romanticizes and trivializes the uncomfortable "catastrophic" story to make it readable. Uncas sacrifices his life for the sake of his beloved just as Hobomok but the sacrifice of the former, death in the battle, is a conventional heroic deed. Uncas, the noble savage, is engaged in the conflict with the "bloodthirsty Indian" Magua, whereas Hobomok's and Corbitant's confrontation is marginal as compared to his sentimental potlatch with Charles Brown.

If Child took a risk to compete with the maître, Cooper seeks compromise between the precarious plot and the literary respectability. He manages to preserve the plot and immortalize it yet at the expense of its radicalness. The chain of "gifts" initiated by *Hobomok* involves Catharine Maria Sedgwick and her *Hope Leslie* as well as Cooper's own *The Wept of Wish-ton-Wish*. However, what I want to stress here is that the unarticulated exchange between Child and Cooper in *Hobomok* and *The Last of the Mohicans* may be described in Child's own metaphoric terms of the fight for the "occupied ground." Child claims her right for the share in the field by opening a new frontier while Cooper restores his ownership by borrowing the plot and converting "the catastrophe of the story" into a conventional formula. Eventually, Cooper outbids Child in their potlatch-like competition of literary gifts, as it were, but he does it in reverse, by stepping back and suggesting a more conformist alternative. It is also noteworthy that Child uses military language framing her narrative—the very opposite of the sentimental language of the gift and sacrifice her antagonist characters adhere to. Violence borders on the sentiment, rivalry comes hand in hand with gallantry. Child's alter ego bows and leaves the "summits" to Cooper yet firmly occupies the American imaginary by forcing upon her readers the inconvenient fantasy of the national past.

As the analysis above has demonstrated, this fantasy is indeed inconvenient: Child, while telling the story of the nation-making as a peaceful consensus achieved through gift-giving, simultaneously leaves the loose ends of this consensus exposed. Giving originates in suppressed warfare; gratitude becomes a symbolic weapon that allows the white character to eliminate the presence of the superior indigenous rival in the realm of memory and discourse. The novel was originally published anonymously, with authorship ascribed to "an American." As we have seen, however, "American" is a loose and fluid category in *Hobomok*, constantly in the process of its making—or, in Hobomok's case, its unmaking. The American identity bestowed on the white settler is not a divine endowment or predestination but a gift of self-removal that a native man offers him in the course of the equal yet deeply miserable potlatch-like exchange. Calling the novel "Hobomok" and insisting on Hobomok's continued presence in the shared memory of the colony as well as in Mary's heart, Child's narrator seeks to repay the debt to Native Americans through acknowledgment, counter to the white character's policy of oblivion. To a modern reader, however, Child's tribute may seem less than compelling: ultimately, the narrative of gift-giving, no matter how dramatic and ambivalent the story behind it, obscures the origins of the nation, which lie in the military extinction and territorial removal of the indigenous population.

WORKS CITED

Anon. 1825. Recent American Novels. *North American Review* 21 (48): 94–95.

———. 1837. Art. V.—*Philothea, a Romance*. By Mrs. Child.... *North American Review* 44 (94): 77–90.

Baym, Nina. 1992. How Men and Women Wrote Indian Stories. In *New Essays on The Last of the Mohicans*, ed. Daniel H. Peck, 67–86. Cambridge: Cambridge University Press.

Bergland, Renée L. 2000. *The National Uncanny: Indian Ghosts and American Subjects*. Hanover, NH: University Press of New England.

Berkhofer, Robert Jr. 1978. *The White Man's Indian: Images of the American Indian from Columbus to the Present*. New York: Knopf.

Bracken, Christopher. 1998. *The Potlatch Papers: A Colonial Case History*. Chicago and London: University of Chicago Press.

Brown, Harry. 2001. "The Horrid Alternative": Miscegenation and Madness in the Frontier Romance. *The Journal of American Culture* 24 (3/4): 137–151.

Carrier, James G. 1995. Maussian Occidentalism: Gift and Commodity Systems. In *Occidentalism: Images of the West*. Oxford: Clarendon.

Child, Lydia Maria. 1824. *Hobomok: A Tale of Early Times*. Boston: Cummings, Hilliard & Co.

Fiedler, Leslie. 1968. *The Return of the Vanishing American*. New York: Stain and Day.

Hage, Ghassan. 2018. Recalling Anti-racism. In *Re-configuring Anti-racism*, ed. Yin Paradies. 123-133. New York: Routledge.

Hénaff, Marcel. 2010. *The Price of Truth: Gift, Money, and Philosophy*. Trans. Jean-Louis Morhange. Stanford: Stanford University Press.

Karcher, Carolyn L. 1994. *The First Woman in the Republic: A Cultural Biography of Lydia Maria Child*. Durham, NC: Duke University Press.

Lévi-Strauss, Claude. 1969. *The Elementary Structures of Kinship*. Trans. John Richard von Sturmer, James Harle Bell, and Rodney Needham. Boston, MA: Beacon Press.

Liebersohn, Harry. 2011. *The Return of the Gift: European History of a Global Idea*. Cambridge: Cambridge University Press.

Lyotard, Jean-François. 2004. *Libidinal Economy*, Trans. Ian Hamilton Grant. London: Continuum.

Mauss, Marcel. 2002. *The Gift: Forms and Functions of Exchange in Archaic Societies*. Trans. W.D. Hall. London: Routledge.

Niemeyer, Mark. 2015. From Savage to Sublime (And Partway Back): Indians and Antiquity in Early Nineteenth-Century American Literature. *Transatlantica* 2:1.

Noble, Marianne. 2000. *The Masochistic Pleasures of Sentimental Literature*. Princeton: Princeton University Press.

Opfermann, Susanne. 1999. Child, Cooper, Sedgwick: A Dialogue on Race, Culture, and Gender. In *Soft Canons: American Women Writers and Masculine Tradition*, ed. Karen L. Kilcup, 27–47. Iowa City: University of Iowa Press.

Palfrey, John Gorham. 1821. Review of Yamoyden, a Tale of the Wars of King Philip, in Six Cantos. *The North-American Review and Miscellaneous Journal* 12 (31): 484–485.

Sahlins, Marshall. 1997. The Spirit of the Gift. In *The Logic of the Gift: Towards an Ethic of Generosity*, ed. A.D. Schrift, 70–99. New York; London: Routledge.

Samuels, Shirley. 2008. Women, Blood, and Contract. *American Literary History* 20 (1–2): 57–75.

Sederholm, Carl. 2006. Dividing Religion from Theology in Lydia Maria Child's Hobomok. *American Transcendental Quarterly* 20 (3): 553–580.

Shreve, Grant. 2014. Fragile Belief: Lydia Maria Child's Hobomok and the Scene of American Secularity. *American Literature* 86 (4): 655–682.

Slotkin, R. 1973. *Regeneration through Violence: The Mythology of the American Frontier, 1600-1860*. Norman: University of Oklahoma Press.

Sundquist, Erik J. 2006. *Empire and Slavery in American Literature, 1820-1865*. Jackson: University Press of Mississippi.

Sweet, Nancy. 2005. Dissent and the Daughter in *A New England Tale* and Hobomok. *Legacy* 22 (2): 107–125.

Tawil, Ezra F. 1998. Domestic Frontier Romance, or, How the Sentimental Heroine Became White. *NOVEL: A Forum on Fiction* 32 (1): 99–124.

———. 2006. *The Making of Racial Sentiment: Slavery and the Birth of the Frontier Romance*. Cambridge: Cambridge University Press.

Wardley, Lynn. 1992. Relic, Fetish, Femmage: The Aesthetics of Sentiment in the Work of Stowe. *The Yale Journal of Criticism* 5 (3): 165–191.

Weiner, Annette. 1992. *Inalienable Possessions: The Paradox of Keeping-While-Giving*. Berkley: University of California Press.

CHAPTER 4

Un-Gendering the Gift Book

4.1 Gift-Giving in the "Era of Annuals"

Two years after the publication of *Hobomok*, American print culture welcomed *The Atlantic Souvenir*, the first national literary annual, or gift book,[1] fashioned after the British *Forget-me-not* and given away in the Christmas season. The *Souvenir* opened up an "era of annuals" as one of their most prominent publishers, Samuel Griswold Goodrich, baptized the period between the 1820s and 1850s (Goodrich 1856: 397) that witnessed an unprecedented number and variety of these elegant and "gaudy" books.[2] Throughout the entire antebellum period, annuals occupied an important segment of the antebellum literary market and played a significant role in promoting US art and literature, both male and female. The first products manufactured and marketed as gifts in the antebellum market (Nissenbaum 1996: 150), these volumes were to epitomize a sentimental idea of what "true" giving should be—pleasing, morally good, free

---

[1] I am using the terms "annual" and "gift book" interchangeably, following the practice of American antebellum authors, editors, and readers, though originally there was, strictly speaking, a "technical" distinction between them (Dickinson 1996: 54). On the generic specificity of gift books, see Urakova (2020b) and" (2020a).
[2] The vogue for gift books, published annually to be given away for Christmas and New Year, came from Great Britain in the mid-1820s. The vogue faded only in the wake of the Civil War, when gift books could no longer meet the public's changing tastes and compete with cheaper monthly magazines.

© The Author(s), under exclusive license to Springer Nature
Switzerland AG 2022
A. Urakova, *Dangerous Giving in Nineteenth-Century American Literature*, American Literature Readings in the 21st Century,
https://doi.org/10.1007/978-3-030-93270-1_4

of self-interest, related to building or maintaining sympathetic relationships—an idea that, often bluntly and crudely, is designed to obscure the commercial strategies of their publishers. Since gift books were often used in courtship rituals and largely targeted at middle-class female audiences, giving had important gender implications.[3] Contrary to Child's challenging vision of sex and gender discussed in the previous chapter, mainstream gift book literature brought readers into the placid Victorian world of fixed gender roles and genteel behavior—a "needlework world," as one turn-of-the-century critic ungenerously tagged it.[4] In this chapter, I uncover an alternative story of gender and gift dynamics in the pages of gift books, addressing three famous gift book publications penned by Sedgwick, Hawthorne, and Poe—"Cacoethes Scribendi" (*The Atlantic Souvenir*, 1829), "The Minister's Black Veil" (*The Token*, 1837), and "The Purloined Letter" (*The Gift*, 1844), respectively.

As fitting objects for the study of the modern gift and its cultural performance as well as of the material culture history of the antebellum period, gift books have been the focus of some critical attention. Existing criticism (Dickinson 1996; Lehuu 2000; McGill 2002; Jackson 2008, etc.) has largely viewed gift books from the perspective of cultural and social studies, with an emphasis on their material and visual aspects. This chapter instead centers on literary texts published in gift books and on how these might have interacted with the framework of these volumes, highlighting the largely overlooked[5] interplay between literature, gift books, and gift-giving. On the one hand, the content of gift books was miscellaneous due to a pragmatic approach to publishing whereby anything that could fill the space was bound into a volume. On the other hand, unlike other periodicals or anthologies, the annual kept its framework of a *sentimental gift* shaped by a peculiar book morphology as well as by recurring rhetorical and formal patterns. Therefore, synecdochically, every story, poem, or plate published in its pages was a gift for the reader. This peculiarity invites us to pay special attention to the self-referential or metatextual elements of gift book publications.

---

[3] Here I am referring to what I call a generic gift book while it is also important to mention that as the market developed, publishers began to fill in narrower niches by addressing specific and diverse audiences: abolitionists, temperance supporters, Masons, juveniles, and so on. Chapter 5 will focus on abolitionist or anti-slavery gift books.

[4] This assessment belongs to Henry A. Beers, a turn-of-the century biographer of Nathaniel Parker Willis. Qtd. In Moore (1994: 6).

[5] With the exception of some studies, for example, Rappoport (2011), or my own: Urakova (2009, 2016; 2020a, 2020b).

A typical or generic gift book had a recognizable appearance. Usually, it had gilt or varnished covers, luxurious—leather, or velvet, or morocco, or paper—binding, and a dozen costly engravings; often, it was miniature in size and came in an elegant slipcase decorated with a ribbon. "Gem-like," it looked like an expensive and exquisite ornament fit for decorating parlor tables (Dickinson 1996: 55; Thompson 1936: 1–2) (Fig. 4.1). Albeit not "lady's books" in the strict sense, these volumes usually tried to appeal to women's tastes, aiming at their target audience; "annuals' authors, editors, publishers, and artists all [presented] some form of the feminine in each volume" (Harris 2005: 622). Telling titles relating to souvenirs, mementos, flowers, or jewelry—common gifts from beaus to belles—added to the feminine flavor associated with these editions. Engravings often portrayed a woman holding or reading a book[6] or contemplating jewels and bouquets. Opening poems or mottos highlighted the romantic aspect of giving as did select poems and tales. As tokens of affection, souvenirs, and forget-me-nots, gift books developed their own, dense metaphoric and conspicuously gendered "dialect" of gift-giving and are intrinsic to the discussion of hierarchical gender roles in antebellum gift culture. Meredith McGill highlights this aspect linking gender hierarchy to the gift book economy:

> Generally purchased by men and given to women—often as part of the courtship process—gift books are situated at a pivot point between economic and affective systems of exchange. As they pass from purchaser to receiver, suitor to woman sought, gift books also need to be transformed from mass-produced commodities into another kind of currency, "tokens of affection" that will be rewarded by a return of the same. One site for this transformation is the engraved presentation plate that scripts a relation between purchaser and receiver even as it allows for the personalization of the gift. (McGill 2002: 34–35)

Such a view of gift books has been challenged by scholars who showed that gift book consumption was not necessarily determined by courtship and romance. As Jill Rappoport claims, basing her argument on Paula

---

[6] These images, not specific to gift books, are the variation of the passive female reader stereotype: a girl languidly musing over a book page. On the passive female reading in the Western nineteenth-century literature see, for example, Felski (2003: 23–56). Sush and similar engravings "promoted an image of the ideal woman as specular, as the object rather than the owner of the gaze" (Mellor 1993: 111).

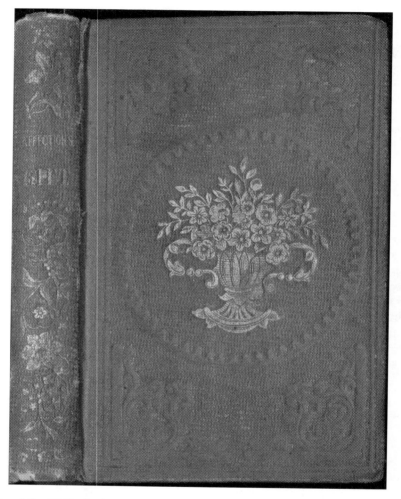

Fig. 4.1 "Affection's Gift." Philadelphia: Henry F. Anners, 1850. Library Company of Philadelphia

D. Feldman's study of gift book inscriptions (Feldman 2006), "annuals were not simply the objects of courtship they were once thought to be, and women were not merely their passive recipients" (Rappoport 2011: 19–22). In her analysis of Victorian gift books, both British and American,

Rappoport emphasizes female givers in gift book literature and the reading community built on the values of mutual giving.

These two approaches, however, seem complementary rather than mutually exclusive.[7] Gift books certainly were not "simply" objects of courtship rituals, yet we cannot not deny or diminish their role in antebellum courtship. Rappoport is correct when she states that *women*, as authors and editors, were largely responsible for the literary content of gift books; women formed the majority of the books' readers and owners. It is no surprise that they introduced the "ethos of generosity" in "an imagined network of gift-giving women" (Rappoport 2011: 22). Yet Victorian women on both sides of the Atlantic, as is well known, were not free from patriarchal stereotypes and heteronormative conventions concerning sex and gender. A good example of such ambivalence is a popular gift book editor and author, Eliza Leslie. Well aware of mainstream needs and demands of gift book marketing, she wrote didactic tales with a happy-marriage-as-a-reward plot, while some of her gift book contributions allow space for the new gift-giving ethos (Rappoport 2011: 22–23) or explosive self-irony and meta-reflexivity (Urakova 2020b: 42–62).

While building on the previous criticism, this chapter takes the third lead and proposes to focus on the transgression of gender boundaries in gift book fiction. The title—un-gendering the gift book—suggests that gender roles represented in gift books were not always as fixed and impenetrable as they seemed to be. By un-gendering, I primarily mean tracing how gift-related patterns circulating in gift books may have been withdrawn from their heteronormative context and re-used in a form of parody, subversion, or critique. While mainstream gift book literature sought to promote the idea of giving or receiving gifts as safe and pleasant, the texts I discuss below invert familiar patterns: a present of gift books becomes a "Pandora's box" that threatens the heroine's femininity and future marital status; a token of love and affection is replaced with a dark, mysterious, and queer symbol; heterosexual romance is challenged by a homosocial exchange of "evil turns." These instances may not necessarily explain the centrality of gift books to antebellum literature nor their appeal to the general readership, yet they invite us to look at the gender of the

---

[7] In a way, these approaches follow the logic of the long-standing "Douglas Tompkins debate" (Douglas 1977; Tompkins 1985) about sentimental literature (here sentimental periodical genre) being either conformist (e.g., Samuels 1992) or subversive (e.g., Showalter 1998).

gift (book)[8] in a new light. Revealing a darker, closeted side to the gift book's libidinal economy opens up an important facet of dangerous giving in nineteenth-century literature, one related to the protest, no matter how tongue-in-cheek or covert, against the gender normativity that genres such as gift books commodified and imposed on their readers. This perspective also allows me to expand our understanding of the gift book itself, long considered as little more than an "emblem of gilded sentimentalism" (Urakova 2020b: 44). In what follows, I suggest seeing the gift book volume as a heterogenous dialogic space where literary texts, including the texts that are now canonical in American literary history, interacted with each other and with the mainstream and commercial culture of giving that gift books represented.

4.2 "Pandora's Box": "Cacoethes Scribendi" and the Virus of Spinsterhood

A story "about writing for annuals, itself written for and published in one of the first examples of the genre" (Fetterley 1985: 3), "Cacoethes Scribendi" (the itch for writing), a renowned tale by Catharine Maria Sedgwick, belongs to the genre of self-referential gift book fiction. Self-conscious about their relation to the broader material/print framework and circulation, self-referential texts reminded the reader that she was reading a gift book—a book that is a gift from a beau, a relative, or a friend. Such stories, poems, or plate articles[9] contributed to the interactive spirit of the genre by including the elements of *mise en abyme* structure. For example, in Sedgwick's story, two annuals—presents of Ralph Hepburn to his pretty cousin Alice that he brings from Boston, "our literary emporium" (Sedgwick 1829: 24)—serve as fictional counterparts of the Philadelphia-based *Atlantic Souvenir*.

"Cacoethes Scribendi" has a conventional love-story framework. In the beginning, the village belle Alice Courland receives a gift from the only available beau, her cousin Ralph Hepburn; in the end, she accepts the hand and the heart of the gallant giver. In between these two events, the lovers, as expected, overcome obstacles to marital happiness. The obstacles in Sedgwick's story, however, get an unexpected ironic twist: the

---

[8] *The Gender of the Gift* is the title of the famous book by Marylin Strathern (1988).
[9] Plate article, a poem or a story, was intended to "illustrate" a gift book engraving.

troublemaker is Alice's widowed mother Mrs. Courland who takes possession of her daughter's gift that turns into a "Pandora's box" for the unsuspecting recipient (24). The box opened by Mrs. Courland frees the virus of "cacoethes scribendi" that not only inspires bad writing but is also believed to be a contagion of eternal maidenhood. What seems at first an unsophisticated narrative about the budding romance between Alice and her cousin becomes a story about the dangers of giving gifts and of reading gift books.

Critics have traditionally read "Cacoethes Scribendi" as a parody of amateur writing and publishing. Mrs. Courland *felt a call*, as Sedgwick ironically emphasizes (25), when she saw the names of her old friends as gift book contributors. The character's writing efforts may be described in terms suggested by a contemporary reviewer: "almost every body was an indifferent good hand at annual-writing" (Thompson 1936: 19). Or, as another reviewer put it praising Sedgwick's story, "we hope ['Cacoethes Scribendi'] will be read by every young lady ambitious of becoming an author" (Anon. 1829: 531). Exploring "what is the difference between the writing of Sedgwick and the writing of Mrs. Courland," Judith Fetterley rightly asserts that Sedgwick, a professional and acknowledged writer, satirized not female authors but bad female authors (Fetterley 1985: 5).

In what follows, I would like to go beyond this rather evident reading and look more attentively at the heteronormative patterns in the story in the context of gift-giving. Alice is a typical "sweetheart" of the sentimental romance, naïve, modest, and sentimental. "Poor simple girl," she sat down to read the annuals brought by Ralph, "as if an annual were meant to be read, and she was honestly interested and charmed" (24). A tongue-in-cheek comment on the volume's allegedly trivial content, Sedgwick's phrase *as if an annual were meant to be read* also refers to the common custom of using gift books as decorative ornaments and souvenirs rather than reading matter.[10] The gift book was first a gift to keep and only then a book to read. It is no surprise that Ralph chooses the annuals not for their literary merits but because they are pretty: "It was the season of peri-

---

[10] "Few people, including those who foolishly spend their money for them, read the annuals ... [A]s the happy custom still prevails of making presents at Christmas and new-year, these books are yet purchased and presented, though seldom read, even by the presentee." ... "Now an annual is bought to look at. No one ever thinks of reading them." John Sartain, *Sartain's Magazine*, 1 (1849); qtd. in Mott (1930: 421).

odical inundation of annuals. He brought two of the prettiest to Alice" (24).

However, although she is "simple girl," Alice reads the annual "correctly," or conventionally:

> Oh the prettiest story, mamma!—two such tried faithful lovers, and married at last! It ends beautifully: I hate love stories that don't end in marriage."
> "And so do I, Alice," exclaimed Ralph, who entered at the moment, and for the first time Alice felt her cheeks tingle at his approach. (24)

The gift book fulfills its purpose: the love-and-marriage story Alice reads in one of the volumes indirectly speaks about the feelings of the giver. The tingle she feels in her cheeks is a sign that the affection is mutual. At the end of the story, Ralph proposes to his cousin by allegedly writing a story for the annual to both please and tease his future mother-in-law. Sedgwick shows that the main purpose of the gift book exchange is making new couples: the nineteenth-century Paolo and Francesca fall in love reading (here: giving and receiving a book and discussing the fictional romance), yet both the book and the love affair are perfectly legitimate. The "prettiest" annual contains the "prettiest" story that is, in fact, the story of Alice and Ralph in utero and also perhaps, a behind-the-scene story of the *Souvenir*'s fair reader.

Alice's "correct" reading of the annual[11] is opposed to that of Mrs. Courland who interrupts the expected itinerary of Ralph's gift suggested by the story Alice reads. Mrs. Courland read the volumes "as perchance no one else ever did, from beginning to end—faithfully. Not a sentence—a sentence! Not a word was skipped. She paused to consider commas, colons, and dashes" (25). Besides the obvious irony concerning the naïve provincial perusal of the Boston-published annuals, this passage is remarkable as a description of transgressive reading practice. Mrs. Courland begins with examining sentences, then moves on to words, and ends up considering "commas, colons, and dashes." Whereas Alice elicits the only "true" meaning that the annuals contain for her—mutual romantic love and marriage—Mrs. Courland literally falls in love with the printed word. Attention to punctuation that has a merely ancillary function in the text

---

[11] On the ambivalence of reading in Victorian time and especially female reading as being both beneficial and dangerous, see Flint (1995); in the antebellum US, for example, Lehuu (2000: 126–155).

and all of a sudden becomes meaningful, overturns the privileged hierarchical position of the content. Decomposing the reading matter into disjoined elements, Mrs. Courland strips it of any coherent meaning and unbounds the contagious "itch" to write and publish. This scene resonates with contemporary fiction about the dangers of reading "intemperance," be it the Gothic frenzied perusal of the scary content or the eroticized solitary skimming of romances.[12]

Mrs. Courland's call is followed by an outburst of generosity as she shares her newly discovered literary "gift" with other unmarried or widowed villagers, converting them into a community of bluestockings. She makes sure that everyone is involved. Mrs. Courland "divided the world in two classes, or rather parts—authors and subjects for authors; the one active, the other passive" (29). When reading the annuals, she pays attention to the ancillary, marginal, and "meaningless" elements of the printed text. Her attitude toward reality is exactly the opposite as everything becomes meaningful and publishable: "There's your journey to New York, Ralph, you might have made three capital articles out of that. The revolutionary officer would have worked up for the 'Legendary;' the mysterious lady for 'The Token;' and the man in black for 'Remember me'" (34). *Legendary*, *The Token*, and *Remember me* are all names of gift books issued the previous year. The fictional world of the annuals transgressed its boundaries and expanded onto the external reality making it "beGemmed" and "beAmuletted," to borrow the ingenious phrase of Alfred Tennyson (Ledbetter 1996: 235). Ralph's gift books keep giving but in an unexpected way, changing the trajectory and endangering the future marital prospects of their original recipient.

Indeed, Alice is the only unhappy person in this carnivalesque,[13] exuberant world. Her friends tease her, calling her a bluestocking because they have "the vulgar notion that every body must be tinged that lived under the same roof with an author" (32). Two years later, in another gift book publication, "A Sketch of a Blue Stocking," Sedgwick debunks popular stereotypes concerning female authors. In the attendance of his mother's female friend, a periodical writer, the male character pictures her as a woman "with rolling black eyes, or deep-set gray ones, a nose like the tower of Lebanon, and cheeks ploughed with lines of thought, and fur-

---

[12] The latter example is anonymously published "Confessions of a Novel Reader" (1839).
[13] On the carnivalesque character of gift books, see Lehuu's Bakhtinian analysis of gift books, Lehuu (2000: 76–101).

rows of reflection." Furthermore, as he says to his friend, "it is absurd to be afraid of a woman, just because she happens to be a *mannish* writer of reviews" (Sedgwick 1831: 36–37). Writing and publishing in periodicals endanger the femininity of the author and decrease her value on the marriage market. When Mrs. Courland and her sisters send Alice's private diary to a periodical seeking to convert her into authorship, the "poor simple girl" has every reason to be horrified. Sedgwick refers to a contemporary prejudice about women's writing as an activity bereft of privacy. For example, Lydia Sigourney's husband asked his wife: "Who wants or would value a wife who is to be the public property of the whole community?" (Qtd. in Richards 2004: 65). A bluestocking is not necessarily a by-word for a spinster but a threatening image of the independent and emancipated woman, a "literary Amazon," lurks behind it. Not only does Mrs. Courland disclose the dangerous potential of the innocent gift (book), she herself becomes an ambivalent giver: while making happy her unmarried or widowed female neighbors by sharing her passion, she upsets and scares her daughter who would prefer to get married rather than becoming an author.

At the end of the story, a timid and well-tempered Alice rebels by throwing a periodical with her unauthorized publication into a blazing fire. The culprit, Ralph Hepburn, who brought the "Pandora's box" to the village, restores harmony and brings "remedy" not only to the daughter but also to the mother. By examining what Ralph calls "a true story— true from beginning to end" (35) that consists only of one sentence, Mrs. Courland goes through the reverse process and restores her "normal," socially accepted role: "Mrs. Courland read and re-read the sentence. She dropped a tear on it. She forgot her literary aspirations for Ralph and Alice—forgot she was herself the author—forgot every thing but the mother" (38). Unlike the excessive and transgressive scene of reading described above, we now encounter a more familiar scene of sentimental engagement ("dropped a tear on it"), more appropriate for both a loving mother and a gift book reader.

The unforeseen transgression of gender roles is easily neutralized by the social power of heteronormativity, and the happy ending re-enforces mainstream values of genteel culture and domesticity. Yet, Sedgwick's story, albeit ironically, implies a possibility of fulfillment, liberation, and plenitude other than sexual and marital, a possibility that opens up as an indirect and unintentional result of gift-giving.[14] Mrs. Courland ungenders the gift book by not complying the rules of its conventional reading, and trivial love gifts, at least temporarily, become "poisoned" with the virus of spinsterhood.

4.3 "A Simple Black Veil": Anti-token of Affection and the Androgynous Self

Hawthorne's collaboration with a famous gift book *The Token*, where he anonymously published many of his early tales, has long become emblematic of his "years of obscurity." Later in his lifetime, Hawthorne would speak about his tales as "rummaged out" "within the shabby morocco-covers of faded Souvenirs," describing "musty and mouse-nibbled leaves of old periodicals, transformed, by the magic arts of [his] friendly publishers, into a new book" (Hawthorne 1982: 1150). The young Nathaniel Hawthorne suffered from the commercial intention of the publisher, Samuel Griswold Goodrich, to publish many pages by one author while making use of established names such as Sedgwick's, one of the favorite gift book authors. At least until Park Benjamin's 1837 review in the *American Monthly Magazine*, Hawthorne's publications in *The Token*, 37 in total, failed to bring their author success or to endow him with a coherent literary identity.

It is likely that in hindsight, Hawthorne believed that his early publications in *The Token* had a "taint of the feminine" he wanted to get rid of later in his career (McGill 2002: 221).[15] His collaboration with *The Token* threatened to compromise his literary masculinity. For example, Margaret Fuller who read Hawthorne's anonymously published "The Gentle Boy" "in a two or three year old Token" sent by a "kind-hearted neighbor" together with "Souvenirs, Gems, and such-like glittering ware" attributed the tale to "a lady" (Fuller 1852: 220). Hawthorne's contributions to *The*

---

[14] Maglina Lubovich shows how Sedgwick elsewhere promoted a positive image of a spinster as an independent woman and a role model (Lubovich 2008: 23–40). While this is not the case in this story, we can nevertheless see that here the daughter's linear, doctrinal, and purposeful attitude is contrasted with unstructured, transgressive, and purposeless (except for the itch to write and publish) pleasure of reading impersonated in the mother's original reading habits.

[15] McGill writes of Hawthorne's "fiction of obscurity" as "a nationalizing tool, part of a large attempt to rid his writing of a taint of the feminine, the childish, the regional, and the foreign" (McGill 2002: 221).

Token invite us to reconsider his homage to sentimental culture and contemporary women's writing,[16] whereas his perhaps most famous short story—"The Minister's Black Veil"—slyly introduces the question of gender ambiguity or androgyny.

It is particularly tempting to recast this Hawthorne's story to the "morocco-covers" of *The Token*: even though "The Minister's Black Veil" was not—unlike "Cacoethes Scribendi" or "The Purloined Letter" I discuss below—originally intended for the annual, it curiously resonates with the gift book's title. A story about a material token published in *The Token* inevitably echoes the symbolic and metaphoric framework of the volume. The minister's black veil is a token in the sense of a material emblem or symbol (Hawthorne uses these terms), not in the sense of a gift or souvenir—quite the contrary, it is the minister's *inalienable property*, as it were. However, the story does raise the question of sacrifice and communality that, in the most perverse way, borders on an extreme form of social alienation. As the analysis below shows, the veil may be interpreted as Hooper's ambivalent offering to the community, the ambivalence manifesting itself on different levels, from its general symbolism to the more marginal but still meaningful "gender trouble" associated with it.

One day, Parson Hooper decides to cover his face with the black veil and refuses to remove it even when his fiancée Elizabeth begs him to do it or when, at the end of the story, he is lying on his deathbed. The veil dramatically alienates Hooper from his congregation and from the woman who loves him, casting doubt and shade on his personality: "No mortal eye will see it withdrawn" (Hawthorne 1835: 307). The meaning of his act remains a mystery to other characters and to generations of the story's readers. Samuel Coale partially summarizes critical interpretations: "The veil … has suggested a symbol for mortal ignorance, a false *signum diabolic*, a demonic object whose effects on the townspeople are such that its very presence vindicates Hooper's behavior" (Coale 1993: 81).

The only explanation that Hooper gives Elizabeth seems to obscure rather than clarify the matter: "this veil is a type or symbol, and I am bound to wear it ever, both in light and darkness, in solitude and before the gaze of multitudes, and as with strangers, so with my familiar friends" (Hawthorne 1835: 312). J. Hillis Miller rephrases Hooper's dialogue with his fiancée as follows.

---

[16] See my lengthy discussion of this in Urakova (2016).

He tells his fiancée Elizabeth that "this veil is a type and symbol," but when she asks in effect the natural next question, "Type and symbol of what?" or rather, to be specific, asks, "What grievous affection hath befallen you ... that you should darken your eyes forever?", he answers only in riddles and enigmas. He speaks in terms of "if" and "perhaps." (Miller 1991: 69)

By contrast, the message of the gift books was at once transparent and translatable. In the volume for 1829, *The Token* published the presentation poem entitled "Gift."

> I come with a gift. 'Tis a simple flower,
> That perhaps may wile a weary hour,
> And a spirit within a magic weaves.
> That may touch your heart from its simple leaves—
> And if these should fail, it at least will be.
> A token of love from me to thee. (Anon. 1829)

The poem unequivocally conveys the annual's meta-message: a "token of love from me to thee" where "me" stands for a male giver and "thee" for female donné.[17] The gift is intended to create a bond between the two and/or to please the recipient, even if the feeling behind it is not reciprocated. Instead, Hooper's gesture puts an end to his affectionate ties. "The dismal shade must separate me from the world: even you, Elizabeth, can never come behind it!" (312). The veil becomes a symbol of self-imposed solitude as Hooper chooses to be a bachelor, a precarious figure of the nineteenth-century literary imagination.[18] While gift books intended to create and sustain social bonds—not only of romantic love but also of parental affection, friendship, or charity—Hooper's "symbol" deprives him of all universal empathetic connections: "love or sympathy could never reach him" (315). The minister himself experiences a great "antipathy to the veil" and cannot look at his own reflection without being frightened (315). As N.S. Boone argues, the "lack of reciprocity" dissociates Hooper from human relationships (Boone 2005: 165–176). The reader is also at a loss: should we sympathize and side with the minister or judge and condemn him?

---

[17] *The Token* more than once republished the lines from the poem as mottos to its subsequent volumes.
[18] As, for example, discussed in Sedgwick Kosofky (1990).

Recasting the story in the gift book, the venue of its first publication, we can see that Hooper's veil indeed functions as an *anti-token* of affection. It is dismal, dark, and gloomy; it alienates and isolates instead of creating sympathetic bonds. The *Token* reader would most likely have understood the tale as a critique of extreme individualistic behavior that dooms Hooper to live and die without human sympathy and marital ties. At the same time, the story suggests an alternative interpretation: Hooper's commitment to wear a veil is an act of sacrifice; he does it for the sake of others; it is a message to community that, albeit obscure and incomprehensible, can change lives and brings souls to God.

> By the aid of this mysterious emblem—for there was no other apparent course—he became a man of awful power over souls that were in agony for sin. His converts always regarded him with a dread peculiar to themselves, affirming, though but figuratively, that, before he brought them to celestial light, they had been with him behind the black veil. Its gloom, indeed, enabled him to sympathize with all dark affections. (315)

The minister's relationship with sinners is described in terms of power; yet this is mimetic power, nonhierarchical by nature. In this sense the veil, Hooper's inalienable possession, is simultaneously a gift for sinners; it creates bonds and ties of sympathy between people marginalized by society and helps them get rid of their own invisible veils. Ultimately, Hooper's emblem brings the sinners to "celestial light." Exposed to everybody and nobody in particular, the message of the token in Hawthorne's story is contingent on circumstances and varies according to the addressee. Appropriate at the funeral, it is disturbing at the wedding. Incomprehensible to most, it becomes meaningful to some through the power of sympathy, breaking anonymity—not unlike the annual that becomes personalized and individualized in the act of bestowal. Yet even when the gift serves its purpose—that of creating a bond between the minister and the sinners—that this is not a happy bond is emphasized by the word choice: "gloom," "agony," "dark affections." Hooper is anything but a pleasing giver; his gift to the sinner is that of a painful conversion through the acknowledgment of one's own vice and the dread of this vice. The ultimate reward of celestial light comes with strings attached, as it were.

The ambivalence of the veil is revealed still further when we examine the story in its immediate surroundings, or rather in dialogue with other gift book entries on the thematic level. The tale contains a direct reference to Hawthorne's own piece, "The Wedding Knell" published in the same volume under the same attribution (by the author of "Sights from a Steeple"): "If ever another wedding were so dismal, it was that famous one where they tolled *the wedding knell*" (309, emphasis mine—A.U.). Sepulchral wedding episodes in both "The Minister's Black Veil" and "The Wedding Knell" rhyme with the melancholy tone of Lydia Sigourney's poem "The Bride." The poem about the wedding ceremony ends with the death of the bride, and "the minister of death" "doth aid or mar the journey of the soul to heaven" (Sigourney 1835 [1836]: 56).

In the same volume of *The Token*, there is a more down-to-earth discussion of mourning rituals in the story "Constance Allerton, or The Mourning Suits" by Miss [Eliza] Leslie. The story explores the legitimacy of not wearing mourning attire if the family does not have the means and the inappropriateness of the mourning fashion that has little to do with grief. One lady, a connoisseur of fashion, advises the bereaved family on the subject of "proper" mourning and recommends, among other items, "double-width crape for the veils" of very superior quality (Leslie 1835: 337). Parson Hooper's black veil is likewise described as consisting "of two folds of crape": "swathed about his forehead, and hanging down over his face, so low as to be shaken by his breath" (303). While this parallel is merely accidental, both tales emphasize materiality, casualty, and even triviality of their tokens, either the emblems of mourning profaned and vulgarized by vanity and fashion in Leslie's story, or the "simple black veil" in Hawthorne's. While lacking the transparency, universality, and applicability of the familiar emblems described in Leslie's story, Hawthorne's token is congenial with their materiality or thing-ness.

Hooper's veil *is* an emblem of mourning but it is a misplaced emblem because Hooper is wearing it all the time and not only on the appropriate occasion. Moreover, as Leslie's story reminds us, the veil is also an attribute of female fashion and dress. This fact is acknowledged in Hawthorne's tale. The villager, a woman, says, "How strange, that a simple black veil, *such as any woman might wear on her bonnet*, should become such a terrible thing on Mr. Hooper's face" (307, emphasis mine.—A.U.). Thus, we encounter a double misplacement: a veil is worn by a man and by a parson, a woman parson being an unimaginable figure in the Calvinist church or in any religious institution of the time. Detached from the bonnet, the veil loses its veiling/unveiling quality and becomes a mask (cf. Hawthorne's 1836 entry in *The American Notebooks*: "An essay on the misery of being always under a mask. A veil may be needful, but never a mask," qtd in Davis 2005: 61). It alters the entire person of the minister. "The black veil, though it covers only our pastor's face, throws its influence over his whole person, and makes him ghost-like from head to foot" (307).

Hawthorne's token, or rather his anti-token, has a conspicuous "taint of the feminine" in the words of McGill cited above. Yet it not only feminizes Hooper but also simultaneously de-feminizes the veil by defamiliarizing it, to use the term of Russian Formalists, or by creating an uncanny effect, in Freudian terms. The "dismal shade" of the veil separates Hooper from his beloved and makes a heteronormative connection impossible. Effeminate and queer under his veil, Hooper singles out and marginalizes himself but also connects with marginalized members of society, unspecified sinners whom universal sympathy cannot reach. He at once Gothicizes the mourning emblem and un-genders a feminine attribute, ultimately making his own gender ambiguous and fluctuating. Hooper becomes "ghost-like," a ghost being de facto alienated and misplaced. The Gothic devices used in the story single out the veil from other emblems described in the gift book literature, including the gift book itself that, its opulent materiality notwithstanding, always came with a surplus of meaning and functioned as a sign in the shared imaginary of its readership.

The "token of love from me to thee" becomes unstripped or, rather, unveiled in Hawthorne's story, hovering between sacrifice and selfishness, sympathy and alienation, devotion and obstinacy but also between the norm and the deviation, the universal and the marginal, the masculine and the feminine, the material and the ghostly. "The Minister's Black Veil" tells an alternative story of giving and bonding that goes beyond the conventional formulas and patterns of the annual—a story doomed to end in Hooper's tragic and irreversible divorce from the general public. If Hooper indeed gives himself away to the community, simultaneously giving up the life of a "normal" man and pastor, it is an example of dangerous giving where the object of danger is the giver himself.

4.4 The Gift Book Turned Inside Out: "The Purloined Letter," *The Gift*, and the Homosocial

Poe's "The Purloined Letter," his third story in the respectable Philadelphian annual *The Gift, A Christmas and New Year's Present*,[19] was published side by side with an engraving of Charles R. Leslie's painting "The Toilette" renamed as "The Necklace" and glossed by a plate poem "The Necklace" by Anne C. Lynch. The engraving shows a girl looking at a luxurious necklace that she has just taken from a parcel (Fig. 4.2) while the plate poem leaves no doubt that the necklace is not a sign of vanity but a "talisman," "Love's own amulet." It is a gift speaking of the lover's feelings and representing him in absence: "As if those jewels cast Love-glances in their rays?" (Lynch 1844: 40). Lynch's poetic adaptation of the image for the annual is a typical product placement. The necklace becomes a pictorial replica of a gift book that functioned as a genteel substitute for jewelry. As Gila Ashtor argues, "this poem/image pair tells a self-referential story about how to use a gift book: the receiver is to relish its beauty as long as it remains tethered to someone else—especially because affective economies and kinship practices suggest the giver of the 'necklace' and gift book is likely the same person" (Ashtor 2012: 63). The pair is also emblematic of the underlying rhetorical strategy of gift books that attempted to disguise their commercial nature with imagery of gratuitously bestowed gifts.

"The Purloined Letter," the third story of the Parisian detective trilogy, is about a secret letter that Minister D purloins from the Queen and that Dupin, Poe's ingenious detective, steals from the Minister and restores to the Prefect who asked him for help. "The Purloined Letter" presents a stark contrast to the neighboring "The Necklace."[20] In Poe's story, the female character, the Queen, is absent, while everything happens "between men": the narrator, the Prefect, and August Dupin. Unlike the necklace, Love's amulet, the precious letter is an object of theft and manipulation; the presumed love correspondence between the Queen and the sender of the letter, Duke S—is pushed to the narrative's margin and plays no

---

[19] On the history of Poe's collaboration with gift books, see Shinn (2013).

[20] This contrast is even sharper if we take into consideration that Poe's tale was published alongside tales by Caroline Kirkland and Nathaniel Parker Willis both with a motif of stolen or dangerous letters. See Urakova (2009).

Fig. 4.2 "The Necklace." Engraved by William Humphrys from a painting by Charles Robert Leslie. Public domain in the United States

significant role in the plot.[21] On the one hand, we have a story of courtship and romance; on the other, a narrative of detection and revenge. On the one hand, a girl contemplates a present from her lover. On the other, Minister D—uses the love letter in question to manipulate a royal woman and Dupin uses it to destroy D—, his old enemy and double. The

---

[21] We do not know from the story whether the letter concerns a secret love affair or a political complot against the King. If it is the former, then Dupin sustains (presumably) adulterous relations, very much at odds with the didactical character of the annual. Dupin who restores the letter to the Queen may be seen as an accomplice in the "crime" against the royalty and, as one might suspect, against the moral.

heterosexual commerce of commodified seduction epitomized by the engraving and the poem contrasts with the homosocial dynamics of the revenge plotline in "The Purloined Letter."

It seems counterintuitive to read "The Purloined Letter" in the context of gift-giving, especially considering that its plot evolves around the opposite act—stealing. However, as my analysis will demonstrate, the relationship of Poe's story to the gift book framework is stronger than it might first seem. In order to specify the place of "The Purloined Letter" in *The Gift* still further, I suggest reading it against the background of the stories with a motif of romantic gift-giving, that, like Lynch's "The Necklace," use a technique of *mise en abyme*. In the two stories published in previous volumes of *The Gift*, well familiar to Poe—one by popular gift book author Maria Griffith and the other by Catharine Maria Sedgwick—a fictional double of the gift book is a letter or a parcel. This particular circumstance invites us reading these texts together.

Sophia Lee, the female character of Griffith's "The Old Valentine" (1838) receives a mysterious valentine and, after recognizing the handwriting of a man she knows, carefully examines it in detective-like fashion:

> [T]here is some mystery about this—pray, when did he write it? It must have been lately, for here is 1837, and yet—stay—I declare there has been an erasure, for I see the top part of a 6 or 5 above the 7, and look here, too, Gift is in paler ink: a word has been scratched out there. It never struck me before, but the paper is not as white as the envelope. (Griffith 1838: 50)

The scratched-out word is, one would guess, the name of the addressee, and suggests that this is an old valentine that has been re-gifted to Sophia.[22] As it finally turns out, Sophia's secret admirer Mr. Day, a "serious man of business" (52), wrote this letter years ago at the request of their mutual friend, who had bad handwriting, and who sent the valentine to Sophia. Although Mr. Day was writing the text "mechanically, without considering the import of the words at all," it is thanks to the "dear little paper" that he reveals his feelings to Sophia (57).

The valentine serves as a substitute for *The Gift* as a volume, since a valentine is already itself something in-between a love letter and a present.

---

[22] What Griffith describes in her tale often happened in the publishing world. It was a common practice to repackage pages "from old gift books in new bindings" or to rebind pages "from unsold periodicals ... as gift books." On the gift book fraud, see Cohen (2012: 8).

The Gift, very much like the valentine in the story, is compiled and designed for nobody in particular. The name that is left blank on the presentation page needs to be filled in, in each individual case. In "The Old Valentine," the true addressee of the valentine—true in a supreme, symbolic sense—is finally discovered. *The Gift* functions in very much the same way, converting depersonalized economic relations of seller-buyer into personalized affective bonds of sender-receiver.

Unlike the happy-ending narrative of Maria Griffith or Sedgwick's own "Cacoethes Scribendi," her "The Unpresuming Mr. Hudson" (1835) printed in the earlier volume of *The Gift* is a didactic story with a moral, "meditating upon the trials of a pretty young girl who is chaperoned to watering-places by a silly, expecting, and credulous mother" (Sedgwick 38). Louise Campbell, traveling with her mother in a stagecoach to the Springs, is courted by the gentlemen who accompany them—with the exception of one Mr. Hudson. He is the only member of the group who does not give the flowers he has collected to Louise. But on the day of departure Louise, going to her cabin in search of something she has left behind, finds there a parcel, "on which was written in pencil, 'To L. C. from C. H.' and under it the trite of quotation from the text-book of lovers, 'The world is divided into two parts—that where she is, and that where she is not'" (35). She unbinds the envelope's blue ribbon "with a fluttering hand":

> It was a blank album, with flowers pressed between its leaves, the very flowers that the "unpresuming Mr. Hudson" had not the courage to offer to Louise on the first day of their acquaintance. Here they were embalmed by love and poetry; for on each page was pencilled a quoted stanza from some popular amorous poet. (35)

Louise, however, misreads both the flower language and the envelope's address. She correctly deciphers the initials "C. H." as "Charles Hudson." But "L. C." is not "Louise Campbell," it is her former schoolmate "Laura Clay," who has just arrived at the same cabin and who presents herself as Hudson's fiancée. When the real addressee is found out, the narrator, Louise's elderly female companion, secretly restores the album "to its right place" (38). Louise's imagination stirred up by her mother's ambitions betrays her. She does not guess that the addressee written on the envelope may be the wrong one, assuming that "L. C." can have only one signified, that is herself.

Like the valentine in Griffith's story, the album functions as the annual's double. Many handwritten albums were bound in the gift book style and entitled "Casket of Thoughts" or "Token of Affection" (Thompson 1936: 20); "albums were often given as holiday presents" (Hayes 2000: 21). Thompson counts "at least fifty" annuals "dealing with flowers and flower-language," "appropriately named 'Flora's Album,' 'Flora's Dial,' 'Flora's Interpreter,' 'Floral Keepsake,' 'Poetry of Flowers,' or 'Flower Garden'" (Thompson 1936: 17). The name of the sender (C.H.) ciphered in the initials was a common way of signing love messages as well as poems in periodicals, including *The Gift*.

The flowers in the album have a special meaning for Louise (Hudson collected the same flowers on the day of their acquaintance). Yet they are not those flowers but just flowers speaking a universal language of love, like the quotation on the envelope labeled as "trite" (here we can detect Sedgwick's tongue-in-cheek irony). Still, what causes disappointment to Louise Campbell gives "a pleasant feeling" to her substitute, Laura Clay, proving to Laura as well as to the readers the love and truthfulness of her fiancé. Louise was determined that "the flowers should not fail to their destination" (24) and they did not. Sedgwick's didactic tale restages the same plot pattern as does Griffith's valentine story: the itinerary of the flower album corresponds to the libidinal nature of gift book circulation. Both stories, in counterpoising love and vanity, advocate a type of giving generally favored in gift books; the gift's prime value is in the feeling it expresses—an unequivocal meta-message that reaches the reader in the form of an elegant mise en abyme narrative.

What happens if we place Poe's tale in the outlined framework? We can see that *The Gift's* reader would expect Dupin to scrutinize the letter, noting the minute details with almost feminine attentiveness, and to decipher the letter's address. The color of the paper proves to Sophia that the valentine was written much earlier than it was sent; "the soiled and torn condition of the paper" that Dupin notices in D—'s study makes the former suspect intentional "design to delude the beholder into an idea of the worthlessness of the document" (Poe 1844: 59). Concealing the letter, D—readdresses and reseals it, forging a correspondence of an obviously intimate nature between himself and a fabricated female addressee; the envelope is "addressed, in a diminutive female hand, to D—, the minister, himself" (58). The credulous Prefect, unlike Dupin and like Louise in Sedgwick's story, reads the clues too straightforwardly, expecting the signifier to coincide with the signified and looking for the letter "with the ducal arms of S—family" (59).

In "The Unpresuming Mr. Hudson" the album, a gift book substitute, is neatly enveloped in white paper bound with a blue ribbon. The card rack of pasteboard where Dupin discovers the purloined letter hangs under the mantelpiece, "dangling by a dirty blue riband" (58; "ribbon" in the now-canonical revision of 1845). In Sedgwick's story, the only line written on the envelope beneath the initials is a "quotation from the text-books of lovers" (35). At the end of "The Purloined Letter," Dupin copies "into the middle of the blank sheet" (61) of his letter a quotation from Crébillon's revenge play and leaves it inside. The letter that D—conceals while leaving it in the open is compared to the glove "turned … inside out" (59). Employing this metaphor to Poe's story itself, we can see that the letter in the story—the gift book's counterpart and antipode—may be interpreted as its inverted image.

On the one hand, Poe's plot is apparently in tune with the symbolic itinerary of letters and parcels in *The Gift*. In all the three stories, "a letter always arrives at its destination," in the words of Jacques Lacan about "The Purloined Letter" (Lacan 1988: 58). The letter/parcel, an object of desire, finds its "true" addressee or returns to its owner. On the other hand, as the analysis below demonstrates, Poe rather inverts and purloins the generic narrative of the gift book. Dupin does return the letter to the Queen via the Prefect. But he does not give him the letter; he asks the Prefect to write him a check first. Poe's character signs the check, not a valentine or a birthday card. Though excluded from affective relations altogether, the returned letter could have still been a token of Dupin's partisanship and loyalty, his admiration, or respect. Instead, a self-proclaimed "partisan of the lady" (60), he prefers simply to be paid for his service, choosing to remain anonymous.

A different type of relation manifests itself near the closure of the tale when Dupin leaves the facsimile of the purloined letter to D—and signs it, breaking his anonymity. His signature is itself a cipher, a quotation, but Dupin has no doubts that D—, well acquainted with his handwriting, will recognize it. The facsimile is thus not a facsimile in the strict sense: when signed and readdressed, it becomes an independent message. This is emphasized in the tale's narrative structure: the story of Dupin's and D—'s past relations has nothing to do with the purloined-letter plot. Dupin says at the end:

To be sure, D—, at Vienna once, did me an evil turn, which I told him, quite good-humouredly, that I should remember. So, as I knew he would feel some curiosity in regard to the identity of the person who had outwitted him, I thought it a pity not to give him a clue. (61)

The allusion to the myth about Atreus and Thyestes in the quotation left by Dupin ("Un dessein si funeste, / S'il n'est digne d'Atrée, est digne de Thyeste" [61]) suggests the motif of blood feud. It also refers to a category of gifts "given by wronged individuals who wreak revenge by tricking their malefactors into unwittingly accepting parts of their deceased loved ones who have been fashioned in jewelry, utensils, or made into food" (Sowerby and Urakova 2022, forthcoming). Not unlike his creator, the "literary Mohawk" Poe,[23] Dupin, mediating revenge with a letter, replaces a violent gesture by a literary quotation. The gift motif thus reappears at the very end of "The Purloined Letter," but, indeed, "turned … inside out" (59).

Placing "The Purloined Letter" in the gift book framework, we can see how Poe mediates the conventional gift book narrative of a heterosexual intrigue by a homosocial one, and thus engages the typical gender economy of the annual. His "androgynous" Dupin is Achilles, who "hid himself among women," as the famous motto to "The Murders in the Rue Morgue" by Thomas Browne might well suggest: "What song the Syrens sang, or what name Achilles assumed when he hid himself among women, although puzzling questions, are not beyond all conjecture" (Poe 1984: 397).[24] "The Purloined Letter" seems to combine analytic powers of detection, commonly attributed to men, with attenuated apprehension of material data commonly attributed to women. Yet Dupin not so much

---

[23] Poe, an astute critic, was called "Our Literary Mohawk" in A.J.H. Duganne's poem "A Mirror for Authors," published in *Holden's Dollar Magazine* 3 (1849), together with a caricature by F.O.C. Darley representing Poe as a ferocious Indian with a tomahawk in his hand. This "assumed almost the status of a critical cliché" in the 1840s (see Jackson 2002: 97). There has been a long tradition of reading "The Purloined Letter" as an autobiographical tale, and of reading this particular final scene as an allusion to Poe's own literary battles. The rivalries, thefts, invasions of privacy, and personal assaults that Poe witnessed during his magazinist career are, indeed, looming behind the plot.

[24] Cynthia Jordan, for example, comments: "The epigraph to the first tale, 'The Murders in the Rue Morgue,' introduces the idea of crossing gender boundaries to recover the now 'dim-remembered story' of female experience." Jordan (1987: 13).

recovers "the second story—'the woman's story'—which has previously gone untold" (Jordan 1987: 5)[25] but purloins it instead.

"The Purloined Letter" redirects the reader's attention from the itinerary of a love message to the dynamics of power; a woman's personal secret is but a "use-value" object in the men's struggle. The tale replaces the "asymmetrical conditions of gift book circulation" with the symmetry of the "round robin" plot. The homoeroticism of "The Purloined Letter"[26] strikingly reveals itself when placed against the background of the gift book tradition, which more or less openly commodified heterosexual conventions. While not a story with a gift motif, Poe's is ultimately a story about dangerous giving, as revealed at the metatextual level. The characters are involved in a series of exchanges or "evil turns" which may be considered, after Avner Offer, as "pathological gift cycles" (Offer 1997: 455)—at odds with the annual's placid gift-giving patterns. D–and Dupin, rivals and doubles, maintain a secret homoerotic bond that is sealed by Dupin's signature upon the facsimile—his final, covert blow.

The three stories—"Cacoethes Scribendi," "The Minister's Black Veil," and "The Purloined Letter"—that I have closely read in the context of their gift book publications, different as they are, share an underlying principle. Not only do they narrate the dangers, real or imaginary, that a misused gift book, a misplaced token, or a misappropriated letter may incur, they all reveal the instability and fluidity of gender roles and conventions. Of the three, only Sedgwick's is a story about an innocent gift that becomes "Pandora's box" for the receiver, as a third party becomes involved. The relation of Hawthorne's and Poe's stories to gift exchange is circumstantial: the publication venue offers a framework that allows us to read the texts in the gift-related context. This context foregrounds the similarities between these two otherwise very different stories. The stories center on material objects that have been removed from their original place: the veil from the woman's bonnet; the letter, "turned, as a glove, inside out" (59) from the royal boudoir, and from the (possible) romantic exchange. Both objects give "the oddest *odor di femina*" to their owners, to borrow Lacan's ingenious comment on "The Purloined Letter" (Lacan 1988: 48). As a result, we get a situation of homosexual panic: Hooper gives up his future marriage; Dupin and D—become engaged in a homosocial

---

[25] Jordan, "Poe's Re-Vision," 5.
[26] On Poe's queer writing see, for example, Person (2008), Greven (2014).

conflict. This panic is echoed in "Cacoethes Scribendi" where the price of a woman's independence is eternal maidenhood.

The veil in Hawthorne's story is Hooper's inalienable possession but also an emblem of his unilateral sacrifice. The letter instead is an object of a series of embedded narratives and exchanges: a treason and love story in question (the Queen and S—); theft and blackmail (D— and the Queen); bargain (Dupin and the Prefect); revenge (Dupin and D—). At the same time, both the veil and the letter, contextually, begin to function as the gift book's *mise en abyme* in reverse: the dark and gloomy veil alienating its owner or the letter being an instrument of manipulation and revenge are the opposite of Love's amulet and the token of affection that the gift book was intended to be.

In each case, irony/humor, Gothic devices, or elements of the new mystery genre/revenge narrative, interacting with the sentimental framework of the gift book, highlight the conventional character of the heterosexual romance embodied in the image of the pure gift. Transgression of gender roles is the result of misreading, displacement, or eversion, narrating an alternative story of gift(-book)-giving. While the examined tales both transcend and fit in the gift book conventions, we should not forget that it is the playful, self-referential meta-structure of the gift book itself that allows deviations from its fictional routine, mainstream ethics, and rhetoric of gift-giving. Gift books undoubtedly epitomized a new sentimental and commercial ethos of the gift, yet they also, in the democratic spirit of the antebellum market, welcomed a heterogeneity of styles and themes and engaged their contributors and readers in an interactive play across words and things, a play that, as we have seen, could take an unforeseen and non-insignificant turn.

WORKS CITED

Anon. 1829. The Gift. In *The Token: A Christmas and New Year's Present* [for 1830]. Boston: Gray and Bowen, 1.

———. 1839. Confessions of a Novel Reader. *Southern Literary Messenger* 5 (3): 179–193.

Ashtor, Gila. 2012. The Gift (Book) That Keeps on Giving: Poe's 'The Purloined Letter,' Rereading, Reprinting, and Detective Fiction. *Poe Studies* 45.2 (3): 57–77.

Boone, N.S. 2005. 'The Minister's Black Veil' and Hawthorne's Ethical Refusal of Reciprocity: A Levianasian Parable. *Renascence: Essays on Values in Literature* 57 (3): 165–176.

Coale, Samuel. 1993. Hawthorne's Black Veil: From Image to Icon. *Critic* 55 (3): 79-87.
Cohen, Lara Langer. 2012. *The Fabrication of American Literature*, 79–87. Philadelphia: University of Pennsylvania Press.
Davis, Clark. 2005. *Hawthorne's Shyness: Ethics, Politics, and the Question of Engagement*. Baltimore: Johns Hopkins University Press.
Dickinson, Cindy. 1996. Creating a World of Books, Friends, and Flowers: Gift Books and Inscriptions, 1825–60. *Winterthur Portfolio* 31 (1): 53–60.
Douglas, Ann. 1977. *The Feminization of American Culture*. New York: Alfred A. Knopf.
Feldman, Paula R. 2006. Introduction. In *The Keepsake for 1829*, ed. Frederic Mansel Reynolds, 7–32. Orchard Park: Broadview Press.
Felski, Rita. 2003. *Literature after Feminism*. Chicago: University of Chicago Press.
Fetterley, Judith. 1985. *Provisions: A Reader from 19th-Century American Women*. Bloomington: Indiana University Press.
Flint, Kate. 1995. *The Woman Reader, 1837–1914*. Oxford: Clarendon.
Fuller, Margaret. 1852. *Memoirs of Margaret Fuller Ossoli*. Vol. 1. London: Richard Bentley.
Goodrich, Samuel Griswold. 1856. *Recollections of a Lifetime; Or, Man and Things I Have Seen*. Vol. 2. New York: Miller, Orton & Milligan.
Greven, David. 2014. *Gender Protest and Same-Sex Desire in Antebellum American Literature: Margaret Fuller, Edgar Allan Poe, Nathaniel Hawthorne, and Herman Melville*. Burlington: Ashgate.
Griffith, M[aria]. 1838. The Old Valentine. In *The Gift: A Christmas and New Year's Present* [for 1839]. Philadelphia: Carey and Hart.
Harris, Katherine D. 2005. Feminizing the Textual Body: Female Readers Consuming the Literary Annual. *The Papers of the Bibliographical Society of America* 99 (4): 573–622.
Hawthorne, Nathaniel. 1982. *Tales and Sketches*. New York: Library of America.
[Hawthorne, Nathaniel]. 1835. The Minister's Black Veil. In *The Token and Atlantic Souvenir: Christmas and New Year's Present* [for 1836]. Boston: Charles Bowen, 302–320.
Hayes, Kevin. 2000. *Poe and the Printed Word*. Cambridge: Cambridge University Press.
Jackson, Leon. 2002. 'Behold Our Literary Mohawk, Poe': Literary Nationalism and the 'Indianation' of Antebellum American Culture. *ESQ: Journal of American Renaissance* 48: 97–133.
———. 2008. *The Business of Letters: Authorial Economies in Antebellum America*. Stanford: Stanford University Press.
Jordan, Cynthia S. 1987. Poe's Revision: The Recovery of the Second Story. *American Literature* 59: 1–19.

Lacan, Jacques. 1988. Lacan's Seminar on 'The Purloined Letter'. Trans. Jeffrey Mehlman. In *The Purloined Poe: Lacan, Derrida and Psychoanalytic Reading*, ed. John P. Muller and William J. Richardson, 55–76. Baltimore: Johns Hopkins University Press.

Ledbetter, Kathryn. 1996. 'Begemmed and Beamuletted': Tennyson and Those 'Vapid' Gift Books. *Victorian Poetry* 34 (2): 235–245.

Lehuu, Isabelle. 2000. *Carnival on the Page: Popular Print Media in Antebellum America*. Chapel Hill: The University of North Carolina Press.

Leslie, [Eliza]. 1835. Constance Allerton, or The Mourning Suits: A Story of Domestic Life. In *The Token and Atlantic Souvenir: Christmas and New Year's Present [for 1836]*, 323–358. Boston: Charles Bowen.

Lubovich, Maglina. 2008. 'Married or Single?': Catharine Maria Sedgwick on Old Maids, Wives, and Marriage. *Legacy* 25 (1): 23–40.

Lynch, Anne C. 1844. The Necklace. In *The Gift: A Christmas, New Year, and Birthday Present* [for 1845]. Philadelphia: Carey and Hart.

McGill, Meredith. 2002. *American Literature and the Culture of Reprinting, 1834–1853*. Philadelphia: University of Pennsylvania Press.

Mellor, Anne K. 1993. *Romanticism and Gender*. New York: Routledge.

Miller, Hillis J. 1991. *Hawthorne and History: Defacing It*. Oxford: Blackwell Publishing.

Moore, Thomas R. 1994. *A Thick and Darksome Veil: The Rhetoric of Hawthorne's Sketches, Prefaces, and Essays*. Boston: Northeastern University Press.

Mott, Frank Luther. 1930. *A History of American Magazines, Volume I: 1741–1850*. New York: Dr. Appleton and Co.

Nissenbaum, Stephen. 1996. *The Battle for Christmas*. New York: Vintage Books.

Offer, Avner. 1997. Between the Gift and the Market: The Economy of Regard. *Economic History Review* 3: 450–476.

Person, Leland S. 2008. Queer Poe: The Tell-Tale Heart of His Fiction. *Poe Studies* 41 (1): 7–30.

Poe, Edgar Allan. 1984. *Poetry and Tales*. Ed. Patrick F. Quinn. New York: Literary Classics of the United States.

Poe, Edgar Allan. 1844. The Purloined Letter. In *The Gift: A Christmas, New Year's and Birthday Present* [for 1845]. Philadelphia: Carey and Hart.

Rappoport, Jill. 2011. *Giving Women: Alliance and Exchange in Victorian Culture*. Oxford: Oxford University Press.

Richards, Eliza. 2004. *Gender and The Poetics of Reception in Poe's Circle*. Cambridge: Cambridge University Press.

Samuels, Shirley. 1992. Introduction. In *The Culture of Sentiment: Race, Gender, and Sentimentality in Nineteenth Century America*, ed. Shirley Samuels, 3–8. Oxford: Oxford University Press.

Sedgwick, Catharine Maria. 1829. Cacoethes Scribendi. In *The Atlantic Souvenir* [for 1830], 17–39. Philadelphia: Carey, Lee & Carey.

———. 1831. A Sketch of a Blue Stocking. In *The Token: A Christmas and New Year's Present* [for 1832], 36–37. Boston: Gray and Bowen.

———. 1835. The Unpresuming Mr. Hudson. In *The Gift: A Christmas and New Year's Present* [for 1836], 2–38. Philadelphia: Carey and Hart.

Sedgwick Kosofsky, Eve. 1990. *Epistemology of the Closet*. Berkeley: University of California Press.

Shinn, Kathryn K. 2013. Gift Books. In *Edgar Allan Poe in Context*, ed. Kevin J. Hayes, 179–187. Cambridge University Press.

Showalter, Elaine. 1998. Introduction. In *Alternative Alcott*, ed. Elaine Showalter, ix–xliii. New Jersey: Rutgers University Press.

Sigourney, Lydia. 1835. The Bride. In *The Token and Atlantic Souvenir: Christmas and New Year's Present* [for 1836]. Boston: Charles Bowen, 56–57.

Sowerby, Tracey, and Alexandra Urakova. 2022, forthcoming. Introduction: Unpacking Dangerous Gifts. In *The Dangers of Gifts from Antiquity to the Digital Age*, ed. Alexandra Urakova, Tracey Sowerby, and Tudor Sala. New York and London: Routledge.

Strathern, Marilyn. 1988. *The Gender of the Gift: Problems with Women and Problems with Society in Melanesia*. Berkeley: University of California Press.

Thompson, Ralph. 1936. *American Literary Annuals and Gift Books, 1825–1865*. New York: H. W. Wilson Co.

Tompkins, Jane. 1985. *Sensational Designs: The Cultural Work of American Fiction, 1790–1860*. New York and Oxford: Oxford University Press.

Urakova, Alexandra. 2009. 'The Purloined Letter' in the Gift Book: Reading Poe in a Contemporary Context. *Nineteenth-Century Literature* 64 (3): 323–346.

———. 2016. Hawthorne's Gifts: Rereading 'Alice Doane's Appeal' and 'The Great Carbuncle' in The Token. *New England Quarterly* 88 (4): 587–613.

———. 2020a. The 'Flower-gemmed' Story: Gift Book Tradition and Poe's 'Eleonora.' In *Anthologizing Poe*, ed. Emron Esplin and Margarida Vale de Gato, 59–72. Bethlehem, PA: Lehigh University Press.

———. 2020b. 'The Ghost-Book' and the Gift Book: Editorial and Marketing Strategies in Eliza Leslie's *The Gift*. *American Periodicals: A Journal of History & Criticism* 30 (1): 42–62.

CHAPTER 5

Racial Identity and the Perils of Giving

5.1 "The Triple Bond" of the Gift of Liberty

The eminent Unitarian writer William N. Channing concludes his piece "A Day in Kentucky" published in the anti-slavery gift book *The Liberty Bell* for 1843 like this: "If, even under slavery, the African race exhibits such heroic and lovely traits, would they not be noble men, if bound to their white fellow-freemen by the triple bond of gratitude, and mutual confidence, and generous emulation?" (Channing 1842: 68). While calling for their emancipation, Channing invites the enslaved Americans to exchange the bonds of slavery for the bond of gratitude that will tie them even more closely to their white fellow freemen. The institution of slavery should give place to affectionate enslavement or sweet bondage secured by the gratitude of Black people and the generosity of white benefactors. Such an idyllic future of the emancipated United States strikingly reveals the paradox of liberty as a gift. While gratitude, unlike forced labor, is voluntary, it is still an obligation according to the higher moral law. The restored liberty becomes a sentimental bond that puts the Black person in eternal debt to someone who happens to be white and free by "nature."[1]

Critics have shown the deep implications of gift relation in the rhetoric of emancipation. As Kenneth S. Greenberg argues, "prior to the abolition of slavery, masters could liberate individual slaves only by awarding them freedom as a gift" so emancipation "that assumed a form of a gift paradoxically reconfirmed the master-slave relationship" and intended to

---

[1] Avner Offer writes about the bond in the meaning of "a *fetter*, as a form of oppression: 'With gifts you make slaves', an Alaskan Inuk is reported as saying" (Offer 455).

© The Author(s), under exclusive license to Springer Nature Switzerland AG 2022
A. Urakova, *Dangerous Giving in Nineteenth-Century American Literature*, American Literature Readings in the 21st Century,
https://doi.org/10.1007/978-3-030-93270-1_5

"destroy the legal institution of slavery without attacking the heart of the dependency relationship" (Greenberg 1996: 66). Marcus Wood puts it even more harshly: "...in the imagination of people who made emancipation prints and marketed emancipation poetry, the people who marketed the gift of freedom, the slave at a certain level would never be free" (Wood 2010: 116). Along the same lines, Susan M. Ryan emphasizes the ambiguity of Lydia Maria Child's mid-century image of an "everlasting slave" and points at Harriet Jacobs' "burden of white benevolence" when the autobiographical character of her *Incidents in the Life of a Slave Girl* felt "bound" to her English benefactress "by 'gratitude' for a service not of her choosing" (Ryan 2003: 2–3).[2] If "slavery was the central paradox in the country devoted to equality" (Sollors 2017: 106), the idea of giving freedom as a gift to restore equality was another paradox of a kind.

Bearing on the existing criticism, I suggest looking at the gift-related rhetoric in the media where such rhetoric was both welcome and expected—in anti-slavery gift books, particularly *The Liberty Bell*.[3] Like their generic counterparts discussed in the previous chapter, these volumes promoted the sentimental idea of the gift as essentially benign and gratuitous but did so within the particular context of slavery and emancipation. A Christmas present and an offering on the altar of emancipation, the anti-slavery gift book was itself a materialized "freedom's gift"[4] distributed at anti-slavery fairs that were held by female abolitionists at Christmas time throughout the antebellum years.

While Teresa A. Goddu justly speaks of these fairs in terms of sentimental consumerism albeit "constituted as gift economies" (Goddu 2020: 92), anti-slavery gift books were also engaged in the web of gift exchanges beyond marketing. Contributions were voluntary donations, or "gifts to the cause," in the words of Mary Weston Chapman (Chapman 1858: 24); not only contributors but also those who "had otherwise aided the Bazaar" received volumes gratuitously (Thompson 1936: 84); the buyers often circulated the annuals instead of keeping them. One abolitionist reader, Eliza F. Meriam, confessed in a private letter that she was tempted to put

---

[2] Ryan quotes Child's 1862 statement: "I *want* to do other things, but *always* there is kneeling before me that everlasting slave, with his hands clasped in supplication." Ryan comments that Child's "ambivalence, at the same time wanting and not wanting to be begged from, suffuses every word" (Ryan 2003: 2).

[3] *Liberty Bell* was the most well-known and long-lived gift book and a platform of the influential Garrisonian movement, which makes it a good representative example.

[4] "Freedom's Gift" was a title of one of the anti-slavery gift books.

the copy of *The Liberty Bell* alongside her "other valuables" but decided to "circulate it, among the good people of Framingham, peradventure some of its tones may awaken their sympathy and interest, for the poor slave" (qtd in Chambers-Schiller 2018: 259). Unlike ordinary gift books with a clear-cut, often gendered division between the giver and the receiver, anti-slavery gift books engaged everyone as a potential donor of the slave reduced to the status of iconographic emblem, or fictional character, or discursive construct. The slaves were absent from the actual exchanges that took place at the anti-slavery fairs but the whole structure of the gift book evolved around this objectified speechless figure.

Predictably, the story of unilateral gift-giving from white abolitionists to their Black brethren was a metanarrative of the anti-slavery annual sold together with sugar bowls, pincushions, and other merchandise decorated by an imprinted figure of Josiah Wedgwood's kneeling slave in chains (Fig. 5.1).[5] Less predictably, some publications questioned the impeccable authority of the white benefactor while others attempted to overturn the

Fig. 5.1 *Am I Not a Man and a Brother?* Medallion by Josiah Wedgwood, 1787. Public domain

---

[5] Josiah Wedgwood was an English abolitionist whose anti-slavery medallion, depicting a kneeling slave in chains, accompanied by inscription "Am I Not a Man and a Brother" (1787) became one of the most widely circulated abolitionist images. Later a twin image of a female figure appeared—"Am I Not a Woman and a Sister?"

hierarchical structure tacitly implied by the story of white benevolence. In this chapter, I focus on how the gift relation and its dynamics reflected in the pages of the anti-slavery gift book contributed to shaping racial identity and what potential perils this practice evoked. Toward the end, I briefly discuss an alternative story: how a free Black community used the sentimental language of the gift inspired by gift book and album culture to find a more positive way of appreciating reciprocity.

5.2 "Everlasting Slave"? Sentimental Rhetoric of the Gift in *The Liberty Bell*

Together with *Autographs for Freedom*, *The Oasis*, *Freedom's Gift*, and *The Star of Emancipation*, *The Liberty Bell* belongs to the class of gift books targeted at the audience sympathetic to the abolitionist movement.[6] For abolitionists, the gift book was a suitable format for fundraising in the holiday time. As Julia Griffith, the British editor of *Autographs for Freedom*, wrote in the letter to Emerson,

> the beauty of its exterior will commend it as a suitable Christmas, or New Year's gift, while its contents, we hope, will abound with earnest and truthful appeals to the humane sentiments and Christian principles of the reader unalloyed with the trifling matter which too often fills the pages of Christmas books. (Qtd in Fritz and Fee 2013: 72)[7]

Griffith advertises her product as both a gift book and an anti-gift book. A beautifully decorated present, it does not have the triviality and frivolity of the ordinary gift book but tackles serious issues in accordance with the values of Christianity and humanism.[8] As Mary Weston Chapman put it in

---

[6] Alongside gift books of general interest, there were numerous volumes addressed to specific audiences (juveniles, anti-immigrants, temperance supporters, Masons, etc.).

[7] Qtd in Meaghan M. Fritz and Frank E. Fee, "To Give the Gift of Freedom: Gift Books and the War on Slavery," *American Periodicals: A Journal of History & Criticism*, 23.1 (2013), 72.

[8] The anti-slavery gift book epitomized the existing tension between the "seriousness of the cause and the necessary frivolity of a fundraising fair" (Gordon 1998: 53). See also Hansen's commentary about Chapman's anti-slavery fairs: "As Chapman herself indicated, her sale was in a good position to take 'advantage of the city market for the benefit of the slave,' and she wisely held the fair in late December to attract buyers of Christmas and New Year's presents. 'Think of the cause,' she entreated in one fair notice, "and for its sake reserve your gift of money till Christmas'" (Hansen 1993: 128).

her 1846 letter to Mary A. Estlin, the American public "must be treated as children, to whom a medicine is made as pleasant as it[s] nature admits. A childish mind desires a small measure of truth in gilt edged, when it would reject it in whitty-brown" (qtd in Chambers-Schiller 2018: 259). Keeping the form and format of their commercial counterparts, anti-slavery annuals were significantly more modest in appearance due to the seriousness of the cause as well as the scarcity of funds (Thompson 1936: 85; Fritz and Fee 2013: 74). While the first five volumes of *The Liberty Bell* contained an ornamental title page and two volumes had expensive silk and leather bindings, they looked poor compared to *The Gift* or *The Token* discussed in the previous chapter: none of the gilt edges Weston referred to; two or three engravings instead of a dozen (Thompson 1936: 85).

Another feature that distinguished these products was the cosmopolitan politics of their editors; *The Liberty Bell* alone was an international platform with numerous European contributors, from the British writer and journalist Harriet Martineau to the Russian essayist Nikolai Turgenev. Anti-slavery gift books also welcomed African American authors—a practice unthinkable in other annuals.[9] The main purpose of abolitionist gift books was anti-slavery propaganda; hence, essays, letters, and sketches prevailed over the fictional genres that formed a large part of the content in their counterparts. As these volumes were meant to encourage fundraising instead of courtship or family gifts, they predictably emphasized acts of benevolence instead of a libidinal gift economy.

The Liberty Bell was published by the American Anti-Slavery Society and edited by an anti-slavery activist, Maria Weston Chapman. *The Liberty Bell* first appeared in 1839, at the Boston anti-slavery fair that Chapman organized together with her two sisters;[10] in all, fifteen volumes were issued between 1839 and 1857. Chapman was a supporter of William Lloyd Garrison and published the annual largely to promote his ideas; while she "resisted labeling herself as editor, instead attributing authorship of the *Bell* to all contributors, or 'Friends of Freedom', of the gift book." (Fritz and Fee 2013: 70), everyone in the abolitionist circle was well aware of her editorial work; she was also a frequent contributor to the gift book. For example, in a poem-manifesto in the first volume of the *Bell* in defense

---

[9] Frederick Douglass contributed to *The Liberty Bell* before his split with the Garrisonians, as did William Wells Brown and Charles Lenox Remond. *Autographs for Freedom*, however, had significantly more African American contributors. See Frank and Fee, 2013: 68.

[10] "The antislavery fair was Chapman's 'invention'" (Gordon 1998: 52).

of her anti-slavery fairs, Chapman used sentimental rhetoric directly appealing to her readers and encouraging them to labor for the sake of freedom:

> The slave is dying in his chain
> Unheeded and alone;
> We see his tears, we feel his pain—
> We make his wrongs our own. (Chapman 1838: 53)

Chapman's stanza reveals the anatomy of sentimental sympathy: we see an enslaved man suffering, "feel his pain," project his condition onto ourselves, and start acting.[11] *The Liberty Bell* was not only "heavily organized through the political cohesion of its contributors that more or less consistently promoted Garrisonian beliefs" but was also "designed specifically to soften Garrisonian radicalism and to make his politics more palatable for moderate readers" (Fritz and Fee 2013: 72). Sentimentality was a major tool to mitigate radical messages as the one we encounter, for example, in Garrison's essay "No Compromise with Slavery": "whether by peaceful or a *bloody* process—slavery must die" (Garrison 1843: 214).

Garrisonians believed freedom to be the inalienable property of every human being. The crime of the enslavers is that "they presumed to alienate what is inalienable… the dearest possession the man can hold—*the possession of himself…*" (May 1850: 76; emphasis in original). French contributor M. Emile Souvestre points at the fact that there was no "voluntary agreement" between the enslaver and the slave: "Slavery is, clearly, the offspring of War… Are you even the owner of this person by virtue of a voluntary agreement? Has he transferred his liberty to you as a return for some benefit…? Not at all! There has been no bargain, no contract, between you!" (Souvestre 1850: 189–190). The origin of American slavery is warfare as the opposite of bargain, or contract, or voluntary agreement, such as a gift of oneself. Therefore, the enslaver is a thief, and the enslaved person owes him nothing (Hopper 1842: 167). The situation is different, however, when the abolitionist comes to the scene and gratuitously helps the suffering brother or sister to return their stolen freedom.

---

[11] For Garrisonians, "pain was no longer the result of divine Providence, but the result of human actions" (Cima 2014: 60). On abolitionist use of sympathy, see also 39–90. As Weston herself wrote in her report, "we began by indulging our sensibilities over an individual slave: and still we follow Sterne's good counsel to present a single case, the better to awaken the first emotion of sympathy" (Weston 1858: 2).

This constitutes a new type of relations based on sympathy, gratitude, and debt.

Lydia Maria Child's well-known "Jan and Zaida" tells the story of a Javan slave taken to auction with his numerous family because the kind-hearted woman who had held him in slavery had died without protecting them. At the auction, Jan does the unthinkable—bids for his and his family's freedom with a golden ducat that his "owner's" neighbor, an English abolitionist, had once given him as a gift. "[D]ropping on his knees," Jan begs the buyers not to bid over him. "Tears dropped from the eyes of many young people; the agent swallowed hard; and even the auctioneer was conscious of a choking feeling in his throat" (Child 1855: 91). The scene culminates in "one of humanity's inspired moments": after the dead silence in the room that lasts more than a minute, Jan becomes the owner of his family and himself. "A trifling keepsake" (77), the ducat is a gift that keeps giving as it converts slaveholders, the agent, and the auctioneer from merciless dealers to sentimental subjects; the word choice is eloquent: tears drop right after Jan drops on his knees.

The true hero of the story, however, is the giver of the ducat: "Was the golden ducat *all* that poor despairing slave owned to the good Englishman? No; that was the smallest part of the debt; for to the moral influence of his conversation, and the books and papers he scattered in the neighborhood, might mainly be attributed the changing public sentiment" (93). Child's kneeling and supplicating slave is a verbal replica of Wedgwood's popular cameo image, a symbol of the anti-slavery fairs. Conversely, a contributor to *The Liberty Bell* or anyone who helps the fair to run becomes "the good Englishman," an abolitionist who changes public sentiment and whose disinterested labors for the anti-slavery cause put the slave in debt.[12]

Child's emotional and heartfelt narrative of white benevolence published in one of the last volumes of *The Liberty Bell* resonates with many fictional and non-fictional texts of the earlier volumes. One such representative example is a sketch "Pater Noster." In a parable-like manner, it tells the story of a hypocritical pastor: after giving a moldy crust of bread to a beggar, he volunteers to teach him divine wisdom. The beggar, who learns that God is our Father, asks the priest why he gave his "brother" only a moldy crust of bread. The author, Amasa Walker, uses the anecdote as a springboard to address the issue of slavery:

---

[12] Child's story is more complex and should not be reduced to the narrative of gift and debt—it also advocates racial integration. See Levy 2007: 150–151.

> And the colored man is in bondage, is robbed of his all, his liberty, his family, and every thing that man holds dear; and now he presents at the door of the white man—and asks for what? For his freedom, for the privilege of taking care of himself... and what answer will the white brother give? Will he turn him off with a mouldy crust? (Walker 1843: 119)

The enslaved person *is* a hungry beggar in Walker's sketch; he is asking for freedom as a beggar would ask for alms.[13] But asking whom? "The slave does not ask his master to set him free. That would be useless, that would only bring upon him additional stripes and severer toil; but he does come to *us* and ask for liberty that is so unjustly and cruelly denied him. Shall we reject his prayer?" (119). The sketch ends up with a direct appeal to the visitor of the anti-slavery fair:

> And now the Liberty Bell calls you to the door of the Christmas Anti-Slavery Fair where your enslaved brother stands shivering with cold, and trembling with fear; with a down-cast, yet hopeful, wishful eye, waiting to see what you will GIVE him to make his heart and the hearts of his wife and little ones rejoice in the blessings of heaven-bestowed freedom. Say, man, woman, child, *will you turn him off with a mouldy crust of bread*? (121; emphasis in original)

Freedom is inalienable property but it is also a heavenly gift; forcefully alienated, it may still be re-given, and it is the mission of *The Liberty Bell* reader to intervene, as the excessive sentimental rhetoric of the cited fragment implies. Unlike Jan in Child's story, the enslaved person in "Pater Noster" is not kneeling but his "hopeful, wishful eye" is downcast, connoting humility. Through a number of displacements, freedom, a legitimate but alienated property, becomes a gift, making the slave an object of benevolence, not a claimer of her rights. In this 1843 piece, we encounter ideas that would enkindle Child's 1855 story demonstrating the consistency of patterns including the reproduction of the fair's iconic symbol, Wedgwood's kneeling man in chains. Generous abolitionist and forever-grateful slave were the annual's stock figures together with a cruel "slaveholder," endangered beautiful "mulatta," grieving mother, or good-hearted but weak owner. These figures were inseparable from the racialized identities of the participants. Considering "the prevalent bodily vocabulary" of

---

[13] Symptomatically, Child's Jan becomes an object of almsgiving as soon as he is free: one of the spectators gives him a florin and collects money on his behalf.

the anti-slavery sentimental fiction "that interprets dark skin as an unvarying sign of slavery," most *Liberty Bell* pieces did not distinguish between "being black" and "being a slave" (Sanchez-Eppler 1988: 39). In a similar manner, the slave's benefactor was a white man or woman by default, despite the fact that free Black activists had an important share in the movement.

A couple of publications in *The Liberty Bell*, however, disrupt the ideal traffic of benevolence from the white givers to the Black donées as they address the subject of well-intended but harmful and dangerous or useless and inconsiderate gifts to the slaves. In her essay "What is Anti-Slavery Work?" (1844), a renowned American abolitionist Lucretia Mott criticizes what she calls "misdirected benevolence" (Mott 1845: 255). The essay is written on a specific occasion: a year before, friends of Freedom in Philadelphia made a fundraising appeal to purchase an enslaved woman who was to be sold away from her relatives and friends as a result of her owner's bankruptcy. Mott cites from the resolution of the Female Anti-Slavery Society she herself attended. The Society decided to decline all pecuniary aid to this cause calling such aid "useless appropriation of money" and "indirect support of slavery" (254).

In her essay written in the form of a letter to a friend, Mott attempts to justify this rejection. She admits it to be a "peculiarly hard" case since it was a "feeling" appeal and the "poor victim of the oppressor's power" needed help. She also confesses that she herself "contributed her mite toward the purchase of slaves" driven by sympathy. However, she claims to have changed her opinion on the subject completely. A gift of individual liberty attained by purchasing a slave from the owner is vicious and harmful because it acknowledges "the right of property in man" (255) and indirectly supports the system. "The sum obtained in this way is often used for the purchase of other slaves" (256). The gift to one person initiates a chain of purchases leading to the enslavement of others. Answering her own question—"What is Anti-Slavery Work?"—Mott suggests a better channel for donations: "If the sums, raised for this object, were appropriated to the enlightenment of the public mind on the enormity of the whole system, how much more effective would it be" (256).

What is remarkable about Mott's essay is her charges against sympathy as the sole and legitimate reason for giving. Mott invites her readers to think in terms of political economy rather than act out of empathetic impulse: "Let us extend our benevolence to the whole class of 'the suffering and the dumb,' rather than expend our means in acts of sympathy towards a few isolated cases" (257). Just as giving alms supports pauperism, according to many European and American philanthropists of the time (Johnson 1818: de Gérando 1832: 9)[14], buying a person's freedom makes the institution of slavery prosper. The essay portrays the enslaved people as "the suffering and the dumb" in accordance with the general line but the abolitionist loses her superior position of the benign giver, siding, even if involuntarily, with the "slaveholder." Supporting Chapman's politics that encouraged donations for the anti-slavery propaganda, Mott's text goes counter many of the annual's sentimental texts plotted around specific and isolated acts of benevolence and counter Weston's own philosophy. As Weston writes in her report, "we began by indulging our sensibilities over an individual slave: and still we follow Sterne's good counsel to present a single case, the better to awaken the first emotion of sympathy" (Weston 1858: 3).

In the volume of *The Liberty Bell* for 1848, we find another discussion of harmful "white" gifts in Frederick Douglass's essay "Bibles for the Slaves." The essay criticizes the initiative to donate money to the American Bible Society so that it can purchase and distribute Bibles among slaves. The initiative comes from the church but "into this enterprize have been drawn some who have been known as advocates for emancipation" (Douglass 1847: 122). Douglass starts with a number of practical questions: "Do they suppose that Slaveholders, in open violation of their wicked laws, will allow their Slaves to have the Bible? How do they mean to get the Bible among the Slaves?... Do they intend to send teachers into the Slave States, with the Bibles, to teach Slaves to read them?" (123–24). The Bible is a useless gift to the slaves because they cannot read—this is one of the Douglass's main points. In the final paragraph, he compares such an offering with a stone given to a hungry man, ice bestowed on a freezing man, and a dollar thrown to a drowning man, drafting a list of essentially cynical and toxic gifts.

The Bible given to the slave is not just useless; it is "a shame, a delusion, and a snare" (125). Collecting money for something that has no practical use but sounds and looks good, pseudo-philanthropists help the system prosper, albeit in a different way than described by Mott. This enterprise "absorb[s] the energies and money in giving to [the slave] the Bible that ought to be used in giving him to *himself*" (126). A Bible becomes the

---

[14] Joseph-Marie de Gérando was a French philosopher whose ideas were popular and influential in the antebellum US.

wrong substitute for the gift of freedom. Moreover, before the slave becomes free, all the gifts are wasted on him, and Bible especially. "The Bible was given to Freemen, and any attempt to give it to the Slave must result only in hollow mockery" (125). Speaking of the unpracticality and inappropriateness of the Bible as a gift to slaves, Douglass finally arrives at the core question of gift-giving and slavery. "The Slave is property. He cannot hold property. He cannot own a Bible. To give him a Bible is but to give his Master a Bible" (126). The problem is not only with the slave's illiteracy, but also with giving *any gift* to someone who does not own "himself."

In the antebellum South, "according to the logic of slave regime ... all transactions involved the giving of gifts; food, clothing, and shelter we supplied as gifts by the master" (Greenberg 1996: 65); some "slaveholders" cynically gave essentials such as clothes to the slaves as Christmas gifts (Nissenbaum 1996: 272–73).[15] Douglass instead defines a slave's identity through her exclusion from the gift relation of any kind. Being a "thing" herself, a slave cannot own "other" things and therefore cannot receive gifts.

The essay is ambivalent. On the one hand, speaking of "giving" the slave "to himself," Douglass follows the familiar pattern that represents freedom as a gift. On the other hand, he conceptualizes the impossibility of the gift given to a slave. Doing that, he overturns the pattern: freedom is not so much the gift as it is the absolute condition of any gift exchange to take place. The only possible gift is the free gift, not in the usual sense of the gift freely bestowed but in the meaning of the gift freely received.[16]

Douglass's essay is an example of an alternative and markedly unsentimental discourse of gift-giving in *The Liberty Bell* as well as one of the earliest nineteenth-century attempts to conceptualize the meaning of the gift seen in the context of slavery, power, and ownership. The essay, using a particular case of misdirected and harmful benevolence, also slyly attacks sentimental religious didacticism that considers the Bible as the best gift under any circumstances. Ironically, as if to counterbalance the radicalism of Douglass's message, *The Liberty Bell* published it alongside a poem entitled "A Christmas Hymn," a translation "from the German of John Tauber" by Theodore Parker, where we read, for example, that the Father's Word "brings great Help to cheer us" (Parker 1847: 118).

---

[15] On the nature and ambivalence of Southern gifts from slaveholders to the slaves see also Luck 2014: 138–187.

[16] There is, however, a difference between Douglass's statement and Kirkland's discussion of the freely received gifts (Chap. 2). Kirkland largely addressing white middle-class readership could not go as far.

A free person can freely receive and own gifts but she also has the privilege to give them. The story of a Black person who becomes a donor or a benefactor instead of a kneeling beggar forms another alternative plotline, challenging the metanarrative of the anti-slavery gift book.

5.3 "The luxury of giving": The Ambiguities of the Black Donor Plot

The narrator of Eliza Lee Follen's "A Morning Walk," a lady walking the streets of a big city, contemplates "the degradation of the extremely poor"—human beings who have immortal souls but whose "extreme poverty almost condemns them to vice and ignorance" (Follen 1840, 102). Yet most importantly, these men and women are deprived of "the joy of doing good, the pleasures of benevolence: they have nothing to give" (103). Among the city poor, she notices a "colored man" "whose dress indicated great poverty" (104). Observing the patches on his clothes, the narrator, however, estimates that the man has a wife and that he has earned his dinner. He is the so-called *worthy poor*.

To the narrator's great surprise, the pedestrian gives alms to a "colored woman" who looks even poorer than he does. The narrator follows the good example, and the "colored man" says to her: "Oh ma'am, we must do something for these poor creatures." The joint act of charity, adds the narrator, "for a time levelled the distinction which society had raised between us" (105). The "colored man" and the narrator end up walking along the same side of the street and talking about different matters. What strikes the narrator most of all is the fact that the almsgiver is not only poor himself but also belongs to the "despised people of color" (106). The story contains a traditional allusion to the Biblical story of the widow's offering: the narrator feels remorse when she realizes that, unlike herself, the "colored man" gave away half of what he had. At the same time, the tale makes an interesting point that seems to go beyond the conventional framework of so-called benevolence literature (Bergman and Bernardi 2005: 1-23). Equality, the narrator suggests, is not in the economic welfare, class, skin color, but in the "luxury of giving." Benefactors walk on the same side of the street, despite their class and race distinctions. A capacity to give what is seen as surplus or excess ("luxury") constitutes the citizen's identity that eventually transcends, even if temporarily, the presumed racial distinction ("despised people of color").

The same volume published Edmund Quincy's story "Dinah Rollins" about the narrator's visit to a poor Black woman who became a benefactor of her white friend. "Dinah Rollins" is of peculiar interest because of its self-referential character.[17] Introducing Dinah, the narrator confesses that "in the course of a pretty extensive and careful circle of studies, including most of the Annuals and Souvenirs of the last dozen years," he does not remember "to have read of a single heroine, whatever might have been the extremity or the variety of her distress, who was reduced to rub down horses and sweep out stables for her support" (Quincy 1840, 129). Later in the story, he calls Dinah "a very different person from the heroines of the generality of 'the hot-pressed darlings', which are annually furnished forth by the 'trade' to friendship and love, as gifts for Christmas and New Year. She would find herself brought acquainted with strange company in the Book of Beauty or the Flowers of Loveliness" (136). Dinah is an anti-gift-book character the same way *The Liberty Bell* is, in many respects, an anti-gift-book, the opposite of "the hot-pressed darlings." Yet, this woman with "an expression of goodness and benevolence" on her face of "the intensest black" (136) is a genuine giver and the true heroine of the true gift book.

The plot of the tale overturns the metanarrative of white benevolence. At first sight, Dinah, a slave who remained without support after the death of her masters, is "an object of interest and good offices to many benevolent individuals" (133). It is no coincidence that the narrator visits her on Thanksgiving; his visit resembles the visit of the poor, a widespread philanthropist practice in the antebellum US. However, contrary to the reader's expectations, Dinah does not ask for help; instead, she gives it.

Dinah supports herself working hard and gives shelter and food to a poor white woman. The woman is old and disabled, and would have ended her days in the Alms-house if not for Dinah's exceptional generosity. Importantly, the woman whom Dinah knew from the past is not her former mistress; she does not "owe" her anything unlike in the stories where former slaves "repay" their former owners for their kindness.[18] Her

---

[17] Quincy was not only a popular contributor to *The Liberty Bell*, like Follen; he was also one of its editors.

[18] In Quincy's own *The Liberty Bell* stories with a motif of insurrection, "Two Nights in St. Domingo" (1843) and "Lewis Herbert" (1844) noble slaves save their masters; in "Lewis Herbert," the slave supports the former master and his daughter when they become penniless. In both stories, it is stressed that the slaved people owe nothing to the enslavers but is also implied that the latter were relatively kind to the former.

hospitality is an act of pure disinterestedness and Christian virtue that is "not limited by color," as the narrator concludes (141).

Both "The Morning Walk" and "Dinah Rollins" are in tune with sentimental notions of gratuity, benevolence, and altruism as Christian or universal virtues and as such do not stand out from the general run of anti-slavery fiction. What makes them distinct is their relation to their publication venue. "The luxury of giving," Follen's term, not only puts the Black characters on the same level as the white ones in the stories; it also puts them in the place of *The Liberty Bell* authors and readers—the place of the giver, or donor. As abolitionists many times claimed, the virtues of Black people make "them" no different from "us" ("Am I not a Man and a Brother?"). However, on the structural level, this equation failed: there is an "us" who give and "them" who need, seek, and receive help. The stories invited readers to reconsider this hierarchy: the unnamed poor Black man and Dinah Rollins are no longer the objects of benevolence; they directly engage with and challenge the privileged position of the white benefactor.

The pioneering message of these two stories, allotting a Black persona with a new social identity as giver, however, remains ambiguous. In Follen's story, in particular, the ambiguity derives from the tacit obligation to reciprocate. At the end of the tale, the narrator tells another anecdote, now about a "colored woman" who after emancipation, is content to live in the family of her former masters as their servant. Every day, she puts on her best clothes and secretly goes to a particular place in the garret. The family members once follow her and see that she folds her hands, makes a low curtsy, and says, "I thank you, God" (Follen 1840: 108–109). In the final paragraph, the narrator fantasizes about freed Black people leaving enslaved labor and kneeling "before the Father of mercies" as they say "we thank you, God" (109). This anecdote not only inadvertently implies that former slaves are better off in the household of their enslavers than in the streets—a populist pro-slavery argument. The collective body of imaginary worshippers also represents the enslaved person as a passive receiver of freedom as God's gift and replicates the familiar iconography of the kneeling slave, albeit now unchained. The tale's finale suggests that the Black old man is "bound" by a moral obligation to reciprocate God's supreme gift of freedom by giving alms. Thanking God, the grateful Black people in the narrator's utopian vision indirectly thank His mediator, an abolitionist to whom the story is addressed.

In "Dinah Rollins," the ambiguity is implied by the dangerous proximity between gift-giving and slave labor in Dinah's case. Dinah hosts and supports the white poor while maintaining racist stereotypes that make the narrator speak of Dinah's "delicacy" in the treatment of her guest.

> Knowing, as she said, 'that white folks don't like to have colored folks to live with them," and having but one room for their joint accommodation, she divided it into two parts by means of a line hung with old clothes, that she might give her guest a separate apartment, in deference to her supposed prejudices. (Quincy 1840: 134)

Despite her superior position as a benefactor, Dinah stresses her racial inferiority to her white guest. The narrator overtly compares Dinah's benevolence with the forced labor of Southern black slaves who work to provide their enslavers, "illustrious paupers," with pocket money and board (140). The difference is that Dinah's charity is, as the narrator puts it, an example of disinterested kindness, being voluntary and cheerful, and the white woman reciprocates with gratitude instead of flogging or selling her benefactor. However, Dinah's stance of racial inferiority casts doubt on this distinction: her gift is both free and bound with prejudice. The narrator's example of Dinah's "delicacy" discloses the humility of the Black servant fantasized by the white author. The notion of slaves as benefactors of their white masters was part of the abolitionist discourse. In his 1844 lecture, Emerson aphoristically calls people in slavery "our benefactors, as they are producers of corn and wine, of coffee, of tobacco, of sugar, of rum, and brandy, gentle and joyous themselves, and produces of comfort and luxury for the civilized world..." (Emerson 2012: 297–98). Like Emersonian "gentle and joyous" slaves, Quincy's "cheerful" and "delicate" Dinah works hard for the comfort of her white guest. The long history of gratuitous slave labor and racialism risks blurring the boundaries between benevolence and servitude that the narrator is so carefully trying to emphasize.

Returning to Douglass's "Bibles for the Slaves," it is no surprise that the Black abolitionist and former slave expressed uneasiness concerning gift-giving. As long as slavery remained a threat, gift-giving in both directions was fraught with the dangers of new enslavement, whether we speak of the bond of gratitude or integration of former slaves into society as its "gentle" members, ready to forgive their oppressors, to render them services and help. The two stories discussed above rewrite the gift book's metanarrative and overturn its hierarchies, but only partially, as Follen's step-back final or Quincy's racial hierarchy demonstrate. Was it possible for the antebellum Black community to model gift exchange as a free, equal, and wholesome practice? To answer this question, in what follows, I briefly discuss an alternative way of imagining gift exchange in the pages of friendship albums that belonged to free Black women of Philadelphia and Amy Matilda Cassey in particular.[19]

5.4 "That love which circles in its chain"[20]: Re-appropriating the Sentimental in Cassey's Album

It is natural to speak of friendship albums alongside gift books due to the affinity between these two textual objects. Leon Jackson calls gift books commercial and mass-produced counterparts of hand-written albums: the former, while they "physically resembled [albums] in form," "came already filled with content" (Jackson 2008: 140). The albums instead circulated in a community of friends and family who filled their pages with "mementos," usually poems, original or copied, and watercolors. Yet empty albums, with their ornate Morocco bindings, were mass-produced; like gift books, they indicated the status of their owners who would expose an elegant volume on the parlor table as a sign of middle-class prestige. Albums were common presents and participated "in a system of reciprocal gifts" (Kete 2000: 60). If the text published in *The Liberty Bell* was a supreme donation to the anti-slavery propaganda, the album entry was a specific gift for the album's owner; most entries contained a dedication but even when they did not, their place in the album implied their exclusivity.

How can we interpret William Lloyd Garrison's piece "The Abolition Cause" (1843) penned for the album of Amy Matilda Cassey, a free Black woman from Philadelphia who, with her husband Joseph Cassey, was an

---

[19] Just as *The Liberty Bell* was the most famous anti-slavery gift book, Cassey's album, as it was known, was the most famous album belonging to the circle of free Black women in Philadelphia that counted many renowned Black and white, female and male contributors. Other known albums belonged to Martina and Mary Anne Dickerson and Mary Virginia Wood Forten.

[20] The lines are from a poem in James Edmeston's *Sacred Poetry* (1848), originally entitled "Written in a Sister's Album" and copied in the album under the signature "E.G." The poem speaks about the connection between the living and the dead but it may be applied to any type of intimate community.

activist in the anti-slavery movement? Garrison is writing about the "disinterestedness" of the abolitionists who undergo numerous hardships in their field but whose goodness is rewarded. "It is the gratitude of the suffering and the oppressed—the approbation of a good consciousness—the blessing of the Most High" (Cassey 1833–1856: 11). Garrison replicates the familiar template of the unilateral abolitionist gift to the "oppressed" rewarded by eternal gratitude. Yet while in the pages of *The Liberty Bell* this template tacitly implies white benevolence, in the album it does not. Garrison's piece is *for* Cassey and, indirectly, for her husband and the whole community of his Black allies. He "emancipates" abolitionist "disinterestedness" from the inevitable association with the skin color.

Garrison's text, lengthy by album standards, was one of the few devoted to anti-slavery matters in Cassey's album. Such texts were in minority if compared to common album entries devoted to the themes of friendship, womanhood, and motherhood. As Jasmine Nichole Cobb neatly puts it, "friendship albums are important examples of early nineteenth-century African American print culture because they evidence free blacks as readers, writers, and artists with no particular focus on slavery or abolition" (Cobb 2015: 30). While the albums were interracial and invited both women and men to participate, most of the contributors were Black female friends of the album owner; their exchange followed sentimental and genteel conventions that the writers borrowed and adopted for their needs from poetic anthologies, gift books, or lady's magazines. Contributors, with few exceptions, used other platforms for anti-slavery propaganda and chose to address more intimate and private matters in the albums.

Recent research has revealed a number of consistent patterns that distinguished the albums belonging to Black women in Philadelphia from the white models and counterparts. Erica R. Armstrong has argued that after getting married, white album owners "found themselves unable to maintain their friendships over the extended periods of time," whereas Black women's albums "represented a network of friends and acquaintances that would not be dismantled, but rather nurtured" (Armstrong 2004: 97). One possible explanation is the precarious status of the Black middle class in the antebellum United States: although many of the free Black people had been free since the Civil War, they lived under the threat of kidnapping and had to face racism on a daily basis. Community was a way to achieve self-support based on reciprocity and affirm shared values including gentility, education, and good manners. Another pattern is the excessive use of sentimental tropes and conventions in the fashion of the albums kept by antebellum white middle-class women. Cobb argues that "although purveyors of sentimentalism excluded Black women from mainstream notions of womanhood and the corollary consumer cultures" (Cobb 2015: 39), the latter nevertheless used popular conventions—for example, the "language of flowers"—as a means to assert their subjectivity and womanhood. Flowers that Black women "gave" to each other by painting them in the pages of the albums expressed their womanhood in the absence of the adequate Black body iconography (39). Mary Kelley in a similar manner shows how the watercolor of a butterfly—a gift of Sarah Mapps Douglass to Amy Matilda Cassey—seeks to express the beauty of the Black womanhood by refusing "to privilege lighter colors... The beauty of Douglass's butterfly is rendered in black" (Kelley 2019: 166). In a word, sentimental language was a sign of social prestige and education, on the one hand, and a form of "camouflage" on the other.

What can gift theory add to the body of the existing criticism on the subject? To begin with, we can clearly see that free Black women were consumers of sentimental literature as their fluency as readers testify. When they copied a familiar sentimental piece into an album, adding a dedication or a watercolor image, they sealed it with a personal inscription removing from the white-associated media and reframing as a gift.[21] Thus, they simultaneously personalized and deracialized a text addressed exclusively to a white audience, despite its claim to speak the universal language of love and friendship. Rather than creating "a new literary product" (Cobb 2015: 38),[22] African American contributors produced a gift of their own making—a practice perfectly legitimized within the album culture. Objectifying sentimental literature as a shareable gift, they constituted their identity as sentimental givers tacitly resisting the sentimental objectification and victimization of their race.[23]

---

[21] Lee Anne Fennell shows how such simple rituals as removing the price tag, wrapping, and inscribing the gift make it illiquid, removing it from the realm of commerce. Wrapping became widespread only by the end of the nineteenth century but the principle remains the same (Fennell 2002: 89).

[22] Owners of albums and scrapbooks typically combined the copied texts with drawings or altered/abridged these texts. I do not think that this practice constitutes an original work as Cobb appears to argue. But it certainly "repackaged" the copied poem as a personalized gift and may be paralleled to inscription in the gift book.

[23] Antebellum sentimental culture was almost exclusively interested in Black people as victims of slavery.

One striking example is Margaretta[24] Forten's gift to Amy Matilda Cassey, a poem "The Forget Me Not" (1834) that she copied from William Gilmore Simms, a Southern poet and a well-known advocate for slavery. Forten transcribed the poem beneath the watercolor of the flower omitting the first stanza that clearly identifies it as a love poem; she made slight changes, clipped a number of lines (most likely for the sake of brevity), changed punctuation, and capitalized different words. She initialed the poem with the last line "Our Love's the flower, 'Forget Me Not.' M F" (Cassey 1833–1856: 14). Even though the size of "M.F." is smaller than the size of the letters in the line and the initial comes after a period that separates it from the text of the poem, the initial as if extends the poetic line or otherwise symbolically inscribes Forten's persona within the poetical space, albeit on its very margin. The love poem by Simms, whose name is omitted, becomes a poem about Forten's friendship with Cassey; the giver of the "sweet token" replaces the author who hardly imagined that his poem would be a means to express the tender feelings of one Black woman to another. The poem thus takes on the new meaning of a personal gift addressed to Cassey: "forget not M.F." (Fig. 5.2).

It is tempting to look at the album-mediated community of Black women and their friends through the lens of terminology suggested by Italian philosopher Roberto Esposito. Esposito traces etymology of the word "community" to *munus*, a particular gift that denotes exchange and is always reciprocal, and distinguishes it from a "potentially unilateral" *donum*. Munus "is the gift that one gives because one *must* give and because one *cannot not* give" (Esposito 2009: 5). The basis of community or *communitas* is not a shared thing, or property (*res publica*) but a subtraction or a lack, one's duty give up something as a community member. Such non-hierarchical gift exchange may indeed be a fit explanatory model. The community of Black album owners and contributors had to organize itself around the void or "landslide" (5) of its transient social status that fluctuated between middle-class prosperity and the constant threat of potential enslavement or abuse.[25] Under the circumstances, circulating the album and filling its pages with poetical "gifts" was a duty that helped maintain the community. A reciprocal act of voluntary com-

---

[24] The Library Company of Philadelphia webpage alternatively attributes the authorship to her sister Mary Forten: https://lcpalbumproject.org/?page_id=245

[25] "For African Americans, middle-class status was often elusive and, if attained, always precarious" (Dunbar 2008: 121).

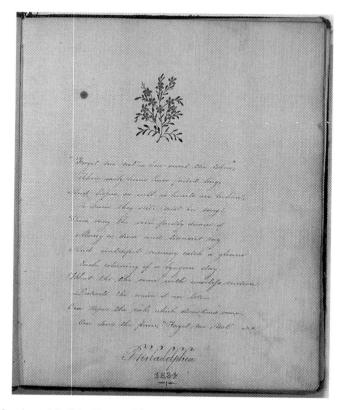

Fig. 5.2 Amy Matilda Cassey Album. Album page containing a drawing of a stem of forget-me-not and a poem about remembrance. By Margaretta or Mary Forten. Library Company of Philadelphia

mitment was free from the burden of the *donum* that dominated interracial relations in the antebellum era. At the same time, we also witness a reverse process. According to Esposito, *munus* implies "removing what is properly one's own… that invests and decenters the proprietary subject, forcing him to take leave… of himself, to alter himself" (6). The Black contributors to albums affirm themselves as communal proprietary subjects precisely in the act of giving, as they share sentimental tokens that carry a stamp of their non-presence within the mainstream genteel culture.

The gift as *munus* is illustrated by what may be called "apology" entries. There are at least two such entries in Cassey's album. In one (dated 1851),

Frederick Douglass confesses feeling "entirely out of [his] sphere... when presuming to write in an album" (Cassey 1833–1856: 35). Speaking of his past in slavery and his current abolitionist activities and metaphorically stressing his preference of "gazing upon huge rocks" to "promenading the most richly cultivated garden and gazing upon the most luxurious flowers" (35), he distinguishes himself from the circle of freeborn Black people who had a much more comfortable background. Yet he simultaneously remains inside the circle being loyal to his "dear friend" as he pens "an apology for not writing something becoming the pages of [her] precious Album" (35). Not only does the gallant apology conform to the rules of gentility, it makes him part of the network, or "chain" of gift-giving within this community.

A similar entry (dated 1834) was by Susan C. Write, presumably a Black female friend of Cassey:

> You ask me on this page to write
> A copy of my heart for you,
> But I thought and words have fled to night.
> Be sure, the original is true. (Cassey 1833–1856: 18)

Refusing to be conventional, Write follows one of the most popular conventions of sentimental and Romantic literature—impossibility of words to convey "true" feelings, sense of the insurmountable gap between the feeling and its expression. What is striking in this short entry is the word "copy." On the one hand, the *copy vs. original* binary is a sentimental convention: the original is always more genuine and precious than the copy. On the other hand, the word choice is likely to be a nod to the prevalent album genre—a copy of the poetical piece withdrawn from the white-dominated media. While Cassey's friends copy poems from anthologies and gift books into the album speaking of their affection, Write does not. Perhaps, she feels challenged by a poet Sarah Louisa Forten, whose poem on the previous page bears a proud title "Original."[26] Or, perhaps, in the absence of the language that could convey the "original" of her heart as a Black woman, she thought that an apology was the best thing to write.

Both Douglass and Write leave their entries in the pages of Cassey's album because they "must give" and "cannot not give," though words fail. They follow genteel rules and conventions even as they refuse to

---

[26] Indicating that the poem was originally composed—common practice in the album.

conform to these conventions; yet the main function of their entries is not self-expression but a communal duty to make love "circle" in its chain, in the meaning of a close circle and network.[27] Antebellum African Americans had all the reasons to feel reserved about the *donum* bestowed upon the Black person, which endangered the receiver by placing her in debt. Even when abolitionist authors like Follen and Quincy attempted to overturn the hierarchy in their stories, it did not quite work. In such context, free Black people had to seek their collective identity not only through resistance to slavery and racism but also through trivial but meaningful acts of gift-giving, simple gestures of attention, support, and solidarity.

In the context of slavery and racial prejudice, gift-giving held the potential to become a powerful tool in defining a racial identity, either through reinstating the status quo (the benefactor is white by default), through questioning/asserting one's freedom to receive or to give gifts (Black slave as donnée / emancipated Black donor), or through re-using, re-giving, and circulating gifts to maintain a network (self-identification of the Black community). We have also seen that the sentimental language of gift-giving may operate in a dual capacity. On the one hand, it simultaneously camouflages and reveals the racial power dynamics of the gift while also prompting an unsentimental counter-discourse that signals dangers or controversies that lurk behind the general tone of disinterestedness or benevolence: giving freedom to an individual potentially jeopardizes the very nature of anti-slavery work; a Bible is harmful when bestowed on the slave; a gift given to the slave is an insult. On the other hand, the language of gift books and friendship albums was used as a resource to create a safe communicative space for participants of color in the face of the precariousness and instability of their status in the slave society.

Works Cited

Armstrong, Erica M. 2004. A Mental and Moral Feast: Reading, Writing, and Sentimentality in Black Philadelphia. *Journal of Women's History* 16 (1): 78–102.

Bergman, Jill, and Debra Bernardi, eds. 2005. *Our Sisters' Keepers: Nineteenth Century Benevolence Literature by American Women*. Tuscaloosa: University of Alabama Press.

Cassey, Amy Matilda. 1833–1856. *Album. MS. African Americana Albums*. Lib. Co. of Philadelphia, Philadelphia.

---

[27] This distinguishes their contributions from album verses perceived as a form of tax by white middle-class Americans (Jackson 2008: 106).

Chambers-Schiller, Lee. 2018. 'A Good Work among the People': The Political Culture of the Boston Antislavery Fair. In *The Abolitionist Sisterhood: Women's Political Culture in Antebellum America*, ed. Jean Fagan Yellin and John C. Van Horne, 249–274. Ithaca: Cornell University Press.

Channing, William N. 1842. A Day in Kentucky. In *The Liberty Bell* [for 1843], 55–67. Boston: National Anti-Slavery Bazaar.

Chapman, Maria Weston. 1838. Lines. In *Liberty Bell* [for 1839], 53–58. Boston: National Anti-Slavery Bazaar.

———. 1858. Report of the Twenty-Fourth National Anti-Slavery Festival. *Maria Weston Chapman Papers*. Schlesinger Library. RIAS, Harvard University.

Child, Lydia Maria. 1855. Jan and Zaida. In *Liberty Bell* [for 1856], 42–93. Boston: National Anti-Slavery Bazaar.

Cima, Gay Gibson. 2014. *Performing Anti-slavery: Activist Women on Antebellum Stages*. Cambridge: Cambridge University Press.

Cobb, Jasmine Nichole. 2015. 'Forget Me Not': Free Black Women and Sentimentality. *MELUS: Multi-Ethnic Literature of the United States* 40 (3): 28–46.

Douglass, Frederick. 1847. Bibles for the Slaves. In *The Liberty Bell* [for 1848], 121–128. Boston: National Anti-Slavery Bazaar.

Dunbar, Erica Armstrong. 2008. *A Fragile Freedom: African American Women and Emancipation in the Antebellum City*. New Haven: Yale University Press.

Emerson, Ralph Waldo. 2012. Address…on the Anniversary of the Emancipation of the Negroes in the British West Indies. In *The Annotated Emerson*, ed. Philip Lopate, 297–298. Cambridge, MA: Harvard University Press.

Esposito, Roberto. 2009. *Communitas: The Origin and Destiny of Community*. Trans. Timothy Campbell. Stanford: Stanford University Press.

Fennell, Lee Anne. 2002. Unpacking the Gift: Illiquid Goods and Empathetic Dialogue. In *The Question of the Gift: Essays Across Disciplines*, ed. Mark Osteen, 85–102. London: Routledge.

Follen, Eliza Lee. 1840. A Morning Walk. In *The Liberty Bell* [for 1841], 101–109. Boston: Massachusetts Anti-Slavery Fair.

Fritz, Meaghan M., and Frank E. Fee. 2013. To Give the Gift of Freedom: Gift Books and the War on Slavery. *American Periodicals: A Journal of History & Criticism* 23 (1): 60–82.

Garrison, Lloyd William. 1843. No Compromise with Slavery. In *The Liberty Bell* [for 1844], 209–222. Boston: Massachusetts Anti-Slavery Fair.

Gérando, Joseph-Marie de. 1832. *The Visitor of the Poor*. Trans. a lady of Boston with introduction by Joseph Tuckerman. Boston: Hilliard, Gray, Little, and Wilkins.

Goddu, Teresa A. 2020. *Selling Antislavery: Abolition and Mass-Media in Antebellum America*. Philadelphia: University of Pennsylvania Press.

Gordon, Beverly. 1998. *Bazaars and Fair Ladies: The History of the American Fundraising Fair*. Knoxville: University of Tennessee Press.

Greenberg, Kenneth S. 1996. *Honor and Slavery: Lies, Duels, Noses, Masks, Dressing as a Woman, Gifts, Strangers, Humanitarianism, Death, Slave Rebellions, the Proslavery Argument, Baseball, Hunters, and Gambling in the Old South.* Princeton: Princeton University Press.

Hansen, Debra Gold. 1993. *Strained Sisterhood: Gender and Class in the Boston Female Anti-Slavery Society.* Boston: University of Massachusetts Press.

Hopper, Isaak. 1842. Story of a Fugitive. In *The Liberty Bell* [for 1843], 163–169. Boston: Massachusetts Anti-Slavery Fair.

Jackson, Leon. 2008. *The Business of Letters: Authorial Economies in Antebellum America.* Stanford: Stanford University Press.

Johnson, Samuel. 1818. *The Table Talk of Samuel Johnson.* London: J. Coxhead.

Kelley, Mary. 2019. 'The difference of colour': Reading and Writing Abolitionism. *Social Dynamics: Authorship and Print Sociability in African and African-American Newspapers* 45 (1): 156–173.

Kete, Mary Louise. 2000. *Sentimental Collaborations: Mourning and Middle-Class Identity in Nineteenth-Century America.* Durham: Duke University Press.

Levy, Valerie. 2007. Lydia Maria Child and The Abolitionist Gift-Book Market. In *Popular Nineteenth-Century American Women Writers and the Literary Marketplace*, ed. Earl Yarington and Mary De Jong. Cambridge: Cambridge Scholars Publishing.

Luck, Chad. 2014. *The Body of Property: Antebellum American Fiction and the Phenomenology of Possession.* New York: Fordham University Press.

May, Samuel J. 1850. The Root of Slavery. In *The Liberty Bell* [for 1851], 73–77. Boston: National Anti-Slavery Bazaar.

Mott, Lucretia. 1845. What Is Anti-Slavery Work? In *The Liberty Bell* [for 1846], 253–257. Boston: Massachusetts Anti-Slavery Fair.

Nissenbaum, Stephen. 1996. *The Battle for Christmas.* New York: Vintage Books.

Quincy, Edmund. 1840. Dinah Rollins. In *The Liberty Bell* [for 1841], 121–141. Boston: Massachusetts Anti-Slavery Fair.

Ryan, Susan M. 2003. *The Grammar of Good Intentions: Race and the Antebellum Culture of Benevolence.* Ithaca: Cornell University Press.

Sanchez-Eppler, Karen. 1988. Bodily Bonds: The Intersecting Rhetoric of Feminism and Abolition. *Representations* 24: 28–59.

Sollors, Werner. 2017. *Challenges of Diversity: Essays on America.* New Brunswick, NJ: Rutgers University Press.

Souvestre, Emile. 1850. Is Slavery Legitimate? In *The Liberty Bell* [for 1851], 189–193. Boston: National Anti-Slavery Bazaar.

Thompson, Ralph. 1936. *American Literary Annuals and Gift Books, 1825-1865.* New York: The H.W. Wilson Company.

Walker, Amasa. 1843. Pater Noster. In *The Liberty Bell* [for 1844], 117–128. Boston: National Anti-Slavery Bazaar.

Wood, Marcus. 2010. *The Horrible Gift of Freedom: Atlantic Slavery and the Representation of Emancipation.* Atlanta: University of Georgia Press.

CHAPTER 6

The Poison of the Gift, the Race of the Gift

6.1 Disinterested, Interested, and Poisonous: Typology of Gifts in *Uncle Tom's Cabin*

In the antebellum United States, one can refer not only to the gender of the gift, in the words of Marylin Strathern (Strathern 1988), but also, as the previous chapter has demonstrated, to the race of the gift. Considering that a Black person in the slave society was an object of various economic and legal transactions, including gift exchange, we may speak about the race of the gift in the literal sense. This chapter will examine the ambivalence involved in *giving a slave as a gift* in nineteenth-century sentimental fiction, focusing on the example of Harriet Beecher's Stowe's *Uncle Tom's Cabin* (1852).

The deathbed scene of little Eva distributing her golden locks among the slaves, a centerpiece of American sentimentalism, has been many times highlighted in the course of the critical reading of Stowe's bestseller novel. The same applies to the other two equally well-studied episodes: Mrs. Bird's charitable sacrifice of her deceased son's clothes for the son of the fugitive slave Eliza, and George Shelby's silver dollar keepsake bestowed on Uncle Tom as the latter was driven away in a slave wagon. All three scenes represent gift transactions that have been discussed in terms of fetishism (Brown 1990: 39–62), a pseudo-religious cult of "sacred relics" (Wardley 1992: 170), or "sentimental collaborations" (Kete 2000: 81–113) and in each instance, used by critics to probe and refine our understanding of the nature of Stowe's sentimentalism. While building on the long-standing tradition of Stowe criticism, I will take a different tack

© The Author(s), under exclusive license to Springer Nature Switzerland AG 2022
A. Urakova, *Dangerous Giving in Nineteenth-Century American Literature*, American Literature Readings in the 21st Century, https://doi.org/10.1007/978-3-030-93270-1_6

in this chapter by asking what happens when a slave himself or herself becomes a gift in the way that Mr. Shelby buys Eliza as a present for his wife, and the way Augustin St. Clare seems to bestow Uncle Tom upon Eva and ultimately gives Topsy to his cousin Ophelia.

Although much has been said about "sentimental property" or "sympathetic ownership" in Stowe, to use Gillian Brown's neat definitions (Brown 1990: 39, 42),[1] the instances of exchanging slaves as gifts in *Uncle Tom's Cabin* have been surprisingly overlooked. Touching upon one of the novel's important and precarious themes—the distinction between people and things—the aforementioned episodes not only contribute to our understanding of the novel's gift economy, they also invite us to revise the interrelation of sentimentality, slavery, and race in *Uncle Tom's Cabin*. I claim here that while pursuing a sentimental ideology of the gift that comes to support racialist implications of its abolitionist rhetoric, Stowe's novel also contains a radical potential of its critique embodied in the image of the poisonous gift of a slave child. Concurring with the critical opinion that Stowe's racism is in the sentiment, I argue that the novel's unsentimental, explicitly racist metaphors paradoxically inform one of Stowe's strongest anti-slavery arguments.

Uncle Tom's Cabin, "the gospel of nineteenth-century sentimental ideology" (Best 2004: 110), was also one of the major antebellum works about slavery and race that exposed itself to the literary market in the wake of the Civil War, and it quickly became one of the most successful commercial enterprises of its time. Simultaneously, it was the author's sincere and well-intended donation to the abolitionist movement, which was, as we have seen in the previous chapter, deeply implemented in the rhetoric of gift-giving. It is not surprising that *Uncle Tom's Cabin* ends with a clear message to the reader illustrated by George Shelby's noble gesture: bestowing freedom on his slaves, the white character acts as a supreme donor. As Stowe herself writes in *A Key to Uncle Tom's Cabin* (1853), "the example of disinterestedness and generosity, in emancipation, might carry with it a generous contagion, until it should become universal" (Stowe 2015: 111).

George Shelby's exemplary deed is also suggestive of the fact that most of the instances of gift-giving in *Uncle Tom's Cabin* are meaningful and have distinct moral implications. The novel's virtuous characters, both

---

[1] For example, possession or property that is inalienable, that should not circulate. Brown writes: "The anti-market task [Stowe] undertakes in *Uncle Tom's Cabin* is to make property relations more sentimental, or truly sentimental—to stop things from circulating" (43–44).

white and Black, alternately participate in the circles of gratuitous giving: from Aunt Chloe's treating young George Shelby with dinner to the hospitality of Birds and Quakers bestowed on Eliza and her family, to Tom's generous help to the sick slave woman in the field that initiated his martyrdom at Legree's plantation. Conversely, proslavery characters have a wrong, misconceived idea about gifts, seeing them exclusively as bribes. For example, Legree promises earrings to Emmeline in exchange for her sexual favors while Haley sincerely believes that a gift of "ear-rings, or a new gown, or some such truck" (Stowe 1982: 15) will adequately assuage Eliza for the loss of her child. Not surprisingly, these characters both represent capitalism at its worst—speculation economy that Stowe feared (Haley)[2] and the Southern, Gothicized version of the Northern industrial competition (Legree).[3] In a word, we encounter a familiar clear-cut distinction between true and false, morally good and morally unacceptable, gratuitous and interested gifts as well as distinctions between giving and trading, charity and bribing, generosity and pragmatism. The more explicitly the gift is represented as an exchange for services or as a form of placation, the more it is seen as false or immoral.

Yet the outlined dialectic is not always as neat and uncomplicated in Stowe's novel as it might appear. First, interested and disinterested exchange, albeit juxtaposed, often do merge in the novel as the supreme gift of *Uncle Tom's Cabin*, George Shelby's emancipation of his slaves illustrates. While a prime example of disinterestedness and generosity, George's gift of freedom simultaneously reminds us of its monetary nature; moreover, it establishes a new economic relation between him and his former slaves that is both interested and alienable: "The place wants as many hands to work it as it did before… I shall pay you wages for your work, such as we shall agree on" (Stowe 1982: 470). The gift (freedom) and commodity (capital) merge in the establishment of a new capitalist entity at Shelby's plantation. It is not a coincidence that the symbol of Shelby's gift is a silver dollar coin bestowed on Tom by the adolescent George in the beginning of the novel. The coin, the medium of market exchange, is transformed into inalienable possession deeply associated

---

[2] On Stowe's deep anxiety about speculation economy, see Best (2004: 101–203).
[3] In the image of Legree, a Northerner by birth, Stowe certainly "demonizes capitalism" (Reynolds 2012: 73) while Stowe's insistence that "a master's self-professed paternal relation to his slave" was "anything but a crass economic relation" (531) was meant to debate and turn against itself the claim of Southern ideologists that "slavery [was] founded upon the household economy" (Riss 1994: 530–31, 526).

with the giver's personality in the act of giving; it becomes valuable as a carrier of sentiment, a word of promise, and a bond of trust. Toward the end of *Uncle Tom's Cabin*, the dollar grows into the symbol of emancipation as it becomes "elevated from a sentimental token into a kind of national promissory note" (Diller 2004: 40). The final scene of the slaves' emancipation, however, returns us to the monetary relations that the dollar seemingly transcended.

Second, the practice of giving slaves as gifts presents a potential threat to the idea of the "morally good" gift (Carrier 1995: 162), since gift-giving, in modern society, tends to oppose persons to things and interest to disinterest (Parry 1986: 458). On the one hand, slaves in *Uncle Tom's Cabin* participate in gift exchange as free agents (albeit with limited means); on the other hand, they are reduced to the status of property and merchandise by the cruel laws of the market—commodities or potential commodities that are sold, bought, inherited, hired, leased, or mortgaged. However, as further analysis will reveal, their status becomes more equivocal as they enter the gray zone where they themselves circulate as gifts "loaded with emotion" (Parry 1986: 466) given or received with well-meaning, charitable intentions. This is a shaky ground that Stowe manages to transcend with the help of sentimental rhetoric but that nonetheless continues to disturb her modern readers.[4]

Finally, Stowe acknowledged the possibility that the gift may be double-edged. In *Dred: A Tale of the Great Dismal Swamp* (1856), she will introduce the theme of the well-meaning gift that eventually becomes harmful to its receivers despite the giver's good intentions. Nina Gordon bestows generous gifts on her enslaved brother and his wife without knowing that the price of these gifts is the wife's freedom: Harry has to spend his savings that would buy his and his wife's freedom to pay off Nina's debts. While in *Uncle Tom's Cabin*, there are no such examples, there are yet gifts that are (1) capable of causing harm to the unworthy, (2) morally ambiguous.

The example of the former is Eva's famous sentimental token. A lock of hair that she gives to Tom as a parting gift on her deathbed functions as a magic charm: it has the power to provide freedom to Cassy and Emmelina

---

[4] Faye Halpern (2018: 633–639) insists on reading *Uncle Tom's Cabin* "unsuspiciously," as her contemporaries would have. While Halpern's approach offers a fresh perspective on the novel, I argue that critical distance does not necessarily mean contempt. One of the critic's tasks can be precisely in understanding the gap between what we as readers find uneasy and disturbing about the novel of the past, on the one hand, and what came as natural or was naturalized at a time when the novel was first read on the other hand.

but, at the same time, causes Legree's mental derangement by "poisoning" him with superstitious fears. Marcel Mauss notes that "it is always a charm anyway (the word "*gift*" has kept this meaning in English) which permanently links those who partake and is always liable to turn against one of them if he would fail to honor the law" (Mauss 1997: 30). Not surprisingly, the superstitious Legree calls the lock a "devilish thing" and tries to get rid of it by burning it. A sacred relic, the lock may be seen as analogous to the Eucharist, "medicine of immortality" that at the early stages of its history was believed to literally poison nonbelievers or sinners.[5]

Conversely, actual poison functions as a deadly gift of motherly love in Stowe's novel. The mixed-race slave, Cassy, commits a crime by poisoning her newborn but in this way she also bestows freedom on her child whom she does not want to see enslaved.[6] Cassy's poison recalls a gift that can "either be good or bad" (Mauss 1997: 31) and is poisonous in the meaning of the ancient *pharmakon*: medicine and/or poison that is alternately harmful and healing, dangerous and wholesome, deadening and redemptive. The Maussian concept of gift as poison, or poisonous gift, challenges the idealist notion of the morally unequivocal, gratuitous, "morally good" gift based on the Christian idea of unconditional generosity. It also "radicalises the critique of *homo economicus*," as Gerald Moore shows, drawing a line from Mauss to Lévi-Strauss and Bataille and eventually to Jacques Lacan, who conceptualized a "gift of shit". Such a gift "ceases to be identifiable as a benign offering and becomes redemptive only in so far as recognised as poison—as that which falls outside and moreover prevents the completion of symbolic exchange" (Moore 2011: 9).

In Derrida, we also encounter the twofold understanding of the gift's poisonousness. On the one hand, as he puts it, "We know that as good, [the gift] can also be bad, poisonous (*Gift, gift*), and this from the moment the gift puts the other in debt" (1992: 12). For Derrida, the gift as debt that initiates a circle of exchange is no gift. Yet, on the other hand, Derrida's own concept of the impossible or pure gift—for example, the gift disrupting a circle of reciprocity—has a "violent, poisonous

---

[5] The Eucharistic analogy is suggested by the novel's Christian typology (Death of Eva = Last Supper; Death of Tom = Crucifixion). The term *pharmakon athanasias* ("medicine of immortality") belongs to Ignatius, an early second-century bishop of Antioch (Ignatius of Antioch, Eph. 20.2); I am thankful to Tudor Sala for this information. On Eva's lock as religious relic and magic fetish, see Wardley (1992: 170–71).

[6] For the detailed discussion of the novel's female poisoner, see Crosby (2005: 165–247).

dimension" to it for "violence is what necessitates the gift's rupture with both consciousness and phenomenology" (Moore 2011: 9). This toxicological logic abides even when applied to women's bodies. In her feminist adaptation of Derrida, Nancy Holland, for example, claims that the woman as an object of gift exchange is "poisoned" with her femininity, "her own subject/self outside the circle of gift and debt" (Holland 2013: 97; see also 93). One can speculate that, in a similar way, the slave given away as a gift is "poisoned" with the surplus of his or her racial otherness that the giver never quite owns and that cannot be traded or exchanged.

In what follows, in my analysis of Stowe's novel, I first discuss the sentimental aspects of slave gifting through the examples of Tom and Eliza, the enslaved characters who participate in the novel's "spiritual transactions," as it were. My focus, however, is on the overlooked example of the poisonous gift in *Uncle Tom's Cabin*—the gift of the slave child Topsy who figures as an unwelcome, wasteful, and repellent present. As I argue, Topsy is the *anti-gift* or *topsy-turvey* gift of the novel that at once directly addresses its embedded racialism and re-inscribes the morale of "pure" giving. The "poison" of this unwanted gift, albeit eventually defused by the "antidote" of sentiment, at least for a brief moment presses the novel's "moral economy" to its limits and places race outside of the sentimental framework.

6.2 "Bound in black morocco": Slavery and Sentimental Exchanges

In *A Key to Uncle Tom's Cabin*, Stowe enumerates economic transactions performed on slaves. She indignantly mentions the right "to buy and sell, lease, hire and mortgage" (Stowe 2015: 206) "lease, sell, mortgage, or hire" (232) men, women, and children, as well as to bequeath them but does not include the slaveholder's right to *give a slave away* gratuitously in this list. The omission of gift exchange is conspicuous, especially since the subject of giving slaves as presents was familiar in abolitionist literature. For example, the narrator of Quincy's "Dinah Rollins" discussed in Chap. 5 mocks the idea of white generosity and gift-giving, rendering an example of the old newspaper advertisement: "TO BE GIVEN AWAY, a likely negro child of five years old; apply to the printer" (Quincy 1840: 126). Such advertisements, he says, no longer appear in the columns of the Southern newspapers:

Now, as generosity is well known to be the inseparable companion of chivalry, it cannot be supposed that the absence of such advertisements is owing to any lack of giving spirit. It must be accounted for either by modesty which shrinks from such a parade of liberal designs, or by a change in the value of the gift, which makes such a proclamation unnecessary in order to find one willing to accept it. (126)

As Quincy argues, further supporting his claim by the counter-example of the Black woman's true generosity, the practice of giving slaves as gifts is "the most indisputable, unimpeachable evidence of the true character of the system" (126).

Igor Kopytoff describes slavery as the "process of social transformation": "Slavery begins with capture or sale, when the individual is stripped of his previous social identity and becomes a non-person, indeed an object, and an actual or potential commodity." Further, he writes, "the slave becomes less of a commodity and more of a singular individual in the process of gradual incorporation into the host society": "the successful phases merge into one another" (Kopytoff 1986: 65). *Uncle Tom's Cabin* neatly illustrates Kopytoff's observation since Stowe was specifically concerned with the fragility of social and human relationships penetrated by the market. However, in the episodes when slaves are given away, "the successful phases" merge into one another even more forcefully, within the limits of a single transaction. Strictly speaking, there is little difference from the moral standpoint between the antebellum practices of selling and giving away human beings; both are unacceptable for the modern sensibility that bears on the distinction between persons and things. In *Uncle Tom's Cabin*, however, both instances of giving slaves as gifts that I analyze here are imbued with sentiment and benevolent feeling. This way, gift exchange simultaneously objectifies and de-commodifies slaves, making the ideology of disinterested giving ethically ambiguous.

This ambiguity is best revealed in the metaphors that accompany transactions or their accounts. When St. Clare bargains with Haley about Uncle Tom whom he is purchasing on Eva's request, he ironically comments about Tom: "All the moral and Christian virtues bound in black morocco, complete!" (179). St. Clare's metaphor "bound in black morocco" most likely alludes not merely to Tom's skin but also to the gift edition of the Bible. In the antebellum United States, a Bible, a sellable commodity, was "the most common book offered as a gift… Giving a Bible was sharing the gift of God" (Lehuu 2000: 82). Seen in this light, Uncle Tom is an embodied "word of God" that has been commodified and that is now given, to Eva by St. Clare but also, figuratively, to St. Clare by Eva; further religious conversion of the planter owes much to Uncle Tom, a walking Gospel, and to Tom's spiritual connection with his angelic daughter. Morocco was also a usual binding of gift books.[7] The morocco metaphor precisely captures Tom's situation: just like a gift book, he is a commodity in transit; his purchase by St. Clare at Eva's request is a an expression of fatherly love for his daughter adding a sentimental value to the object of transaction. Uncle Tom will make a bond between the father and the daughter even stronger as we know from the rest of the story.

Another gift-related metaphor attributed to Tom is far less elevated than that of the Bible or the gift book. Eva tells St. Clare, "Papa, do buy him!" and declares: "I want him." Her much-discussed and nearly scandalous (in the misogynous context) "I want him" sounds like the cry of a spoilt child begging a parent to buy a toy or a candy. Predictably, St. Clare interprets it exactly this way: "What for, pussy? Are you going to use him for a rattle-box, or a rocking-horse, or what?" Eva responds: "I want to make him happy" (180). Eva's benevolent attitude (giving happiness to Tom) contrasts but also dovetails with the toyshop image of consumption. Tom and Eva's friendship begins with the gift exchange of candies and toys on the steamboat and results, paradoxically, in converting Tom himself into "a rocking-horse" that a loving and generous father buys for his daughter. In this scene, Stowe clearly demonstrates the racist prejudices of St. Clare and the moral superiority of his daughter, who sees Tom not as a thing (a toy) but as a person worthy of happiness. But inadvertently, the scene also reveals Eva's spiritual consumerism. Eva wants to possess everyone as she guides souls to the Gospel until she herself dies of consumption. She has no right to make Tom happy by any moral law yet takes this right for granted. To make someone happy means to give someone "happiness" (whatever this might mean), but, in this particular case, giving is inseparable from taking and keeping: a subject of benevolence and an objectified "gift" are the same. Tom's story is a good example of the "spiritual transaction" at work. Gift exchanges among father and daughter,

---

[7] Some of these, like the famous *The Opal, a Pure Gift for the Holy Days*, were religious in character. Ironically, *Uncle Tom's Cabin* was itself published in 1852 as a gift book Christmas edition stylistically resembling a Bible. "The fancy gift book even looked like a Bible. The cover was pebbled deep crimson and adorned with a gold-embossed imprint of Christ… the pages were gilt-edged; and tiny imprints of angels, praying figures, and doves decorated the chapters endings" (Jo-Ann Morgan 2007: 75).

daughter and father, angelic slaveholder and slave mediate between Tom's "thingness," which is implied in the toy metaphors, and his supreme, universal personhood manifested in his religiosity, goodness, and Christ-like suffering.

The story of Eliza told retrospectively is another "gift story" of the novel. As we learn from George Shelby's account on the steamboat, Eliza was bought at a Louisiana slave market at the age of eight or nine as a present from his father to his mother. Arthur Shelby paid an "extravagant sum" for the exceptionally beautiful, white-skinned child who became a favorite pet servant of his wife. When Madame de Thoux, who turned out to be an ex-slave and the sister of George Harris, asks George Shelby "What sort of a girl?" about Eliza, he replies: "A treasure ... a beautiful, intelligent, amiable girl. Very pious. My mother had brought her up, and trained her as carefully, almost, as a daughter. She could read and write, embroider and sew, beautifully; and was a beautiful singer" (495–96). The word "treasure" placed side by side with "extravagant sum" in the next paragraph is equivocal in the outlined context. Eliza is a treasure of a human being, not the least because her best natural qualities were cultivated under the kind guidance of Mrs. Shelby, a grateful receiver and keeper of the gift. Yet the word "treasure" also connotes Eliza's value as a luxurious present that a generous husband bestows on his wife.

Eliza's case even more explicitly reveals the mechanism of generating inalienable sentimental property. However, it is important to stress that Eliza's case is different from other sentimental human "belongings" of Mrs. Shelby since she is the only slave who will not be sold. Arthur Shelby himself, who finds it morally acceptable to sell the devoted and trusty Tom or separate the child from his mother, firmly resists Haley's more than generous offer to buy Eliza: "'Mr. Haley, she is not to be sold,' said Shelby. 'My wife would not part with her for her weight in gold'" (15). A beautiful mixed-race Eliza would cost a fortune in New Orleans but she is worth more than "her weight in gold" for Mrs. Shelby because of a special kind of attachment between the owner and her possession. In his turn, Shelby acts as a Southern "man of honor" who would not take back the gift he bestowed on his wife.[8] What makes the entire passage disturbing is the fact that the distinction between personal and inalienable gifts, on the one hand, and impersonal and alienable commodities, on the other, is tacitly applied to define the value of a human being. Eliza's status in Shelby's

---

[8] On the rituals of gift-giving and Southern honor, see Greenberg (1996: 51–87).

family is unique not only because she is white-skinned, beautiful, and educated but also because she is a gift that is by definition dearer than any gold to a sensitive heart.

Shelby's metaphor, "My wife would not part with her for her weight in gold," anticipates the "treasure" metaphor in his son's account. Both Tom and Eliza, as exceptionally gifted, supreme human beings, make good gifts in the same way (ironically) they make good commodities, because virtue has a high market price, as abolitionists including Stowe many times indignantly pointed out. Stowe seemingly has a trouble with listing gift-giving together with buying, selling, leasing, and other "purely" economic transactions, and she makes an effort to sentimentalize the otherwise scandalous exchange: the gift *of* a slave simultaneously becomes a gift *to* a slave. But this substitution confuses the opposition between persons and things and jeopardizes the idea of pure gratuity. It also reveals deeper racial assumptions of *Uncle Tom's Cabin* that have been at the core of the novel's critique ever since James Baldwin's "Everybody's Protest Novel" (1949): the novel advocates a patronizing, possessive attitude to the people of a different skin color in disguise of disinterestedness (Baldwin 1998). The ideology of a disinterested gift works to support Stowe's racism in that it allows her to naturalize ethically incompatible social attitudes. At the same time, *Uncle Tom's Cabin* models an alternative scene of gift exchange that resists and challenges such naturalization.

6.3 The Poison of the Gift and Its Antidote

When St. Clare makes a present of a Black child called Topsy to his Vermont cousin Ophelia, he performs a putatively benevolent act toward the object of this exchange, the same way Eva does when she asks him to buy Uncle Tom, or that Mrs. Shelby does when treating her husband's "present" with care. We learn that St. Clare saved the girl from cruel owners who had been constantly flogging her and gives her to his cousin for missionary purposes. At the same time, he sees in Topsy a little more than a "fine specimen of Jim Crow," and sees the entire saga of her education as an amusing experiment; Topsy serves as "a rattle-box, or a rocking-horse" for him, as Tom, in his opinion, might serve for Eva. Structurally, we encounter a similarly ambiguous mixture of sentiment and power, benevolence and entertainment. And yet there is a stark contrast between the scene of Topsy's bestowal and the two gifting episodes of Tom and Eliza. Unlike Eliza, Topsy is not a beautiful, well-spirited child. Ophelia is reluctant to receive the present of a slave girl saying to St. Clare: "*I* don't want her, I am sure" (279). Ophelia's reply, "I don't want her," is the exact opposite of little Eva's demand, "I want him." In contrast to Eliza and Tom, Topsy is a gift that is both worthless and unwelcome.

The "thingness" that the transaction inevitably imposes on Tom and Eliza is at least partly transcended by sympathy and benevolent attitude, since both are at once gifts to keep and people to protect and "make happy." By contrast, in Topsy's case, it is blatantly manifested: "Augustine, what in the world have you brought that **thing** here for?" (278) (emphasis added). Ophelia calls Topsy a "thing" despite her proclaimed anti-slavery ideas and Christian beliefs. We know that St. Clare's Vermont cousin treats colored people with an almost physical sense of disgust, the innate racism of the Northerner being the critical target of the novel. And yet Ophelia's slip is more than a marker of her racism within the context outlined above. It discloses a bare fact: you cannot give a person as a gift; you can exchange a thing, and if a person becomes the object of such a transaction, then it *is* a thing in this transaction. The thing may become personalized, inalienable, and memorable, but it is still a thing.[9]

Ophelia's anxiety is further strengthened by Topsy's own scandalous self-representation: "Never was born...never had no father nor mother, nor nothin'. I was raised by a speculator, with lots of others. Old Aunt Sue used to take car on us" (282). At Ophelia's question whether she heard anything about God and knew who made her, Topsy answers: "I spect I grow'd. Don't think nobody never made me" (282). Having no mother and no father and therefore having never been born, Topsy is a true *thing* as well as a commodity in the hands of a speculator; she "personifies the very principles of finance capitalism ... a miraculous fertility that appears capable of making something out of nothing; an infinite fungibility and asset liquidity" (Best 2004: 192–93). Topsy appears to be a sheer symbol of market economy, its simulacrum. In *A Key to Uncle Tom's Cabin*, Stowe particularly emphasizes the "atrocious" and "sacrilegious" character of "breeding human beings" conducted as business (Stowe 2015: 151). To Stowe, breeding is the very opposite of sentimental education, or rather its uncanny counterpart. Instead of cultivating faith and feelings, it mechanically reproduces merchandise for sale.

---

[9] Elizabeth Young observes that "Topsy is represented [by Stowe] as an inhuman 'thing.' Her 'black, glassy eyes' are to be seen rather than to see, and her voice makes 'odd guttural sounds' rather than intelligible speech" (Young 1999: 32).

Yet Topsy is represented as a very specific "commodity," since her purchase (unlike Tom's and Eliza's) is wasteful. To Ophelia, St. Clare's gesture appears both impractical and meaningless: "Your house is so full of these little plagues, now, that a body can't set down their foot without treading on 'em" (Stowe 1986: 279). As Tavia Nyong'o neatly asserts, "Topsy is part of a disturbing and disgusting surplus" (Nyong'o 2002: 376). Even "the violence done upon her" when Ophelia flogs her for misbehavior is "the performance of waste": Topsy continues disobeying her mentor because she is "wicked" as she says herself. Nyong'o links Topsy's wastefulness to Georges Bataille's "general economy," "which for Bataille is founded not upon the problem of scarcity, but rather, the problematics of excess: excess of resources, excess of people" (n 14). The allusion to Bataille in respect to Topsy does not strike me as counterintuitive. Bataille's theory of expenditure works well to explain not only Topsy's precarious position in Stowe's novel but also her status as a gift. While the idea of waste reflects the general state of things in St. Clare's house and also alludes to a common Southern practice of giving away slaves that had or no longer had market value, it also makes a difference as far as gift-giving is concerned. Topsy conspicuously stands out of the similar episodes of "human" gift exchange in that she transcends or denies utility and epitomizes meaningless, or unproductive expenditure that sustains the concept of the true or pure gift in Bataille (1988).

Yet Topsy is not just a wasteful offering; metaphorically, she evokes a topos of a dangerous or poisonous gift. Miss Ophelia "approached her new subject very much as a person might be supposed to approach a black spider, supposing them to have benevolent designs toward it" (Stowe 1982: 280). A black spider is both repulsive and poisonous as it is potentially dangerous. The metaphor is of course ironic and picks at Ophelia's implicit racism. But again, it has deeper implications than just that in the context of gift exchange: the metaphor is disturbing and racist, as is the entire, racially colored scene of Topsy's bestowal—as if Stowe walks us to the very limits of our sensitivity. How does it feel to receive a black spider as a gift? Especially if the spider is given with best intentions? The "spider" suddenly re-inscribes the metaphor of a "thing": it is a thing in the meaning of a creature, but hardly a commodifiable thing. Unlike gold, or a rattle-box, or a Bible, the spider cannot be commodified or fetishized, or elicit sympathy, or have any sentimental value. It does not represent the sentiment of a well-meaning and loving giver (and St. Clare is certainly the one), nor is it inalienable with his personality. It is impossible to imagine a poisonous spider as a token or keepsake. Topsy's alleged "inhumanness," danger, or "poison" free her from sentiment and, therefore, from the ambiguity inherent in the similar episodes with Eliza and Tom.

I argue that what makes this scene so explicitly racist also makes it potentially redemptive. The metaphor of a poisonous black spider, racist as it is, comes close to the impossible gift in a Derridean sense and as such resists the novel's sentimental ideology. How can one challenge the system where the spiritual gifts of a person are also marketable commodities, where persons and things may become hardly distinguishable? Perhaps by giving something that resists the very idea of possession and transcends the binary between disinterested giving and interested exchange. Topsy whose name alone connotes carnivalesque, grotesque subversion, is not only the novel's subversive character as has been many times pointed out, but she is also its anti-gift or topsy-turvy gift, as it were.

Stowe does not stop with the spider metaphor: Topsy is the only black character in the novel repeatedly compared with repulsive or poisonous insects and reptiles. The "serpent" metaphor, for example, forms part of Stowe's notoriously racist juxtaposition of a white, educated, and angelic Eva and a Black, wicked, and devilish Topsy: Eva "is fascinated by [Topsy's] wild diablerie, as a dove is sometimes charmed by a glittering serpent" (289). This comparison contains blatant Biblical allusions to the story of Eve's seduction by the serpent (inverted in the novel's plotline) and continues the "demonic" theme related to Topsy, but it also reveals Stowe's general uneasiness about the poisonous or pestilent potential of the Black race, the very opposite of the "generous contagion" associated with white benevolence. Stowe writes extensively about such perils in *A Key to Uncle Tom's Cabin*, and in *Uncle Tom's Cabin*, she puts her ideas in St. Clare's mouth when he compares the Black influence with the spiritual "small-pox":

> They are in our houses; they are the associates of our children, and they form their minds faster than we can; for they are a race that children always will cling to and assimilate with. If Eva, now, was not more angel than ordinary, she would be ruined. We might as well allow the small-pox to run among them, and think our children would not take it, as to let them be uninstructed and vicious, and think our children will not be affected by that. (272)

St. Clare aligns "uninstructed" and "vicious": a Black person is vicious without education (read: white guidance) and Topsy, who famously calls herself "wicked," is a prime example of this danger. This is not to say that Topsy is actually dangerous or repulsive; a comic character modeled on the picanniny and the readers' favorite, "her frolics and tricks were themselves absorbed into a tradition of 'nigger' entertainment" (Wood 2000: 194). And yet, on the metaphorical level of the novel, Topsy *is* a "virus," her viral and vicious qualities being the other side of her amusing vitality.

Stowe's overall design about Topsy's function in *Uncle Tom's Cabin* is well-known and has been much discussed. St. Clare gives Topsy to Ophelia with the intention to see how far Ophelia's missionary zeal would go, but, more important, Eva's evangelical mission is realized through the Topsy plot. Stowe demonstrates that Topsy's sentimental education via Eva's ministrations proves to be more efficacious than Ophelia's Calvinist methods: Eva's spiritual love and compassion confers a soul and a capacity to feel to the "inhuman" Topsy and converts Ophelia into a better Christian, or "Miss Feely." Christopher Diller emphasizes that both Topsy and Ophelia stand out among the novel's characters: "whereas Tom, Eva, and Eliza reveal their existing sentimental natures through heroic action, and characters like Mr. Bird or even Tom Loker revert to underlying sentimental natures under feminine suasion, Topsy and Ophelia must significantly change to forge new and more sympathetic identities" (34). My point, however, is that they are exceptional in a different way than radical transformations of character, though that may be symptomatic of the problems of gift exchange I have been delineating. The entire narrative of Topsy's "salvation" can be read as a story of how the "sentimental" gift trumps the dangerous one.

In the chapter symptomatically titled "The Little Evangelist," Eva addresses Topsy in her paternalistic manner: "O, Topsy, poor child, *I* love you!" (330). Graphically, Eva's "*I* love you" with the italicized "I" is another counter-replica of Ophelia's "*I* don't want her." The word of love comes together "with a sudden burst of feeling" and a touch as Eva "lay[s] her little thin, white hand on Topsy's shoulder" (330). St. Clare's gift of an unwanted human being is countered by Eva's gift of a kind word.[10] By uttering the word of love, Eva starts the circle of exchange that requires

---

[10] Stowe treated words as gifts, as is demonstrated for example in the episode when the dying Eva is giving locks of her hair to the slaves as "a last mark of her love," whereas the slaves "poured forth words of endearment, mingled in prayers and blessings" in return (339). In *Dred*, Stowe is even more explicit, in a scene when Nina Gordon calls Tiff's little mistress "Miss Fanny": "If Nina had heaped Tiff with presents, she could have not conferred the inexpressible obligation conveyed in these words" (Stowe 1856: 290).

Topsy's reciprocity: "I love you, and I want you to be good... I wish you would try to be good, for my sake;—it's only a little while I shall be with you" (331). The scene produces a revolution in Topsy's mind and heart as she bursts into tears of gratitude. Moreover, her every subsequent appearance in the novel is accompanied with images of gratuitous, disinterested giving. In the next chapter, Topsy comes to Eva's room with a bouquet she picked for her in the garden. Topsy's bouquet stands for her "better," elevated self; it is an expression of her changed, sentimentalized person. In the next scene, Topsy appears in Eva's room again, now begging for a memorable lock of hair that Eva generously bestows on the girl, while reminding her of her obligation: "every time you look at that, think that I love you, and wanted you to be a good girl!" (340). In the next episode, Topsy brings a flower to Eva's deathbed; in yet another, she is "caught" with a theft that turns out to be a prayer book and a lock of hair given to her by Eva that she piously and fondly cherishes.

Anthropologically speaking, Eva and Topsy become dependent actors exchanging inalienable tokens that constitute their new relationship.[11] Eva's gift obliges Topsy to reciprocate and in this sense her gift is never "terminal" (Kopytoff 1986: 69). It both "disembodies"[12] Topsy from her status of "inhuman" commodity and defuses her "poison," but, ironically, such reciprocity of dependent yet freely acting agents results in making Topsy herself a better gift. Stowe rewrites the initial scene of her bestowal when Ophelia wisely asks St. Clare to make the gift of Topsy a legal transaction:

> "There, now, she's yours, body and soul," said St. Clare, handing the paper.
> "No more mine now than she was before," said Miss Ophelia. "Nobody but God has a right to give her to me; but I can protect her now." (361)

The same Ophelia who had unwillingly accepted Topsy as a "thing," now receives her as if anew, legally from St. Clare but truly from the hands of God, who entrusts the "darky" to her motherly care and protection.

---

[11] For example, anthropologist Chris Gregory, distinguishing the gift from commodity, claims that the gift "presupposes reciprocal dependence and inalienability" (Gregory 1982: 24).

[12] Since most of the modern gifts are commodities and yet need to be disinterested and pure, the "ideology of the perfect gift" accommodates this contradiction by "disembodying the object given, by asserting that the sentiment that the gift carries is important while the object itself, the vehicle, is insignificant" (Carrier 1995: 15).

The racist underpinnings of this episode are self-evident: God has no more right to give Topsy to Ophelia than does St. Clare. Ophelia, who did not "want" Topsy the way she was, insists on "holding" the girl who now meets the standards of a sentimental female character having become pious, sensitive, and submissive.

"Humanizing" and "sentimentalizing" Topsy through a series of exchanges (of feelings, tears, and gifts), Stowe retreats from the radical step she made when introducing her in the novel for the first time. The ending of Topsy's narrative—sending her along with other former slaves to teach the Gospel in Liberia—is yet another conformist step back. Susan Ryan is correct, however, when she argues that Stowe's newly born missionaries have different reasons to move to Africa. George Harris, for example, chooses one of his two adopted racial identities (Ryan 2000: 764; being white-skinned, he could have stayed in the country of his father instead of moving to the lost motherland, his mother's land). Topsy does not have a similar choice; she is phenotypically determined to go and stay "with her own people" and ideologically determined to fulfil Eva's evangelical mission. Topsy reciprocates by spreading the word of God among Liberians in return for Eva's kind word of love.

At the same time, the ending may also reflect Stowe's deeper uneasiness about Topsy's racial otherness and is indicative of the fact that she conceived the Black race as a dangerous and trying gift of God to the whites that they should neutralize and disarm, but that would be still safer to remove. The final act literalizes St. Clare's metaphor when he says to his cousin, anticipating Topsy's appearance,[13] that she loathes Black people as she would "a snake or a toad" and would willingly send them "to Africa, out of your sight and smell" (211). Topsy's eventual removal in reverse (instead of sending a missionary to the Blacks, a Black person is sent away as a missionary) is suggestive of the fact that Stowe feared that race itself, rather than "ignorance" or "vice," may be "poisonous."

While the pattern of Topsy story reveals that the sentimental ideology of the gift that Stowe professed has racialist, conformist, and repressive elements, the episode of Topsy's unwelcome bestowal is evidence of the fact that not everything in *Uncle Tom's Cabin* is under control of Stowe's sentiment—that she intuitively and perhaps subconsciously tested the limits of sentimentality. This scene, as I have argued, suggests a possibility,

---

[13] On the connection between this episode and its metaphors and Topsy's story, see Otter (2008: 22–23).

a glimpse of a different, non-sentimental rendering of the subject, a tacit if unintended criticism of the novel's own premises. It also suggests a strong anti-slavery argument that allows us (albeit briefly) to imagine giving a gift that cannot be possessed.

Reading *Uncle Tom's Cabin* in anthropological perspective has shown that Stowe's novel effectively uses the ideology of disinterested, "morally good" giving to its own ends. This ideology is both conformist and comforting, and, like many of her contemporaries, Stowe makes a considerable effort to bypass all the acute angles it entails. Sentimental exchanges of personalized things grow uncomfortable when trading in objectified persons, and yet Stowe pushes her concept in this direction in order to demonstrate practically how sentimental modes of exchange can achieve a balance between interest and disinterest, and between benevolence and control. The thing and value-related metaphors betray the ethical controversy of such a strategy and help to explain why modern readers may feel uneasy with Stowe's policies.

As the analysis has shown, Stowe constitutes a dense metaphoric language of the gift that is ambiguous and equivocal: it takes us away from the "gift" versus "commodity," giving versus trading binaries to a more complex understanding of the gift that eventually, as a virus, becomes potentially capable of possessing instead of being possessed. This language betrays the novel's unambiguous moral message and registers the deeply troubled meanings that the gift of race, or of the racial other, may imply. If the race *is* poison, then unless neutralized or removed, it is capable of altering both the "giver" and the "receiver," of telling another, non-conventional story.

Topsy's case seems to run counter to this general tendency, and despite Stowe's efforts to naturalize her unruly character via a series of reciprocal exchanges of gifts, words, and tears, her "poison" is out there as a sign of viral, vital, and vibrant potential of both the character and the book. The final triumph of the sentimental racial conformism notwithstanding, Topsy's viral quality shunned in Stowe's narrative becomes projected on *Uncle Tom's Cabin* itself, promptly labeled as "poisonous" reading by its opponents.

It is symptomatic that Stowe, as Elizabeth Young has demonstrated, shared with Topsy her "demoniac rage" and transgressiveness in Southern reviews, where the author of *Uncle Tom's Cabin* was called a "monster," "a devil," and "the man Harriet" (Young 1999: 54). A proslavery reviewer, George Frederick Holmes, went so far as to employ Stowe's own metaphorical language to debase her novel. In *The Southern Literary Messenger*, Holmes compares "the emblems of fiction" in *Uncle Tom's Cabin* with creatures that sing sweet Siren's songs and have a skin "as sleek and slimy and glistening as that of the serpent which tempted Eve." He advises his readers to "repel them from [their] intimacy and from [their] dwellings, which their presence would contaminate," and to "reject them with disgust" (Holmes 1852: 721). What strikes me in this example is the similarity between Holmes' characterization and Stowe's description of Topsy as a "glittering serpent" charming the innocent Eva. Calling books poisonous and harmful was a commonplace practice in antebellum prescriptive literature, but redeploying the racist metaphors that *Uncle Tom's Cabin* trades in, Holmes places its author and her character in a similar position, if not exactly the same boat.

Indeed, in the wake of the Civil War, Stowe's contemporaries tended to see *Uncle Tom's Cabin* as a poisonous gift that functioned, as a *pharmakon*, that is, in a twofold way. Proslavery writers accused Stowe of sowing discord between neighbors, while her fellow abolitionists praised this discord as healing and redeeming. When Abraham Lincoln allegedly called Stowe the "little lady who made the big war,"[14] it is hard not to suspect that this patronizing compliment playfully concealed the image of a mythical Pandora—a divine gift to humankind whose famous box released disagreements and wars.

Works Cited

Baldwin, James. 1998. Everybody's Protest Novel. In Baldwin, James. *Collected Essays*, 11–19. Library of America.
Bataille, George. 1988. *The Accursed Share: An Essay on General Economy*. Trans. Robert Hurley. New York: Zone Books.
Best, Stephen M. 2004. *The Fugitive Properties: Law and the Poetics of Possession*. Chicago and London: The University of Chicago Press.
Brown, Gillian. 1990. *Domestic Individualism: Imagining Self in Nineteenth-Century America*. Berkeley: University of California Press.
Carrier, James G. 1995. *Gifts and Commodities: Exchange and Western Capitalism Since 1700*. London: Routledge.

---

[14] As has been many times pointed out, there is no textual evidence to support this popular anecdote.

Crosby, Sara Lynn. 2005. *Poisonous Mixtures: Gender, Race, Empire, and Cultural Authority in Antebellum Female Poisoner Literature*. Diss. Notre Dame (IN): University of Notre Dame.

Derrida, Jacques. 1992. *Given Time: I. Counterfeit Money*. Trans. Peggy Kamuf. Chicago: University of Chicago Press.

Diller, Christopher. 2004. Sentimental Types and Social Reform in *Uncle Tom's Cabin*. *Studies in American Fiction* 32 (1): 21–48.

Greenberg, Kenneth S. 1996. *Honor and Slavery. Lies, Duels, Noses, Masks, Dressing … in the Old South*. Princeton: Princeton University Press.

Gregory, Christian. 1982. *Gifts and Commodities*. London: Academic Press Inc.

Halpern, Faye. 2018. Beyond Contempt: Ways to Read *Uncle Tom's Cabin*. *PMLA* 133 (3): 633–639.

Holland, Nancy J. 2013. 'Everything comes back to it.' Woman as Gift in Derrida. In *Woman and the Gift. Beyond the Given and All-Giving*, ed. Morny Joy, 92–100. Bloomington: Indiana University Press.

Holmes, George Frederic. 1852. Rev. of *Uncle Tom's Cabin*. *Southern Literary Messenger* 18 (12): 721–731.

Kete, Mary Louise. 2000. *Sentimental Collaborations: Mourning and Middle-Class Identity in Nineteenth-Century America*. Durham: Duke University Press.

Kopytoff, Igor. 1986. The Cultural Biography of Things: Commoditization as a Process. In *The Social Life of Things: Commodities in Cultural Perspective*, ed. Arjun Appadurai, 64–95. Cambridge: Cambridge University Press.

Lehuu, Isabelle. 2000. *Carnival on the Page: Popular Print Media in Antebellum America*. Chapel Hill: The University of North Carolina Press.

Mauss, Marcel. 1997. Gift, Gift. In *The Logic of the Gift: Towards an Ethic of Generosity*, ed. Alan D. Schrift, 28–33. New York; London: Routledge.

Moore, Gerald. 2011. *Politics of the Gift: Exchanges in Poststructuralism*. Edinburgh: Edinburgh University Press.

Morgan, Jo-Ann. 2007. *Uncle Tom's Cabin as Visual Culture*. Minnesota: University of Missouri Press.

Nyong'o, Tavia. 2002. Racial Kitsch and Black Performance. *The Yale Journal of Criticism* 15 (2): 371–391.

Otter, Samuel. 2008. Samuel Otter on the Race Question: Uncle Tom, Topsy, and Miss Ophelia. In *Bloom's Guides: Harriet Beecher Stowe's* Uncle Tom's Cabin, ed. Harold Bloom. New York: Infobase Publishing.

Parry, Jonathan. 1986. The Gift, the Indian Gift, and the 'Indian Gift'. *Man* 21 (3): 453–473.

Quincy, Edmund. 1840. Dinah Rollins. In *The Liberty Bell* [for 1841], 121–141. Boston: Massachusetts Anti-Slavery Fair.

Reynolds, David S. 2012. *Mightier Than the Sword*: Uncle Tom's Cabin *and the Battle for America*. New York: W. W. Norton & Company.

Riss, Arthur. 1994. Racial Essentialism and Family Values in 'Uncle Tom's Cabin'. *American Quarterly* 46 (4): 513–544.

Ryan, Susan M. 2000. Charity Begins at Home: Stowe's Antislavery Novels and the Forms of Benevolent Citizenship. *American Literature* 72 (4): 751–782.

Stowe, Harriet Beecher. 1856. *Dred, A Tale of the Great Dismal Swamp*. Vol. I. Boston: Phillips, Samson.

———. 1982. *Uncle Tom's Cabin; Or Life among the Lowly*, in Stowe, Harriet Beecher. *Three Novels*, ed. Kathryn Kish Sklar. New York: Library of America.

———. 2015. *A Key to Uncle Tom's Cabin: Presenting the Original Facts and Documents upon Which the Story Is Founded*. New York: Dover Publications.

Strathern, Marilyn. 1988. *The Gender of the Gift: Problems with Women and Problems with Society in Melanesia*. Berkeley: University of California Press.

Wardley, Lynn. 1992. Relic, Fetish, Femmage: The Aesthetics of Sentiment in the Work of Stowe. *The Yale Journal of Criticism* 5 (3): 168–191.

Wood, Marcus. 2000. *Blind Memory: Visual Representations of Slavery in England and America, 1780–1865*. Manchester: Manchester University Press.

Young, Elizabeth. 1999. *Disarming the Nation: Women's Writing and the American Civil War*. Chicago: University of Chicago Press.

CHAPTER 7

Pure Tokens and Venomous Bodies

7.1 "None Are *Poisonous*"? A Bouquet to the Reader

In the preface to *Forget-me-Not, or the Philipena* (1852), a gift book that she edited, Mrs. J.S.F. [Joanna Skelton Fosdick] Lunt compares her "little volume" to a nosegay of flowers, quoting from Montaigne who said, "I have here only a nosegay of culled flowers, and have brought nothing of my own but the thread that ties them." Expanding on this metaphor, Lunt offers the volume to the reader as a gift in the hope that, "to the eye accustomed to appreciate beauty wherever it is found, and loving the simple wild flower as well as the stately rose, none of them appear utterly valueless." She adds that "of one thing [I am] certain—none are *poisonous*. The nosegay, such as it is, is offered to the public, with the hope that it may prove a not wholly unacceptable GIFT" (Lunt 1853: n/p; emphasis in the original.—A.U.).

The words "poisonous" and "gift," both emphasized in Lunt's original text, seem to be mutually exclusive: to be acceptable, the bouquet must not be poisonous; imperfection can be forgiven but malice never. The "unpracticed fingers" of the gift book compiler, as Lunt calls herself, may collect "unworthy" flowers but not poisonous ones (Lunt 1853: n/p). Lunt does not specify what exactly she means by "poisonous," but we may assume it represents "sinful," "polluted," "corrupted," "immoral," "vicious," or "licentious" in the general line of the "poisonous books" rhetoric from which her metaphor stems. The gift of selected poems adheres to the dualistic logic of poisonous versus pure or benign, harmful versus wholesome. Gift-giving, in Lunt's interpretation, *is* a moral act; for the gift to be pure or true, it should be free from any taint of corruption or vice.

© The Author(s), under exclusive license to Springer Nature Switzerland AG 2022
A. Urakova, *Dangerous Giving in Nineteenth-Century American Literature*, American Literature Readings in the 21st Century, https://doi.org/10.1007/978-3-030-93270-1_7

In "The Old Manse," a preface to *The Mosses of the Old Manse*, Hawthorne compares his stories to "idle weeds and withering blossoms" that together with the "old, faded things, reminding [him] of flowers pressed between the leaves of a book" form a bouquet that he offers to the reader (Hawthorne 1982: 1148–49). Just as Mrs. Lunt was to do six years later, Hawthorne modestly suggests that his "flowers" may be "unworthy" ("weeds," "old, faded things") but tacitly avoids moral questions concerning purity and poison. The reader fluent in the metaphorical language of the time, however, might have noticed that one of the "flowers" in the "bouquet"—"Rappaccini's Daughter," previously published in the *Democratic Review* (1844)—is a story about a garden full of poisonous plants. Rappaccini's daughter is a pure maiden who has grown up in this garden: like a beautiful but poisonous flower. The narrator's name, M. de l'Aubépine (hawthorn in French), is a double pun referring both to Hawthorne and to hawthorn, the author and the flower. Is Hawthorne's own offering—the story about the woman-flower—"pure" or "poisonous"?

This chapter expands on the previous discussion of the ambivalence associated with the notion of the "poisonous" gift and of the related terms "antidote" and "pharmakon"; however, this time the discussion is situated in a different framework and deals with the poisonous gift primarily on the level of the motif or plot. The three texts I will analyze below, ranging chronologically from the 1840s (as I return to Hawthorne) and moving from there toward the end of the nineteenth century, exhibit archetypal patterns of poisoning via gift-giving, be this the giving of a poisonous gift of a woman or a gift of poisoned food. The relativity of these archetypes is revealed in the modern context, especially when they interact with the emerging consumer culture, while at the same time they contribute to challenging the simplistic didacticism of authors such as Mrs. Lunt, which envisions a gift as exclusively wholesome, benign, and pleasing.

To demonstrate the ambiguity of the pure versus poisonous binary, this chapter will focus on how bodies, conceived of as venomous or polluted, become exteriorized in gifts and tokens as well as in the counter process, when impure thoughts or words materialize as poisonous droplets or hideous creatures. While dealing primarily with the physical threat that the gift (allegedly) poses to health or life, the texts I will discuss simultaneously reveal the strong metaphorical potential of the "poisonous," the very boundaries between the material and the immaterial, the bodily and the spiritual being fluid and traversable. This allows me to cover a rather wide spectrum of toxic or gifts presumed to be toxic, such as flowers, liquids, food, or words.

The material or corporeal aspect of giving highlighted in this chapter brings forward the question of gender. In "Rappaccini's Daughter" as well as in *Elsie Venner* (1861) by Oliver Wendell Holmes, also looked at in some detail in this chapter, we are dealing mainly with the archetypal vision of the "dangerous impure" female body, both texts recalling and revising ancient tales about "poisonous maidens whose tissues were impregnated with toxins and who thus killed any youth they seduced" (Crosby 2016: 134).[1] An alternative interpretation that at once echoes and overturns the masculinist approach can be drawn from the example of a short story titled "Brother Dunstan and the Crabs" (1898) by an obscure late-nineteenth-century author Caroline Wilder Paradise; in this, the final text considered in this chapter, gifts emanate from the communal *male* body and are implicitly associated with male sexuality.

With this double anthropological and gender focus in mind, I will examine the hitherto overlooked dynamics of gift exchange in familiar narratives by Hawthorne and Holmes, including in the exhaustively analyzed "Rappaccini's Daughter," and will introduce the heretofore obscure story "Brother Dunstan and the Crabs," which allows me to trace the recurrence of the poisonous/impure gift imagery both within the canon and at its margins.

7.2 "Touch It Not!" Pernicious Transactions in "Rappaccini's Daughter"

While "Rappaccini's Daughter" has attracted extensive critical attention, especially within postwar New Criticism but also in feminist criticism and gender studies, the function of gifts in the story remains a peripheral concern. Critics usually focus on Beatrice's sacrifice as part of her general victimization[2] or discuss the embedded story of the poisonous woman given to Alexander the Great as a gift,[3] not necessarily connecting these episodes

---

[1] The female body has been associated with poison and danger in different eras: see Lyons (2013; Groebner 2002).

[2] See, for example, Easton who in summarizing widespread critical opinion writes: Beatrice dies, "sacrificing [herself] for men demonstrably undeserving of such inordinate devotion" (Easton 2004: 83).

[3] On Alexander's gift, see specifically Brenzo (1976: 153, 164).

to other instances of gift-giving in the story. Similarly, much has been said about poison in the story and about its figurative or metaphorical dimensions—for example, the significance of the poisonous plant imagery and the figure of the female poisoner—but once again without directly relating these themes to gift-giving (e.g. Kloeckner 1966; Brenzo 1976; Hallissy 1982; Bensick 1985: 83–84; Roger 1997; Crosby 2016: 127–143). In what follows, I will outline a structure of gift exchange in the story, which will allow us to see how giving and poison are interconnected.

Gift exchanges in "Rappaccini's Daughter" both form a non-verbal language and constitute the story's metaphorical language. Giovanni declares his admiration by giving Beatrice a bouquet; Beatrice accepts the floral offering and expresses a desire to reciprocate with a flower from her garden. Professor Baglioni, Giovanni's senior advisor and Rappaccini's rival, cites an ancient story about a fatal gift—in which an Indian prince sends a poisonous woman to Alexander the Great with the intention of killing him; Alexander is alerted and saved by a physician—to explain the "terrible secret" (Hawthorne 1982: 996) of Rappaccini's daughter, who has also "nourished" with poison since childhood. He refers to the antidote that he passes on to Giovanni to administer to Beatrice as a precious gift: "the little silver vase" that contains the medicine is "well-worthy to be a love-gift to the fairest dame in Italy" (998). Giovanni, at first incredulous, eventually changes his opinion and offers the antidote to Beatrice. Rappaccini then appears and orders Beatrice to give a flower to Giovanni as a sign of their union but she disobeys and soon after dies, killed by the antidote that was, in the end, lethal.

Gifts in Hawthorne's story are simultaneously signs and tokens that are meaningful in various ways. They speak a language of power, control, and manipulation (e.g., in the cases of Rappaccini, Baglioni, the Indian prince) on the one hand, and a language of courtship and love (Giovanni) on the other. The latter is conspicuously impersonal: the bouquet is bought at the florist's; the vase wrought by Cellini together with its contents belongs to Baglioni. Responding to the courtship, Beatrice acts coquettishly: "I accept your gift, and would fain recompense it with this precious purple flower; but if I toss it into the air, it will not reach you. So Signor Guasconti must even content himself with my thanks" (986). Concealing from him that the flower is poisonous (Easton: 84), she teases Giovanni into a romantic affair where he will have to content himself with words and gazes. Yet in contrast to Giovanni's commercial bouquet, Beatrice's counter-gift is "the portion" of herself (Emerson 1983: 536), both metonymically (the flower from her bosom) and metaphorically (at least in Giovanni's eyes, Beatrice herself looks like one of the flowers in the garden). She plucks the flower from the deadly shrub she addresses as "sister"; she has an intimate and passionate, almost lesbian (Tambling 2004: 6) attachment to the plant. While being simultaneously a symbol of Beatrice's fatal self-alienation (where her body is a projection of male ambitions and fantasies), the flower that she offers to Giovanni speaks of her genuine intention to give her uttermost self to the one she chooses.

The initial exchange between the lovers, which draws on the contrast between Giovanni's trivial but harmless bouquet and Beatrice's exquisite and unique but poisonous flower, is both conventional and subversive. For example, Giovanni, "'installed in a high and gloomy chamber' that overlooks the garden ... occupies the structural position of the maiden in the fairy tale" (Greven 2012: 146). Indeed, he throws the bouquet down from the window, just as a "dame in Italy" (Hawthorne 1982: 998) would do in granting her admirer a sign of attention. Giovanni's bouquet is one of the tokens of his androgynous/passive character that manifests itself in the story's homosexual iconography. In Freudian terms, it is a phallic sign of his "heterosexual failure and male terror over female sexuality": the bouquet withers in Beatrice's "grasp" (Greven 2012: 161–62). The seemingly clichéd scene of flower exchange signals that the love story between Giovanni and Beatrice is doomed to fail, that their union is impossible.

Even more ambiguity surrounds Giovanni's second gift, the antidote. At the end of the story, Beatrice dramatically accuses Giovanni: "Oh, was there not, from the first, more poison in thy nature than in mine?" (1005). If she is correct,[4] then the antidote may be associated with Giovanni in a more personal or intimate way than it first seems, the "precious liquid" (998) being "poisoned" with his inner, "figurative" venom (which appears to be more deadly than the actual poison of the antidote (Roger 1997: 433)) as the vase passes through his hands. In such a case, the antidote would be a mirror image of Beatrice's flower: it is at once an alienated gift (the vase belongs to Baglioni) and an expression of the giver, his "portion" (in Giovanni's case, the exteriorized venom of his nature). The difference between the two acts of gift-giving is that Beatrice withdraws the offered flower to protect Giovanni while Giovanni prompts Beatrice to take a risk in accepting his offering.

[4] There are critics, among them Miller (1991), who interpret Beatrice's accusation of Giovanni as one of the numerous "false ends" of the story.

The inversion that accompanies the ultimate and lethal act of gift-giving—when the medicine turns out to be a poison—resonates with the male language of the gift throughout the story. All the male characters wholeheartedly proclaim the innocence or harmlessness of their offerings. Giovanni's bouquet, which initiates the fatal acquaintance, is the first in the series of purportedly pure and, as he calls it, "healthful" offerings: "Signora," says Giovanni, 'here are pure and healthful flowers. Wear them for the sake of Giovanni Guasconti!'" (984). Baglioni uses the word "innocuous" when endorsing his antidote: "One little sip of this antidote would have rendered the most virulent poisons of the Borgias innocuous" (998). Ordering Beatrice to give Giovanni a flower from the most dangerous plant in the garden, Rappaccini claims: "It will not harm him now!" (1004).[5] Hawthorne's story contains a clear message: do not trust the male donor! As Brenzo compellingly argues, the parallel between the main narrative and its *mise en abyme*, a legend about Alexander the Great told by Baglioni, is inverted. The three male characters—Rappaccini (Indian prince), Giovanni (Alexander), and Baglioni (sage physician)—eventually all play the part of the poisoner/treacherous giver, the Indian prince (Brenzo 1976: 164).[6]

"Touch it not!" cries Beatrice when Giovanni, reminding her of the promised "reward," the ungiven gift, tries to pluck the deadly flower (993). This eroticized episode, with its connotations of deflowering, provokes a reflection on Beatrice's protective role in the story. She protects Giovanni from the poisonous gift, just as the physician in the embedded narrative protected Alexander—with the exception that this is her own gift that imperils Giovanni. Her story simultaneously echoes that of Alexander as she too receives a gift of deadly poison. She then involuntarily passes on the venom of her body to her lover, as the Indian woman

---

[5] While what Rappaccini says is the truth, his words sound ominous since the flower, although no longer harmful, is nonetheless the symbol of the damage he has caused to Beatrice and later to Giovanni, who becomes "infected" with Beatrice's poison and thus immune, like her and against his will, to the poison of the flower.

[6] In *American Notebooks*, Hawthorne mentions a similar plot, namely, Montaigne's story of Ladislaus, a King of Naples, who demanded that the inhabitants of the besieged city of Florence deliver to him a beautiful virgin, the daughter of a physician. The father gave his daughter a perfumed handkerchief that turns out to be poisoned and the two died in each other's arms. In this story, there is no theme of gift-giving (the woman is offered as the spoils of war) but there is similar objectification: all the citizens adorn her "in the richest manner" as if she were an artifact. Instead of gift-giving, there is bargain: Ladislaus will show mercy in exchange for the delivery to him of the virgin (Hawthorne 1972: 241).

almost does. Her structural role in the story is more complex than the image that Baglioni's misogynous narrative seeks to impose on us, for example, that Beatrice *is* the Indian woman.

However, the parallel between Beatrice and the woman in the embedded story does exist on the structural or symbolic level of "Rappaccini's Daughter"; it should not be underestimated. Beatrice is not "offered" or "given" to Giovanni in the literal sense yet the objectifying (and commodifying) male gaze aligns her with the Indian woman who is a diplomatic gift bestowed on Alexander, as a jar of precious wine or a piece of jewelry might be. Rappaccini's plan coupled with Giovanni's male fantasy turns Beatrice into a licentious spectacle, simultaneously elusive and hyperreal in its intensity.[7] Beatrice is not just beautiful; her beauty is "glowing," "brilliant," and "vivid," while the garden with its rich vegetation and luxurious, exotic flowers frames it to her advantage.

Giovanni's story, like that of Alexander, is a story of unsatisfied desire. Even after he gains access to the garden by bribing the old dame, Lizabetta, he and Beatrice remain separated as if by an invisible glass wall: "He had never touched one of the gleaming ringlets of her hair; her garment—so marked was the physical barrier between them—had never been waved against him by a breeze" (995). Beatrice resembles a commodity seen behind the glass window of the closed shop—both near and distant, desirable, and inaccessible. Giovanni, an Alexander of our time, indeed acts as a typical modern consumer might: he is fascinated with what he sees, his imagination stimulated by the unusual combination of beauty and terror and by Beatrice's inaccessibility. The consumer wants to gain the object of his desire in the safest possible way. When Beatrice's poison invades his system, Giovanni is filled with spite and will not tolerate any loss of control. The only way to possess Beatrice is to rid her body of poison.

What sets Beatrice apart from the Indian woman is her ability to transcend the status of object assigned to her by offering Giovanni the immaterial gift of love. Remarkably ignoring contemporary issues of slavery, Hawthorne relegates the notion of enslavement of the female body to a legend of olden times.[8] His Beatrice, although "enslaved" in the garden,

---

[7] On the story as an allegory of a middle-class addiction akin to alcoholism, as Giovanni hovers between his obsession with Beatrice and the idea of normalcy, see Temple (2014: 405–425).

[8] On Hawthorne's avoidance of a direct discussion of slavery, see, for example, Arac (1986: 261).

is a victim of patriarchy, not of slavery, and Rappaccini's crime is in abusing his parental power, not in the power itself.[9] Unknowingly, Beatrice helps implement her father's plan yet she also acts out of free will when falling in love and conducting what she believes to be a secret romantic relationship with Giovanni—a luxury that her mythological counterpart, a slave, would not have been allowed.

Beatrice voices a prejudice concerning the virtue of a woman giving herself away in love and marriage.[10] She declares that she "would fain have been loved, not feared" (1005); rebelling against her father's power, she defends the values of the sentimentalized version of the patriarchal family where the father bestows his daughter on a suitor to whom she is sentimentally attached. Beatrice is a giver inasmuch as she is a gift. Giving oneself and giving one's love is the same thing for Hawthorne's female character, whose sublime self-sacrificial plotline runs counter to the objectifying strategies of the male characters.

The drama is in the fact that Beatrice's *gift of self* cannot be bestowed in any conventional, legitimate way; therefore, like the poisonous flower—a symbol of her sexuality?[11]—it is simultaneously given (offered) and not given (withdrawn). Aware of this inevitability, she nevertheless hopes that Giovanni accepts this controversial offering unconditionally. When he fails to do so, she resorts to a desperate gesture by taking the antidote—a "love-gift" she suspects to be poisoned with Giovanni's inner venom. On Beatrice's side, there is a hazardous action leading to suicide, on Giovanni's, the prudence of the consumer aiming for self-preservation and hoping to

---

[9] Beatrice Cenci, who was abused by her father in a famous case from late Renaissance Rome, is a particularly important prototype for Beatrice Rappaccini and her story sheds light on the "thwarted nature" of the father/daughter relationship; some critics speculate that Hawthorne's story is about incest. See, for example, Evans (1964).

[10] Here we can also see the overlap of what Morny Joy considers as two major stereotypes about women as the "given" and as the "all-giving" (Joy 2013). While there is a strong general tendency to see Hawthorne as a proto-feminist author (especially Baym 1982, 2005; also Elbert 2008; Greven 2012), some critics express skepticism toward his feminism (e.g., Medoro 2009; Crosby 2016). I agree with Easton that "there is evidence of both feminist and misogynist views in [Hawthorne's] imaginative and non-fictional writings which have been hotly debated" (Easton 2004: 80).

[11] There is a long-standing critical tradition of reading Beatrice's poison figuratively or allegorically in terms of sexuality. See, for example, Crews 1964: 407–408; Brenzo 1976; Hallissy 1982: 231–32. As Brickhouse puts it, "the positing of lethal toxicity in female sexuality predictably conforms to the nineteenth-century American literary convention of the femme fatal" (Brickhouse 1998: 231).

gain at a low cost to himself. This dualism serves to illuminate the ambivalent, non-dualistic nature of the poison of Beatrice's gift.

The last lines of the story—uttered by Baglioni—assign the blame for Beatrice's death to Doctor Rappaccini, a Romantic "mad scientist." Rappaccini commits a crime against the very core principles of sentimental culture by making sympathy and feelings tools of virology: in loving Giovanni, Beatrice cannot avoid infecting him with her "thwarted" or poisonous nature. The author of "Rappaccini's Daughter" shares with his malicious character this experimental zeal, combining as he does sentimental sensitivity and didacticism with the biased archetype of the "impure" and "dangerous" female nature. As a result, we are confronted with an unresolvable paradox: the only pure and true gift in the story is Beatrice's poisonous gift of self; the only gift that should be unconditionally accepted, according to the ethical imperative of romantic love, is a gift that cannot safely be possessed. "Rappaccini's Daughter" is a story about dangerous giving that manifests on different levels: from the giver's poisonous touch to the recipient's toxic thoughts; from the physical threat of contamination to the risks of the sublime and ethically required act.

Returning to Hawthorne's metaphor of the bouquet, the language of the gift in the tale may also be read as the language of authorship and literary skill. In his now classic study, Michael T. Gilmore demonstrates that "Rappaccini's Daughter" is in fact "a fictionalized version of Hawthorne's literary circumstances in 1844 and an allegory of the common reader's inability to read him rightly" (Gilmore 1985: 64). The proxy for the common reader is the consumer in the story, Giovanni, both influenced by the two groups outlined in the preface—transcendentalists (Rappaccini) and the "pen-and-ink men" appealing to the general public (Baglioni)—while "the most dazzling creation in the garden, Beatrice is intended as an allegorical representation of Hawthorne's writing" (64). Just as Beatrice died of "misreading," Hawthorne presents himself as the innocent victim of textual misunderstanding, "a writer deprived of an audience because the public persists in mistaking his grim exterior for his inner character" (64).

The general line of Gilmore's argument is compelling: projected onto the literary craft, the word "poisonous" is more likely to signify grim, disturbing, or uncomfortable than sinful or corrupt.[12] However, I cannot

---

[12] The image of art as *pharmakon* links "Rappaccini's Daughter" from the 1840s and Hawthorne's earlier work from the 1830s (see Urakova 2016), including "The Minister's Black Veil" discussed in Chap. 4. Yet we also witness an important shift in the rhetoric of

agree with the clear-cut dualistic logic that Gilmore attributes to Hawthorne: that "Rappaccini's Daughter" is a cry out to the reader that "the 'real' Hawthorne is conventional, sentimental, longs to 'open an intercourse with the world,'" just as Beatrice seeks to have an ordinary life (Gilmore 1985: 68). The analysis above suggests that Hawthorne insists on both meanings: his art is pure not despite its being disturbing or dark but because it is both. The dualism of the poisonous and the benign that works perfectly for rhetoricians such as Mrs. Lunt is here replaced with the ambivalent logic of "*and*" instead of "*or*." I would agree with Magnus Ullén who, while also reading the story as an allegory of art, argues that the lethally poisonous Beatrice could have been "the mediating link to a fuller reality, had her young lover not been so anxious to cure her of the toxin that is also her lifeblood ... [T]o the extent that art is capable of performing redemptive—or socially cohesive—work at all, it does so insofar as the reader is able to believe in the ideal aspirations of the artist, in spite of the work's imperfections" (Ullén 2017: 275).

Beatrice paradoxically owes her exquisite beauty, vivacity, and strangeness to her sublimely poisonous "nature" while being at the same time sincere, sensitive, and loving. The poison gives the power of influence or possession over an ordinary consumer/"reader" such as Giovanni (it gets into his system, whether he wants it or not!), while her inner purity and female vulnerability make her gift of love both human and moral. The story's paradoxes are plausible when understood in the supreme poetical sense that incorporates literal and figurative meanings and invites ambiguities.

7.3 "Subtle Poisons": Gifts and Metaphorical Venom in *Elsie Venner*

In her comparative analysis of "Rappaccini's Daughter" and *Elsie Venner*, Kathleen Gallagher draws attention to the serpentine imagery in the former: from the flowers in the garden that are described as "serpent-like" to the "lustrous purple and crimson tones of Beatrice's dress and the plants," "the exotic colors of Lamia in serpent form" (Gallagher 1975: 55). While Beatrice's serpentine connection is merely metaphorical (she is poisonous, like the poisonous "serpent-like" flower: 978), Elsie's kinship with

literary self-marketing between these two stories: while the Minister's symbol is a "simple black veil," Berenice is associated with excessively beautiful, albeit toxic and evil, flowers.

rattlesnakes in *Elsie Venner* has its origins in a prenatal accident: when her mother was bitten by a snake, the venom entered Elsie's system in utero.[13] Holmes's "medicated novel" as he later called it (Holmes 1892: ix), allegedly based on scientific evidence, invites us to believe that Elsie *is* a girl-snake with a double, human/ophidian nature.[14] Critics persuasively demonstrated that both texts, sharing a common source, Keats's *Lamia*, have numerous parallels, even though Holmes never acknowledged his debt to "Rappaccini's Daughter" (Gallagher 1975; Hallissy 1985).

It is indeed possible to read *Elsie Venner* (published in *The Atlantic Monthly* in 1859 and then in book form in 1861) as a sophisticated rewrite of Hawthorne's story. Both female characters, femme fatales, are doomed because their "nature" is poisonous. Both involuntarily kill innocent and unsuspecting creatures (Beatrice—insects and a lizard, Elsie—a bird) and have an intimate, sympathetic connection with poisonous plants (Beatrice) or rattlesnakes (Elsie). Both are dangerous to humans. They leave marks on the skin of others (Beatrice when she touches Giovanni; Elsie when she bites her cousin as a child) and cause them physical damage, illness, or even death (while Beatrice gives her venom as a "virus" to Giovanni, Elsie's evil eye is believed to have caused the death and illness of her wet nurse and governess, respectively). Both are compared with the poisonous Indian woman gifted to Alexander the Great. Both fall in love with a handsome young student of medicine and, broken-hearted, die from the antidote offered by him as a gift.

At the same time, Holmes intensifies, expands, or alters some of the Hawthornesque motifs he appears to have borrowed. Elsie's envenomed blood affects her more profoundly and systematically than it does Beatrice: she is wild, unruly, unconventional, and incapable of human empathy, the very opposite of the meek and angelic Beatrice. Holmes moves the setting

---

[13] Holmes's interest in poisons, including in poison as medicine, manifests itself in his medical essays when he discusses homeopathy or speaks of medicine in terms of small doses of poison. See Holmes (1891).

[14] In an 1842 notebook entry, Hawthorne cites Frances Calderon de la Barca who speaks of "persons who have been inoculated with the venom of rattlesnakes" and are "thus secured forever after against the bite of any venomous reptile"; their "own bite becomes poisonous." "Thus a part of the serpent's nature appears to be transfused into them" (Hawthorne 1972: 238). Brickhouse, after other scholars, suggests that this was a possible inspiration for "Rappaccini's Daughter" (Brickhouse 1998: 230). In his turn, Holmes, criticizing homeopathy, refers to "the old barbarous notion that sick people should feed on poisons [Lachesis, arrow-poison, obtained from a serpent (Pulte). Crotalus horridus, rattlesnake's venom (Neidhard)" (Holmes 1891: x).

of the story from exotic Italy to a New England village and gives Elsie an appearance that is alien and foreign: half-Spanish (a "flaw" from the racially purist perspective that Holmes develops throughout the story), she combines "Spanish" impulsiveness with a snake-like coldness. The dangers of mixed-blood associated with Elsie have more explicit racial connotations (Davis 2002; Crosby 2005: 247–324) than in the significantly more equivocal case of Beatrice whose envenomed blood could be read as encoding racial impurity (Brickhouse 1998: 238; Crosby 2016: 136). Unlike Giovanni, the main male character in *Elsie Venner*, Bernard Langdon, is not in love with Elsie, though his feelings toward her, a mixture of fascination and repulsion, are similar. His gift of the antidote, sent without a second thought, kills *and* "purifies" her, albeit for a brief period of time. On her deathbed, Elsie abandons her "lower nature" (444) and becomes a "true" sentimental heroine which demonstrates that Holmes adheres to the didactic binarism of the pure versus poisonous that Hawthorne attempted to resist or transcend in the image of Beatrice.

While Hawthorne expresses a distaste for the medical profession (Gross 1981; Bensick 1985; Temple 2014), Holmes's novel honors medicine as both science and corporation. Forged around the biblical theme of original sin and experimentally combining literature and medicine, his novel is, above all, a story of the medical student's initiation into the so-called cast of Brahmins (Holmes's term: 1–6)—a New England elite of white male academics. An aspiring scholar experiencing difficult circumstances, forced to earn his living as a village schoolmaster, Bernard eventually enters the supreme academic community, thanks to his talents but also with the aid of female investments: Elsie "invests" herself as scientific material (Bernard's article about her case brings him recognition), while his fiancée Letty Forrester endorses him with financial capital. Holmes's instrumental vision of the sentiment is an ideological shift from the romantic absolutism of love, which Hawthorne places above the safe ethics of self-preservation; in this and other respects, *Elsie Venner* conspicuously defuses Hawthorne's radicalism.

What makes Holmes's novel interesting in the context of dangerous giving is not so much its underlying ideological pattern, with its sexist and racist connotations lying close to the surface (Parker 1972; Traister 1999; Davis 2002), as it is the countermovement that can be identified on the metaphorical level. Concurring with this general line in Holmes's criticism that considers the novel as a sample of mid-century masculinist sentimentality, this chapter suggests shifting the focus and looking at *Elsie Venner* as being trapped between the literal and the figurative meanings of the poisonous/ophidian. Bodies, objects, and words become intricately entangled in the novel, in a manner that is at odds with its general and linear framework.

With the exception of Bernard's fatal offering, dangerous giving in *Elsie Venner* is associated exclusively with Elsie. Unlike Beatrice who offers Giovanni a flower but never actually gives it, Elsie imposes her unwelcome presents—rare alpine flowers—first on her schoolteacher Miss Helen Darley and then, inverting gender-prescribed roles, on Bernard. For Elsie who seems more at ease in the company of rattlesnakes than of her fellow villagers, non-verbal communication via gifts is a way to reach out to others and to demonstrate her sympathy to those she likes. The communicative aspect of gift-giving is captured in the quotation from Virgil's *Aeneid*—"Incipit effari, mediaque in voce resistit" [she begins to speak, and stops mid-sentence: 176]; the flower that Bernard finds in his copy of his book is lying precisely on this line. Elsie's gifts, her first step toward "human" sensitivity, fall mid-way between the ophidian silence and the language of sentiment that she does not (yet) master; they are tokens of sympathy closely associated with her body and self.

The reaction of both receivers to the gifts is, however, far from what Elsie might have expected. Helen Darley does not dare to refuse the gift but she immediately tries to get rid of it.

> She made an excuse for quitting the schoolroom soon afterwards. The first thing she did was to fling the flower into her fireplace and rake the ashes over it. The second was to wash the tips of her fingers, as if she had been another Lady Macbeth. A poor, over-tasked, nervous creature,—we must not think too much of her fancies. (78–79)

Miss Darley's terror and repulsion derive from her inability to separate Elsie's offering from her "impure" body and draw on a metonymical relationship—as if Elsie indeed had venom on her cold fingers. By washing the fingertips that Elsie touched when giving her the flower and burning the flower itself, Miss Darley engages in a double act of purification. She tries to wash the imaginary poison from her hands just as Lady Macbeth had tried to wash imaginary blood from her own. Despite the narrator's ironic attitude (his comment about Miss Darley being a nervous creature anticipates the late-nineteenth-century discussions of female hysteria), Miss Darley's reaction is deeply rooted in the shared prejudice against Elsie:

Elsie's evil eye and dangerous touch—a theme of village gossip—affect everything that comes into contact with her. At the same time, the ironic comparison of the spotless character of Miss Darley with Lady Macbeth emphasizes the ambiguity of her reaction to the presumably toxic gift: afraid that she will be poisoned by Elsie's touch, in her act of washing her hands Darley is compared to the villain who poisoned the guards with drugs and thus allowed Macbeth to kill the king.

Holmes's idealized male character, Bernard Langdon, exercises more self-control when receiving Elsie's flower, yet his reaction is similar to Miss Darley's. Bernard discovers a fresh mountain flower "between the leaves of the Virgil which lay upon his desk." "He looked at Elsie, instinctively, involuntarily. She had another such flower on her breast. A young girl's graceful compliment,—that is all,—no doubt,—no doubt." Bernard, under the spell of the flower, tries the Sortes Virgilianae by allowing the Virgil to fall open at random. The book opens on the story of Laocoon: "He read with a strange feeling of unwilling fascination, from 'Horresco referees' to 'Bis medium amplexi,' and flung the book from him, as if its leaves had been steeped in the subtle poisons that princes die of" (176).

This metonymical transfer of "poison" (from the fingertips to the flower, from the flower to the book) is echoed by a metaphorical transfer: *Aeneid* contains a legend about deadly snakes; snake-like, Elsie presents a danger similar to that of the legend.[15] The leaves of the book become poisonous as if they were the leaves of the envenomed flower; the snake poison in the text of the poem mixes with Elise's imaginary poison. Bernard reads the story of Laocoon with "unwilling fascination" as if the book hypnotizes him, as a snake might.

Not only does Bernard behave irrationally, he also seems to be misreading the classical text and its message. The Virgil is opened on a page of the fourth chapter that in telling the tragic story of Dido abandoned by Æneas foreshadows Elsie's tragic fate: soon after, she will bluntly demand: "*Love me!*" of Bernard (423) and, after his polite but firm rejection, will grow fatally ill. The author's hint or prophesy remains unnoticed because Bernard finds in his reading precisely that which he expects or fears, following an associative chain: the flower—Elsie—snake—Laocoon—poison.

Elsie's flowers, unlike Beatrice's, are not poisonous per se; their "subtle" metaphorical poison does not appear to be deadly: the gifts that

---

[15] Elsie's connection with the Laocoon myth is emphasized in another chapter when it says that she "was taken up in studying the stereoscopic Laocoon" (313).

horrify and repel the recipients cause no apparent harm to either of them. We may also wonder if this is due to precautions undertaken out of superstition, like the burning of the flower and the washing of hands in Darley's case, or if Elsie's good intentions override the magnetic influence that her ophidian body exerts on people and things. If the latter is true, can we think of the flowers allegedly tainted by Elsie's "impure" touch as pure tokens of sympathy or love?

The novel contains an example of the reverse: a well-intended token that becomes toxic and causes lethal harm. Bernard's offering to his ailing friend worsens Elsie's condition and precipitates her death. He contributes the leaves of the white ash to the handmade basket of autumnal flowers that the local schoolgirls send to the ill Elsie among other "little tokens of good-will and kind remembrance" (439). Bernard does so seemingly unaware of the fact that white ash is deadly for snakes—a belief the plot draws upon.

> The school-girls' basket was brought in with its messages of love and hopes for speedy recovery ... Elsie began looking at the flowers, and taking them from the basket, that she might see the leaves ... She took out the flowers, one by one, her breathing growing hurried, her eyes staring, her hands trembling,—till, as she came near the bottom of the basket, she flung out all the rest with a hasty movement. (439–440)

Bernard's gift, bestowed with the best intentions and with no ill or venomous thoughts, seems to be a reflection of Elsie's flower, albeit counter in function or effect. Just as Elsie picks the rare alpine flower in the untrodden mountain path, Bernard collects the colorfully tinted leaves of the white ash during his long solitary walks; the plant is rare and difficult to find in the area. Elsie hides her gift in the book; Bernard's leaves decorate the bottom of the basket that is full of flowers and "messages of love." Elsie's flower deeply disturbs Bernard's imagination while the leaves of the white ash render Elsie "paralyzed" and "senseless," her faint cry chilling the blood of "the startled listeners at her bedside" (440)—a creepy metaphor especially when we remember that Elsie herself has a snake's cold blood in her veins. That the narrator uses the same vocabulary in both instances ("flung") emphasizes the similarity of Bernard's and Elsie's reactions to the gift. The difference, however, is that Bernard remains unharmed while Elsie dies, making us wonder: Can a deadly gift ever be pure?

Ironically, purity is already encoded in the symbolic underpinnings of the white ash. Is Bernard returning to Elsie her virginity, which she had offered him earlier, the white connoting innocence, as Hallissy wittily suggests, or should we think of the white ash in terms of racial purity? Are the leaves of white ash comparable to the white leaves of the book, a sentimental counter-story that dooms Elsie to die? The leaves are purple like the flames; are they capable of "purifying" the female body and soul of its prenatal defilement with the vigor of Calvinist faith? Was Elsie, in the end, cured/killed by the power of metaphor?

The figurative language that Holmes employs indeed sets a trap by creating an alternative yet tangible reality that simultaneously supports and jeopardizes the entire ideological construct of Brahmin superiority. Elsie is ophidian because, according to the plot, the venom "altered her biochemical constitution" raising the question of "whether she is biologically a woman anymore" (Spinner 2015: 442). Yet she is coldhearted *like* the snake and vicious *like* the biblical snake but also, metonymically, sinful and feminine like Eve, seduced by the snake with whom she associates herself.[16] The "subtle" poisons of Elsie's gifts are so haunting because her ophidian nature is half-biological, half-fictional. Metaphorical—rather than literal or verifiable or science-based—meanings lie beneath the narrative structure of the novel, and cast a shadow on the final triumph of positivism, rationality, and pragmatism.

No surprise that *Elsie Venner* ends with a story of Elsie's parting gift that is no longer conceived of as harmful. It is a snake-shaped golden bracelet that she bestows on Bernard from her deathbed and that the narrator spots on the wrist of Bernard's young wife some time after Elsie's death. When Elsie wore the bracelet before her illness, it functioned as a symbol of her disturbing nature, like her castanets and extravagant scarfs. Now, a token of her new, "purified" sentimental identity, the bracelet connotes the masochistic act of self-sacrifice: she gives the gift to Bernard *for* his fiancée Letty, her substitute:

> At that moment the young lady lifted her arm accidentally in such a way that the light fell upon the clasp of a chain which encircled her wrist. My eyes

---

[16] It is interesting to note how Holmes, when referring to Elsie's possible prototype, Margaret Fuller whom he had known since their school years, shows the relativity of such judgment: "one who loved her" would compare her "long, flexible neck" "to those of a swan, and one who loved her not to those of the ophidian who tempted our common mother" (Holmes 1878: 242).

filled with tears as I read upon the clasp, in sharp-cut Italic letters, *E. V.* They were tears at once of sad remembrance and of joyous anticipation; for the ornament on which I looked was the double pledge of a dead sorrow and a living affection. It was the golden bracelet,—the parting-gift of Elsie Venner. (486–87)

Elsie finally manages to give a "portion" of herself that the recipient is happy to keep. The bracelet, a conventional keepsake, metaphorically epitomizes the character's tamed character and vanished Lamian identity in its safe, socially acceptable form. "The double pledge of a dead sorrow and a living affection" eliciting tears of sorrow and joy, it eventually functions as a fit token of the eponymous "medicated" novel intended for a sentimentally educated reader. In the end, the snake-like bracelet becomes a symbol of Elsie's spiritual rebirth and, as a symbol of Asclepius, of medicine itself (Traister 1999: 224).

The bracelet, however, can also be seen as a token of the novel's internal ambiguity, representing the entangled cluster of meanings which do not easily translate into the young Brahmin's success story. On the one hand, the pure and the poisonous cannot co-exist in Elsie's body; on the other, the novel, via the chain of tropes, suggests that the pure and the poisonous are not as mutually exclusive as they seem. Elsie's bracelet is a pure gift, yet its "sharp-cut" letters and the encircling, snake-like chain may be seen as a residue of Elsie's uncomfortable identity that is indissociable from the now-perfect keepsake. The bracelet's inscription, Elsie Venner—also the character's name, the novel's title, and the last words in the novel—suggests that Elsie will be a lasting presence after all and that the collective effort of getting rid of her and her gifts has at least partially failed. Written on the verge of the Civil War, the novel signals the looming crisis of antebellum sensibility and almost desperately offers, as its ultimate resort, a sentimental antidote against the "venom" of the social and metaphysical controversies that it lays bare, in the form of a bizarre story about a woman-snake.

7.4 GIFTS, TOKENS, AND SINS IN "BROTHER DUNSTAN AND THE CRABS"

In both Hawthorne and Holmes, the female characters cannot escape the "poisonous vessels" that their bodies are or are imagined to be and the gifts they offer have a taint of this grotesque, excessive corporeality: a touch that pollutes, a breath that poisons. In the last section of this chapter, I discuss a text where the venomous body is that of a male community of monks, while the gifts given—crabs—are embodiments of sins in the literal sense: they both correspond to the abstract catalogue of human vices and emanate directly from the sinners. The text emerged from the pen of the late nineteenth-century female author Caroline Walker Paradise and was published in the 1898 volume of *Godey's Lady's Book*. Walker does not use words "poisonous" or "venomous" but clearly works with the related categories of pure and polluted, innocent and vicious, safe and dangerous. The layout of the story in the magazine publication graphically emphasizes this relationship: the first letter of the story—the letter "T"—is in the shape of a snake. The illustration at the bottom is also curious: it depicts crabs in a net but one resembles a spider in a web, another a scorpion—a hint that the monks are "caught" or "entrapped" at the end of the tale (Fig. 7.1).

"Brother Dunstan and the Crabs" belongs to the genre of *Godey's* didactic short stories that maintained a certain generic consistency throughout the century; although written at the end of the nineteenth century, it is noticeably Hawthornesque in style. Set in an unnamed, presumably French, village (and thus contributing to the anti-Catholic literary tradition in American nineteenth-century fiction), the story raises the theme of sin but does so in a much more conventional way than *Elsie Venner*: "Brother Dunstan and the Crabs" is a parable about the inability to rid oneself of one's sins and the inescapability of punishment. By a miracle, at vespers Father Superior transforms the sins of the monks—"all the unholy things that existed among the only partially sanctified"—into

Fig. 7.1 Illustration to the story. Paradise, Caroline Wilder Fellowes. "Brother Dunstan and the Crabs," *Godey's Lady's Book*, 1898, 136, p. 206. Public domain. (Courtesy of HathiTrust)

"an army of fighting, scuttling, diabolic crabs" (Paradise: 209). The monks send Brother Dunstan to the village to get "rid of them for good" (209); while Brother Dunstan initially manages to do so, the crabs are re-gifted and return to the monastery, where they spread out inside the building. This conventional parabolic plot, however, gains an interesting anthropological dimension that reveals itself in the motif of gift exchange: crabs can only be given away as gifts; the success of the enterprise relies on whether the gift will be accepted; the logic of the gift eventually undoes the plan of the monks.

The story begins with the unusual night visit of Brother Dunstan, believed to be "the very flower of sanctity" (203), to Giles Aubry, a pious village man. "I have not come to accuse you of sin," he says to calm the frightened man down, and adds "with some embarrassment": "I have brought you with my hand a little gift. I beg you to accept from me a lot of very fine crabs nearly out of the water" (204). While Giles is dying to have delicious crabs in his soup-pot, he does not accept the gift because he is fasting as penance for venial sin, and the monk leaves the house with his mission as yet unaccomplished. Although venerated as a saint, Brother Dunstan acts as a devil would, not only in trying to tempt the poor soul of the naïve villager with his "diabolic" gift but also in deceiving him: the gifts were not taken from the water, they come directly from within the monastery walls. The problem is that the monks cannot boil and eat the crabs themselves since they embody the "unholy things" within their community—including spite, envy, malice, evil-speaking, jealousy, suspicion, backbiting, irreverence, and so on. Eating your own "sin" symbolically means taking it inside your body, absorbing it. The monks who know the genesis of the crabs see them as "hateful creatures" personifying their own vicious, sinful selves, the evil concentrated in their communal social body. A gift of poisonous food lurks behind the monks' offering to the villagers.

The story goes on to describe the other visits by Brother Dunstan. As the narrative proceeds, we enter the realm of relativity: the meaning of the gift is contingent on the recipient's perspective. Dame Jessamy, the "cheeriest" old woman in the kingdom (205), cannot accept the crabs because her son was drowned and she cannot eat anything that comes from the sea. While Giles Aubry associates crabs with pleasure and temptation, Dame Jessamy associates them with death. Newly married Rouben and Isabel finally accept the "simple gift" but when they open the basket, Isabel no longer wants it: she sees the crabs as "poor creatures" and is unwilling to put them into the cooking pot while still alive. The couple sell the crabs for a crown to a 16-year-old boy, Peter Simple. This bargain proves fatal for the monks. The crabs end up with Peter's mother, "a pious, grateful soul, to whom the pleasures of the palate were nothing if one might do a deed of generosity and grace" (206). She instructs Peter to carry the basket to the monks as a "token of gratitude" for teaching him his letters; he does so, "with gloom in his heart" and leaves his "burden" unguarded at the monastery because he is reluctant to disturb the monks during their prayers (206). Peter's mother, driven by generosity, gratitude, and goodness, does not assign any specific meaning to the crabs but sees the precious basket as something she can give away. The gift-as-a-burden all of a sudden becomes a "token of gratitude."

The theme of gift-giving makes the story of the sinners who failed to pass on their sins to others more sophisticated than a didactic story about crime and punishment. By giving the crabs away, the monks are seeking to rid themselves of a burden, but the story does not make it obvious whether they intend to "poison" or harm their congregation. In such a case, can sins make a good gift? Is the monks' plan beneficial to everyone—the villagers will be fed, the sins will disappear—as they tacitly seem to believe? Here we have a curious and certainly unintended inversion of the Indian tradition of religious gifts described in anthropology. In his seminal work, Jonathan Parry analyzes a well-known ritual practiced in India where "the gift is held to embody the sins of the donor, whom it rids of evil by transferring the dangerous and demeaning burden of death and impurity to the recipient" (Parry 1986: 459). The recipients of these gifts are Brahman priests who "see themselves as endlessly accumulating the sin they accept with the gifts of the pilgrims and mourners who visit the city." Gift exchange presents danger to both parties. While the priest "contracts leprosy and rots" and "dies a terrible and premature death and then faces the torments of hell," the donor "too is an endangered being, for if the priest misuses his gift for some evil purpose he shares in the sin." The receiver must be a "worthy vessel" and perform purifying rituals (Parry 1986: 460). In Paradise's story, it is the priests—the holy fathers—who bestow their sins transformed into "the bodies of hideous, crawling things" (206) on the unsuspecting and trusty congregation in the form of a generous present. Instead of offering the villagers communion that would purify body and soul, they want them to consume something that emanated from their own polluted bodies and souls, by this perhaps even magnifying their sins and spreading them in the world.

When Peter Simple's mother steps in, the situation gets even more complex. As the only donor with pure intentions, she saves the community from the sins by returning these to the sinners. However, it is worth noting that she sends the offering to the monks as a token of gratitude for the good things they did for her son. According to the logic of the gift, the gift keeps giving and is "always on the move," as Lewis Hyde phrased it (Hyde 1983). The woman's "token" is a returned gift, generosity that repays generosity. Ironically, the monks get the crabs back not only because the sin always finds the sinner and one cannot be rid of it by simply passing it on to others but also because their goodness is being rewarded.

The story raises a number of anthropological issues beyond the conventional didacticism of its message. For Paradise, the "poison" appears to be in the gift itself but if the meaning of the gift is contingent on how we perceive it, we may wonder whether it can envenom and pollute anyone but the donor. At the same time, the pure intention appears not to be sufficient to purify the gift that has already been contaminated by the sin or that is, literally, the sin itself. The story leaves this and related questions provocatively open-ended while at the same time exploiting the potential of its underlying metaphor on the affective level. The crabs are "diabolic," "evil," and "hideous"; they seem to have excessive vitality as they scuttle, hide, scramble, battle with each other, and multiply in number (the 50 crabs "seemed to be one thousand"). The way they are described is suggestive of the final inevitability: the monks are doomed to be trapped. At the same time, the story preserves and sentimentalizes the belief in general goodness: the monks have their sins returned to them because of the virtues of the villagers who resist temptation, feel sympathy toward the crabs as living creatures, and give them away as tokens of gratitude. Ironically, the kind woman's innocent act of giving unintentionally (re)poisons the community of monks with their own vices.

The question of gender, too, is of interest here. In "Brother Dunstan and the Crabs," contrary to Hawthorne's story and to Holmes's novel, the impure gift is associated with male, not female sexuality. In the catalogue of vices that crabs embody—spite, envy, malice, evil-speaking, jealousy, suspicion, backbiting, irreverence, laziness, and so on—lust is omitted. However, this unnamed sin is implied in the story of Brother Dunstan who is trying to rid himself of the sin of self-love. When the Brother visits the newlywed couple, he feels particularly uneasy. He is unconsciously envious of the idyllic honeymoon he witnesses, for he himself "had never ever touched the girl's slight fingers." He feels "curious pain and jealousy" and is "lost in a dream, his fresh young manhood, which the frock could only conceal, not kill, all astir" (205). Paradise gets as near to the description of the male erection as one can while remaining within the conventional narrative framework of a lady's magazine. It is telling that Dunstan leaves the basket at the threshold as if the very air in the house of the newlyweds were poisonous to him.

Brother Dunstan has the reputation of a saint, yet the story emphasizes that there is something about his body that suggests a lack of self-control. For example, his face is "unworldly" (205), "honest, pure, and abstracted" (204) but his wavy locks are unruly; the summer breeze takes "profane liberties" with them (204). The final passages of the story describe how "the biggest and the most malignant" of the crabs "caught Brother Dunstan by the skirt, as he passed, rapt in devotion, to his cell" (206). No matter how pious, pure, and abstracted is Dunstan, his baser instincts get hold of him; "self-love" may be interpreted as the "sin" of masturbation to which the monk succumbs, as his "fresh young manhood" overcomes his devotion. Seeing the crabs, in all their carnality, as symbols of repressed male sexuality may shed light on the story's ending: in the end, the gift endangers the donor who, locked up in the monastery, loses control of his body and desires. Male sexuality, when considered in the nineteenth-century tradition of anti-masturbation doctrines, is at its most dangerous when inverted on itself, since it is taken that there is but one step from self-love to sodomy, another common and widespread, albeit unnamed, "vice" within communities of monks.[17]

Paradise's story replicates common elements of nineteenth-century discourses of normalcy and sexuality. Yet the suggested association of impure and poisonous gifts with the male body is a way of challenging the more traditional line that Hawthorne and Holmes follow in demonizing the female body, sexuality, and femininity. Paradise relocates the eroticized "venom," as she refers to the repressed male sexual desire, in terms of a self-inverted dangerous gift.

The three texts examined in this chapter demonstrate that the notion of the poisonous gift—in contrast to the opposite, the gift that is wholesome, benign, or pure—captivated nineteenth-century literary imagination. The aspect of gender is crucial for its understanding not least because in all three narratives, the notions of "poisonous" or "sinful" have implicit associations with sexuality, either female sexuality, which is believed to be

[17] See, for example, Mason (2008: 75–78).

dangerous in itself, or male sexuality, which becomes a source of danger only in particular contexts, such as those of solitary confinement and homosocial communality. In a word, we are dealing with persistent prejudices that determine the relationship between sexes and gifts. At the same time, the array of tentative meanings that the poisonous or sinful gift opens up is much broader and eventually what "poison" does becomes as, or even more, important than what it means. Due to the indeterminacy of what is, after all, a poisonous gift, we encounter a vision of giving as a complex and multi-component act contingent on various internal and external circumstances. The dialectics of the pure and the poisonous that is present in all three texts is simultaneously challenged or complemented by the gift's intrinsic ambiguity, which the sentimental ideology of disinterested giving tended to ignore. This ambiguity enhances rather than mitigates the emotional effect of the gift-related rhetoric that hovers between the literal and the figurative, the "real" and the allegorical, the body and the token.

WORKS CITED

Arac, Jonathan. 1986. The Politics of *The Scarlet Letter*. In *Ideology and Classic American Literature*, ed. Sacvan Bercovitch and Myra Jehlen, 247–266. Cambridge: Cambridge University Press.

Baym, Nina. 1982. Thwarted Nature: Nathaniel Hawthorne as Feminist. In *American Novels Revisited: Essays in Feminism Criticism*, ed. Fritz Fleischmann, 58–77. Boston: Hall.

———. 2005. Revisiting Hawthorne's Feminism. In *Hawthorne and the Real: Bicentennial Essays*, ed. Millicent Bell, 74–102. Columbus: Ohio State University Press.

Bensick, Carol Marie. 1985. *La Nouvelle Beatrice: Renaissance and Romance in 'Rappaccinis Daughter'*. Brunswick, NJ: Rutgers University Press.

Brenzo, Richard. 1976. Beatrice Rappaccini: A Victim of Male Love and Horror. *American Literature* 48 (2): 152–164.

Brickhouse, Amy. 1998. Hawthorne in the Americas: Frances Calderón de la Barca, Octavio Paz, and the Mexican Genealogy of 'Rappaccini's Daughter'. *PMLA* 13 (2): 227–242.

Crews, Frederick C. 1964. Giovanni's Garden. *American Quarterly* 16: 402–418.

Crosby, Sarah L. 2005. *Poisonous Mixtures: Gender, Class, Empire, and Cultural Authority in Antebellum Female Poisoner Literature*. Diss. University of Notre-Dame, Notre-Dame, Indiana.

———. 2016. *Poisonous Muse: The Female Poisoner and the Framing of Popular Authorship in Jacksonian America.* Iowa City: University of Iowa Press.

Davis, Cynthia J. 2002. The Doctor Is In: Medical Insight, Oliver Wendell Holmes, and *Elsie Venner. Nineteenth-Century Contexts* 24 (2): 177–193.

Easton, Alison. 2004. Hawthorne and the Question of Women. In *The Cambridge Companion to Nathaniel Hawthorne*, ed. Richard H. Millington, 79–98. Cambridge: Cambridge University Press.

Elbert, Monica. 2008. 'Dying to Be Heard': Morality and Aesthetics in Alcott's and Hawthorne's Tableaux Mort. In *Death Becomes Her: Cultural Narratives of Femininity and Death in Nineteenth-Century America*, ed. Elizabeth Dill and Sheri Weinstein, 19–46. Newcastle, UK: Cambridge Scholars Publishing.

Emerson, Ralph Waldo. 1983. *Essays and Lectures (Essays: First and Second, Representative Men, English Traits, and the Conduct of Life).* New York: Library of America.

Evans, Oliver. 1964. Allegory and Incest in 'Rappaccini's Daughter'. *Nineteenth-Century Fiction* 19 (2): 185–195.

Gallagher, Kathleen. 1975. The Art of Snake Handling: Lamia, *Elsie Venner*, and 'Rappaccini's Daughter'. *Studies in American Fiction* 3 (1): 51–64.

Gilmore, Michael T. 1985. *Romanticism and the Marketplace.* Chicago: University of Chicago Press.

Greven, David. 2012. *The Fragility of Manhood: Hawthorne, Freud, and the Politics of Gender.* Columbus: Ohio State University Press.

Groebner, Valentin. 2002. *Liquid Assets, Dangerous Gifts: Presents and Politics at the End of the Middle Ages.* Trans. P.E. Selwyn. Philadelphia: University of Pennsylvania Press.

Gross, Seymour. 1981. 'Rappaccini's Daughter' and the Nineteenth-Century Physician. In *Ruined Eden of the Present: Hawthorne, Melville and Poe*, ed. G.R. Thompson and Virgil Lokke, 129–142. West Lafayette: Purdue University Press.

Hallissy, Margaret. 1982. Hawthorne's Venomous Beatrice. *Studies in Short Fiction* 19 (3): 231–239.

———. 1985. Poisonous Creature: Holmes's 'Elsie Venner'. *Studies in the Novel* 17 (4): 406–419.

Hawthorne, Nathaniel. 1972. *The American Notebooks.* Ed. Claude M. Simpson. Cleveland: Ohio State University Press.

———. 1982. *Tales and Sketches.* New York: Library of America.

Holmes, Oliver Wendell. 1878. Cinders from the Ashes. In Holmes, Oliver Wendell. *Pages from an Old Volume of Life: A Collection of Essays 1857–1881*, 239–259. Boston and New York Houghton: Mifflin and Company.

———. 1891. Medical Essays, 1842–1882. In *The Works of Oliver Wendell Holmes* in 13 Volumes. Vol. 9. London: Sampson Low.

———. 1892. *Elsie Venner: A Romance of Destiny*. In *The Works of Oliver Wendell Holmes* in 13 Volumes. Vol. 5. Boston and New Tork Houghton, Mifflin and Company.

Hyde, Lewis. 1983. *The Gift: Creativity and the Artist in the Modern World*. New York: Vintage.

Joy, Morny. 2013. Introduction. In *Women and The Gift: Beyond the Given and All-Giving*, ed. Morny Joy, 1–52. Bloomington: Indiana Unversity Press.

Kloeckner, Alfred J. 1966. The Flower and the Fountain: Hawthorne's Chief Symbols in 'Rappaccini's Daughter'. *American Literature: A Journal of Literary History, Criticism, and Bibliography* 38 (3): 323–336.

Lunt, Joanna Skelton Fosdick. 1853. Preface. In *Forget-me-Not, or the Philipena*. Philadelphia: Dayton & Wentworth.

Lyons, Debora. 2013. Pandora and the Ambiguous Works of Women: All-Taking or All-Giving? In *Women and the Gift: Beyond the Given and All-Giving*, ed. Morny Joy, 53–71. Bloomington: Indiana University Press.

Mason, Diane. 2008. *The Secret Vice: Masturbation in Victorian Fiction and Medical Culture*. Manchester: Manchester University Press.

Medoro, Dana. 2009. 'Looking into Their Inmost Nature': The Speculum and Sexual Selection in 'Rappaccini's Daughter'. *Nathaniel Hawthorne Review* 35 (1): 70–86.

Miller, John N. 1991. Fideism vs Allegory in 'Rappaccini's Daughter'. *Nineteenth-Century Literature* 46 (2): 223–244.

Paradise, Caroline Wilder Fellowes. 1898. Brother Dunstan and the Crabs. *Godey's Lady's Book* 136: 203–206.

Parker, Gail T. 1972. Sex, Sentiment, and Oliver Wendell Holmes. *Women's Studies. An Inter-Disciplinary Journal* 1 (1): 47–63.

Parry, Jonathan. 1986. The Gift, the Indian Gift, and the 'Indian Gift.' *Man* 21 (3): 453–473.

Roger, Patricia M. 1997. Taking a Perspective: Hawthorne's Concept of Language and Nineteenth-Century Language Theory. *Nineteenth-Century Literature* 51 (4): 433–454.

Spinner, Cheryl. 2015. The Spell and the Scalpel: Scientific Sight in Early 3D Photography. *J19: The Journal of Nineteenth-Century Americanists* 3 (2): 436–445.

Tambling, Jeremy. 2004. The Language of Flowers: James, Hawthorne, Allegory. *Literature Compass* 1: 1–17.

Temple, Gale M. 2014. 'Affrighted at the Eager Enjoyment': Hawthorne, Nymphomania, and Medical Manhood. *Textual Practice* 28 (3): 405–425.

Traister, Bryce. 1999. Sentimental Medicine: Oliver Wendell Holmes and the Construction of Masculinity. *Studies in American Fiction* 27 (2): 205–227.

Ullén, Magnus. 2017. The Problem of Modernity: Hawthorne Criticism, Faith, and the Literary Situation. *Orbis Litterarum* 72 (4): 265–293.

Urakova, Alexandra. 2016. Hawthorne's Gifts: Re-Reading 'Alice Doane's Appeal' and 'The Great Carbuncle' in *The Token*. *New England Quarterly* 88 (4): 587–613.

CHAPTER 8

The Gift/s of Death

8.1 Death in Terms of Gift-Giving

In Mark Twain's parable "The Five Boons of Life" (1902), a fairy approaches a young man with a basket full of gifts, informing him that only one of the gifts within is truly valuable and inviting him to make his choice. Picking first pleasure then love, fame, and riches, as the youth grows old, he remains bitterly disappointed in life. When he finally decides to choose the fifth gift from the basket—death—it is too late: the fairy has already given this gift to a little child who had trusted the fairy in making the decision, "asking [her] to choose for it." The main character, who is now doomed to endure all the hardships of old age, laments his lot: "The fairy said true; in all her store there was but one gift which was precious, only one that was not valueless"; other gifts were "poor and cheap and mean." These other gifts, he contends, are "mockeries," "gilded lies," and "merely lendings" because they are not exempt from bargain and trade; one always has to pay for the material or spiritual benefits one receives. For example, "for each hour of happiness the treacherous trader, Love, has sold me I have paid a thousand hours of grief." Death, instead, does not lend anything but "steeps in dreamless and enduring sleep the pains that persecute the body, and the shames and griefs that eat the mind and heart" (Twain 1973: 100). It is an "absolutely free gift," to use Twain's own term (see Chap. 2).

The belief that death is a release from life, as articulated by Twain in the passage cited above, is a truism since antiquity ("not to have been born at all… is the best thing for mortals"[1]). Looking deeper into Twain's text, however, one can find an original configuration bringing together death and concerns typical of modernity, including trading, consumption, and sentiment. This chapter continues to explore the complex relation between the dangerous and the perfect or pure gift in narratives that describe death as a gift or as a condition of gifting—focusing on Twain's *The Mysterious Stranger* manuscripts and Henry James's *The Wings of the Dove*.

Should we be open to considering death as a gift, it would be difficult to see it as anything other than an a priori dangerous—tautologically, murderous—one. The vision of death as a divine gift stems from the Bible, where all God's "gifts," including death and calamities, are believed to be perfect: "Every good and perfect gift is from above" (James 1:17). Beyond the religious context, the concept of the gift of death is familiar to the reader fluent in gift theory from Jacques Derrida's seminal study *Donner la mort* (1995; originally published in 1993) where he introduces the term that gives the book its title, "to give death." In this study, Derrida emphasizes the inevitable "asymmetry" of giving death—understood as either the "mysterium tremendum" of God's will or as the sacrifice of one's life for the sake of another ("dying for the other"). Such asymmetry entails "instability" as opposed to the "feeling of security" that the economy of exchange gives us via "the law of the *oikos* [home]"[2] (Derrida 1995: 95). While acknowledging the importance of the asymmetrical structure of giving death as conceptualized by Derrida, this chapter follows Twain's own phraseology and sees the gift-of-death motif in Twain's late work as a passage or a missing link between traditional religious belief and (post)modern theoretical thinking.[3]

Another thematic focus of this chapter is the gift *of* death, for example, a gift touched or marked by mortality and conditioned solely by the premature and inevitable end of the character's life—a plotline we encounter in Twain and, even more markedly, in James. A parting gift from a dying person—a common sentimental trope as epitomized, for example, by little Eva's lock of hair in *Uncle Tom's Cabin*—was an important part of the

---

[1] Words attributed to Theognis of Megara.

[2] For example, "dying for the other" that Derrida primarily focuses on is an impossible transaction because the singularity of one's existence resists the idea of an equivalent exchange that the structure of exchange tacitly implies.

[3] To my knowledge, the concept and the motif of the gift of death in Twain has not received much critical attention. Michael J. Kiskis mentions its importance but solely in passing. See Kiskis (2011: 22).

culture of mourning and of "sentimental collaboration" (Kete 2000) in the face of death. The difference in the examples I discuss below is in the fact that death itself becomes the absolute condition of pure giving; gift exchange is structured by and around finitude. In the case of James, the gift that is the outcome of such giving lacks the consolation typical of sentimental relics but instead sows discord and haunts the recipient as a token of lost opportunity.

Twain and James, renowned antagonists in the postbellum literary scene,[4] shared a distaste for sentimental clichés and melodrama, with Twain the author of perhaps the most famous parody of major sentimental poet Lydia Sigourney[5] and James in his criticism systematically sneering at sentimentality. Paradoxically, however, both inadvertently paid tribute to the sentimental tradition in their own work, which has led critics to refer to both Twain (Camfield 1994; Kiskis 2011) and James (Smith-Gordon 2013)[6] as "sentimental." What interests me here is the revision or modernization of the sentimental concept of the gift as free from self-interest and/or related to community building in the turn-of-the-century texts by Twain and James, a revision and modernization that simultaneously elaborates on and challenges familiar patterns of pure, disinterested giving, paving the way for future theoretical approaches.

8.2 A Perfect Gift from Above, or Sharing Death in *The Chronicle of Young Satan*

The religious concept of death as a "perfect gift from above" is present in a number of nineteenth-century spiritual narratives. Following the Second Great Awakening (1790–1840), religious life in the United States had become syncretic and diverse while sentimental religiosity attempted to smoothen both the Calvinist heritage and the controversial, conflicting beliefs within new congregations. Before turning to Twain, I will briefly discuss two sentimental novels—narratives of conversion written in

---

[4] Leon Edel, for example, observes that "they were by nature never destined to be intimate. ... No two American geniuses were more dissimilar" (Edel 1972: 37–8). It is known that Twain and James did not have a high opinion of each other's work.

[5] In the character of Emmeline Grangerford in *The Adventures of Huckleberry Finn* (1884).

[6] Peter Brooks contributed to the discussion of Jamesian "melodramatic imagination" (Brooks 1976) while Jonathan Flatley studied the techniques of affect in his work (Flatley 2008).

mid-century—to illustrate two different approaches to death as God's gift to humanity.

The Wide, Wide World (1850) by Susan Warner is a sentimental novel that nonetheless "incorporates a Calvinist faith... that affects... its narrative and rhetorical craft" (Kim 2003: 785). It is from Warner's "sentimental Calvinism" (Noble 2000: 62)—a contradiction in terms considering that sentimental literature was generally non- or anti-Calvinist—that her ambivalent interpretation of death as "unspeakable gift" of God arises. The story of an adolescent girl, Ellen Montgomery, and her spiritual pilgrimage, modeled on Bunyan's *The Pilgrim's Progress*, the novel imagines death as a "sweet home" in the tradition of sentimental domesticity and at the same time suggests that this "home" is accessible only to the elect. In a marginal but meaningful episode, a little Irish boy quotes from the second letter to the *Corinthians* on his deathbed: "Thanks be to God unto for his unspeakable gift!" (Warner 1851, 1: 334). Though Paul in his letter refers to the gift of grace and not to death (2 Corinthians 9:15), the particular circumstances in which the line is quoted in *The Wide, Wide World* suggest that grace is in this context a euphemism of death. Warner strategically places the episode against the background of Christmas festivities and gift-giving. Set against the author's direct and indirect critique of Christmas consumption, the episode emphasizes that the boy is about to receive the most precious gift of all—the epithet "unspeakable" meaning "unknowable and hard to accept" (Hoeller 2012: 85) but also inestimable, superior to others. The boy is the elect, and those present at his deathbed are stood in still and silent in "awe" instead of shedding tears. In Calvinism, the idea of grace is at the heart of the doctrine of predestination that involves an asymmetrical exchange between God and the believer who is never able to reciprocate the divine gift (Hénaff 2003: 313). Instead, the latter learns to be the perfect recipient of anything that comes along, including one's own death or that of a loved one. All the believer can do is learn how best to accept this ultimate gift should she receive it—by accepting with gratitude every manifestation of the divine will, including the loss of loved ones. The asymmetrical structure allows Warner to distinguish between vertical and horizontal exchanges, counterpoising the "unspeakable" gift of death not only to commodities but also to keepsakes that create and sustain affectionate ties in the novel.

The Gates Ajar (1868), a novel by Elizabeth Stuart Phelps, one of the younger generation of sentimental authors, develops a very different attitude by portraying God as a supreme sentimental giver, who satisfies through death the material and spiritual needs of devoted Christians. Death materializes in a number of gifts and rewards intended to compensate for the scarcity of earthly benefits: a girl who cannot afford a piano will have one in paradise; an old maid will get a husband; families will reunite, and so on. Phelps uses sentimental language to describe God's offerings, comparing them with "little keepsakes"—"a lock of hair to curl about our fingers; a picture that has caught the trick of his eyes or smile; a book, a flower, a letter" (Phelps 2019: 115). Death opens the "gates" to even greater gifts that one is granted unconditionally. Phelps develops a vision of death as God's most valuable gift to humankind but takes a different task than Warner: Phelps's novel, written in a time of a rise of religious sectarianism and populism and in the spirit of liberal theology, engages God in a sentimental exchange that borders on consumerist ethics. No longer the *mysterium tremendum* of the Calvinist faith, death here *is* a portal to material and spiritual goods that one can choose in advance, furnishing one's own afterlife while living.

Despite the contrasting vision of death in these two novels, both work within a traditional religious belief in the afterlife, which in the nineteenth-century sentimental novel becomes a "domesticated" paradise or a sweet home; the earthly existence, in both works, is nothing but the preparation for a superior life at the other side of the grave. Twain's idea of death radically departs from this tradition: rebelling against church and religion and professing views that were sometimes atheist, sometimes deist, he rejects the idea of a reward in the afterlife. Unlike Warner and Phelps, who both use euphemistic Biblical language or sentimental "keepsake" rhetoric, he explicitly calls death a gift: it is a gift valuable in itself and not because it represents something else. At the same time, placing Twain against the background of sentimental spiritual novels does not seem counterintuitive, considering that his attitude to religion was ambiguous as much as it was iconoclastic. The liberal theology of the second half of the nineteenth century influenced his own "religious experience"[7] while his Calvinist upbringing affected both his life and work, as provocatively shown by Van Vick Brooks (1920). Developing the concept of the gift of death in the later phase of his work,[8] Twain creates what is at once a secular and apoc-

---

[7] See on this specifically Eutsey (2005: 53–66). On Twain's controversial attitude to religion, see also Brodwin (2003: 220–48); Bush Jr. (2002: 55–94).
[8] This period marked by darkness and gloom and a pessimistic attitude to human nature is often related to Twain's personal circumstances at the time, including financial mishaps and

ryphal version of the religious doctrine. The giver is a supernatural agent or divine substitute—a fairy or a satanic figure; death is a vertical and asymmetrical gift bestowed from above, as it were, but God is absent from this transaction.

Twain's late phase is marked by his interest in apocryphal Biblical history and in the figure of Satan in particular. Unlike the conventional fairy, this satanic character who bestows the gift of death is complex, ambiguous, and syncretic.[9] Philip Traum, a son/nephew of the Biblical Satan in the drafts known as *Mysterious Stranger* manuscripts, combines the traits of the "human God" of liberal theology (Michelson 1980: 47) with those of the deist divinity and a "Calvinist God of wrath" (Camfield 1997: 102). He is a playmate of three boys living in the fictional village Eseldorf/contemporary America—a "divine, omnipotent, playful Tom Sawyer" (Michelson 1980: 47) who also works miracles and preaches as Christ did (Brodwin 1973: 617).[10] At the same time, he is indifferent to those humans he despises; as a demiurge, he has no sympathy for the little men and women he makes from clay and later mercilessly destroys (the anti-Calvinist streak of the novel).

Reflecting Twain's own complex religious views and expressing his growing skepticism about human nature, Traum appears to be neither good nor bad and, as such, is a perfectly disinterested giver. Unlike his infernal uncle, Satan, he does not trade in human souls; despite his preaching, he has little interest in converting the village boys to his faith. While God gives the gift of death by taking the soul to heaven, Traum does not take anything nor does he demand faith or obedience in return. Traum is an unsentimental giver, yet his existential indifference coupled with omnipotence guarantees a disinterestedness of transaction; moreover, his intention is benign even if difficult to comprehend.

---

family deaths. Critics however warn against the oversimplification that such biographical determinism entails. While it is "tempting" to read "all of his late stories as messages of despair," "it is not clear just how much those events necessarily influenced his fiction, a point which is open for speculation" (Rohman 1999: 77). There is also a critical tendency to speak of this period as stimulating and productive rather than regressive, see Fisher Fishkin and Robinson (2005: 1–6).

[9] For discussion of Twain's Satan, see, for example, Brodwin (1973: 206–27); Michelson (1980: 44–56).

[10] The title "mysterious strange" contains allusion to Christ; cf. "They also will answer, 'Lord, when did we see you hungry or thirsty or a *stranger* or needing clothes or sick or in prison, and did not help you?'" (Matthew 25: 44–46).

In the earliest version of *The Mysterious Stranger* manuscripts, *The Chronicle of Young Satan* (1897–1900), Traum becomes friends with three boys who live in a fictional Austrian village in the early eighteenth century. One day he confesses to the narrator, a boy called Theodore, that he wants to do something good for his little friend Nikolaus. "You will be sure to do generously by him," says the narrator. "It is my intention," Traum responds but when Theodore learns what kind of gift Traum intends for his friend, it makes him feel "creepy" (Twain 1969: 117). Traum arranges for Nikolaus, previously destined to live for 62 years, to die in 12 days while rescuing a little girl, Lisa Brandt, from drowning. Theodore pleads with Traum to withdraw his favor and to save Nikolaus from this early death but Traum explains that this would cause more damage to the boy:

> But for my intervention he would do his brave deed twelve days from now—a deed begun and ended in six minutes—and get for all reward those forty-six years of sorrow and suffering I told you of ... sometimes an act which brings the actor an hour's happiness and self-satisfaction is paid for— or punished—by years of suffering. (Twain 1969: 118)[11]

We encounter the same economic logic as in "The Five Boons of Life" cited above, showing consistency in Twain's thought. "An hour's happiness" is not to be given freely; one must pay for it, whether with years of mourning or with years of physical suffering. Death, a gift of time in reverse, spares a person from debt; this gift is unilateral—Nikolaus cannot reciprocate it, he does not know anything about the "benefit" he is to receive—and comes with no strings attached. What makes this gift ambivalent is the human perspective that is present in the novel: no matter how reasonable Traum's arguments are, the boys—Theodore and his friend Seppi—experience fear and grief; until the last moment, they hope for miraculous salvation. When Nikolaus praises Traum's generosity, he

---

[11] There is an autobiographic story behind this episode: Samuel Clemens was haunted by the memory of his boyhood friend Tom Nash who became deaf at the age of 15 after they both fell under the ice of the Mississippi river while skating (Gibson 1969: 20). In *No. 44, The Mysterious Stranger*, Twain includes a story of Jonathan Brinken: a boy saves the drowning Father Adolf and becomes paralyzed as a result; this story replaces the gift-of-death episode of the earlier manuscript, which clearly suggests that the latter had the same autobiographic source.

forgets that the satanic character is a dangerous donor whose bestowals and rewards are far from what a human might expect.

The boys do not quite realize that the gift of death to Nikolaus comes with a gift of time for them: the 12 days of suspense between Traum's decision to grant the gift of death and Nikolaus receiving this death reveal the truth of their being-together with their friend. The revelation is possible because Nikolaus is both living and is *already* dead. "Twelve days— only twelve days. It was awful to think of. I noticed that in my thoughts I was not calling him by his familiar names, Nick and Nicky, but was speaking of him by his full name, and reverently, as one speaks of the dead." Nikolaus, who is perfectly healthy and unsuspecting but destined to die, looks like a "ghost" to the boys: "it was like meeting the dead" (Twain 1969: 122). The feeling of fear and awe comes together with remorse. Theodore laments how dishonest and unfair he was to his friend—for example by stealing an apple Nikolaus had wanted to give to his little sister—in the spirit of the didactical stories for children that Twain, author of *The Adventures of Tom Sawyer*, famously detested. The boys use these last 12 days to compensate for their previous petty and mean behavior:

> [W]e were constantly doing him deferential little offices of courtesy, and saying, "Wait, let me do that for you," and that pleased him, too. I gave him seven fish-hooks—all I had—and made him take them; and Seppi gave him his new knife and a humming-top painted red and yellow—atonements for swindles practised upon him formerly, as I learned later, and probably no longer remembered by Nikolaus now. These things touched him, and he could not have believed that we loved him so; and his pride in it and gratefulness for it cut us to the heart, we were so undeserving of them. When we parted at last, he was radiant, and said he had never had such a happy day. (Twain 1969: 123)

Traum's gift sets in motion a series of gifts that transcend the *do ut des* principle that underlies most human transactions. While the boys act as they do in order to ease their remorse and therefore, according to Twain's skeptical reasoning, pursue their self-interest, their story still explores the potential of disinterested giving. Nikolaus's gratefulness does not give the boys the satisfaction that they might usually experience but instead "cuts them to the heart": they know that they would not have acted in the same way if they had not known about their friend's destiny; they also know that Nikolaus has no time to reciprocate their offerings and favors. The twelve days of suspense—the gift to Nikolaus is already given; the giving was the moment of Traum's decision—is a period characterized by a finitude that leaves the mark of mortality on every item bestowed. Traum's gift is free from even the shadow of self-interest but it is also free from sentiment. By contrast, Theodore's and Seppi's little tokens and favors to their friend are sentimentally charged. Twain uses the emphatically sentimental language of the gift in the passage cited above: "touched," "loved," "gratefulness," "undeserving," and so on. For 12 days, the otherwise selfish and naughty boys love their friend unconditionally, their sentimental nature released by the fact of his approaching death; a non-commodifiable gift, death puts an end to all sorts of earthly or otherworldly trade and replaces bargain with sharing:

> It was an awful eleven days; and yet, with a lifetime stretching back between to-day and then, they are still a grateful memory to me, and beautiful. In effect they were days of companionship with one's sacred dead, and I have known no comradeship that was so close or so precious. We clung to the hours and the minutes, counting them as they wasted away, and parting with them with that pain and bereavement which a miser feels who sees his hoard filched from him coin by coin by robbers and is helpless to prevent it (Twain 1969: 123).

The transient union between the boys and Nikolaus is an example of what French philosopher Jean-Luc Nancy calls an "inoperative community," a community that may be defined in its relation to death, or rather that acknowledges itself in the face of "death as sharing and as exposure." "It is not death as work... it is death as the unworking that unites us because it interrupts our communication and our communion" (Nancy 1991: 67).[12] Nancy's concept is quite applicable to the consideration of Twain's understanding, in this passage of his manuscript, of death as a gift. The paradoxical logic of death is that it generates a feeling of community precisely because it creates an interruption or a gap. The interruption takes the veil of life away and makes the community face the liminality of its existence, which has nothing to do with "working," for example, productivity and gain. In fact, Theodore says that they—and in this he

---

[12] Jean-Luc Nancy was a student of Derrida. See, for example, in Derrida: "Death would be the name of whatever suspends every experience of *giving* and *taking*. But to say that is far from excluding the fact that it is only on the basis of death, and in its name, that *giving* and *taking* become possible" (Derrida 1995: 45).

includes Nikolaus—have "stolen" time from work and other duties, "costing the three of [them] some sharp scoldings, and some threats of punishment." As Nancy writes, "...to reach one another, to touch one another, is to touch the limit where being itself, where being-in-common conceals us one from the other, and, in concealing us, in withdrawing us from the other before the other, exposes us to him or her." Traum's gift of death "exposes" Nikolaus to Theodore and Seppi and engages them in sharing the experience of his approaching end. After Nikolaus dies, the boys return to their usual selves; Traum's gift has an expiration date, as it were: it prompts a chain of pure gestures and gifts but only for a limited short period.

Elaborating on the idea of death as a supreme benefit, an idea that had a sentimental and religious aspect for his contemporaries, Twain brings this idea to its logical limit: the liminality of the gift of death is a direct cause of its perfection. Breaking with the religiosity and didacticism that dominated in sentimental spiritual novels such as those of Warner and Phelps, Twain re-sentimentalizes death in his description of the relationship singled out by mortality. At the same time, for all its purity and perfection, the idea of giving death as a gift remains "creepy": the boys can never fully accept it and begin to appreciate the gift of Nikolaus's death to them personally only many years after. Twain would omit this element of the plot in the later variants in which his satanic character grows more Christ-like; it reappeared only in Payne and Daineca's postmortem edition, published in 1918 under the title *The Mysterious Stranger*. The concept itself, however, is to be found elsewhere in his work, both in his fiction and his *Autobiography*.

In the autobiographical entry "The Death of Jean," Twain calls his daughter's sudden and premature death "the most precious of all gifts—that gift which makes all other gifts mean and poor" (249). The entry is structured around the contrast between murderous Christmas gifts and death as a benign gift. Twain believes that gifts kill Jean: she dies as the result of the "fatigue" caused by the preparing of Christmas presents. The presents she prepares for others turn out to be deadly for her. At the same time, death itself *is* a gift as Samuel Clemens, after losing his second daughter, unambiguously claims, adding that he would not have given it back, even should it have been in his power. Twain's late work, including "The Death of Jean," written by a grief-stricken father, signals both the return of the sentimental language of the gift and an irreversible break from its rhetorical patterns that operated within a Biblical framework: it is no surprise that this language becomes "poisoned" with melancholia.

8.3 "I GIVE AND GIVE AND GIVE": ETHEREAL GIVING IN *THE WINGS OF THE DOVE*

A recognition of its combination of death and the gift, dying and giving, is crucial in understanding *The Wings of The Dove*, a novel by Henry James that, as with Twain's later works, has a personal prehistory. James immortalized his beloved and lost cousin Minnie Temple in the character of Milly Theale, a rich heiress doomed to die prematurely of an unnamed disease. Unlike Milly, Minnie—who died of consumption at a young age—had limited means; by "endowing" her literary counterpart with an enormous fortune, James makes Milly a donor by default: in the absence of close relatives, she is expected to bequeath her money to whomever she chooses.

On the one hand, "death is so pervasive in *The Wings of the Dove* that almost anything you can say about the novel can also be developed into saying something about how it represents death" (Cutting 2005: 82). The novel's major focus is on Milly's "living-towards-death" (Cutting 2005: 96), which defines her unique experience. On the other hand, the plot centers on Milly's fortune—the object of a conspiracy by Milly's English friend Kate Croy and Kate's lover Merton Densher. Kate wants Densher to marry Milly so that he will become her heir; Densher consents to the plan but only on the condition that Kate consummates their relationship. Milly withdraws from her budding romance with Densher and stops all communication between them after she learns about his secret engagement to Kate and discovers Kate's intentions but nonetheless leaves him a large sum of money upon her death. Milly's bequest is revealed on Christmas Eve, in "the season of gifts," as Kate names it (James 1946, 2: 416).

The meaning of Milly's gesture—the climax of the novel—has been the focus of particular critical attention. The debates around it can be summarized by identifying two polar perspectives. On the one hand, Milly acts out of a spirit of disinterestedness, generosity, and Christ-like self-sacrifice; her bequest is a true or a pure gift. A representative example of such an interpretation is Alfred Habbeger's article "Reciprocity and the Market Place in *The Wings of the Dove* and *What Maisie Knew*" (1972), where he argues that "*The Wings of the Dove*... reveals with particular clarity one of the central distinctions in James's ethical awareness—the distinction between the contract and the gift" (458). All characters except for Milly are engaged in the "heartless and commercial world" of "pacts, bargains, contracts, and business deals" (463).[13] Milly, a "dove" as Kate calls her, "gives everything to Densher with no strings attached" and indirectly prompts him to remove himself "from the world of selfish commercial bargain" (458). In other readings, Milly is *la belle dame sans merci*—mean, dark, and manipulative (Friedman 1993: 224); her bequest is a self-interested transaction that destroys Kate's and Densher's relationship. In "Branding Milly Theale: The Capital Case of the *Wings of the Dove*" (2003), Michael M. Martin argues that Milly is not in essence a "dove" but rather brands herself "with the attributes of dovishness—gentleness, generosity, innocence, and vulnerability" (103). Capital allows her to "establish... a transcendental aura that will exercise power long after the comparatively limited physical being known as Milly Theale has ceased to exist" (123). Her postmortem gift is a triumph of capital: it "constrains" and burdens Merton and Kate by "covering them with the fluttering wings of millions and millions of 1$ bills" (106).

The difference between these perspectives recalls the familiar binary of gift and commodity, or rather that of the "true" gift and the gift as a "commodity in sheep's clothing" (Osteen 2002: 231)—an irresolvable dilemma when it concerns the modern, capitalist-bound ideology of the gift; in a capitalist society, self-sacrifice is often seen as self-interest in disguise. For example, Emily Schiller claims that "critics who consider Milly's financial bequest a free and generous 'gift' demonstrate how much they accept the market-place mentality they condemn in Kate and the other characters" (Schiller 1996: 211). What these opposing approaches do share, however, is a set of "characterological" questions, to use Kenneth Reinhard's term: "is [Milly's bequeath] intended as a true gift? to redeem Densher? as revenge? as an attempt to be posthumously loved?" (Reinhard 1997: 136). The gift, by default, expresses the giver's personality—a premise rooted in nineteenth-century intellectual history. Therefore, if we agree that Milly is generous and forgiving, her gift then expresses generosity and forgiveness. If we choose to see her as a manipulator—demonic rather than angelic, corrupt rather than pure, the eagle rather than the dove—then the money is bequeathed with the intention of empowering,

---

[13] There are two much-quoted statements from the novel to support this argument. The first is an utterance by Lord Mark, the second a comment by Kate: "Nobody here, you know, does anything for nothing"; "Everyone who had anything to give, made the sharpest bargain for it."

avenging, or destroying. In eluding the discussion of Milly's motives, the novel seems to invite both critical stances.

In what follows, I intend to go beyond a "characterological" approach, to use Reinhard's term: instead of speculating about Milly's intention, I will explore the connection between her gift and death. Describing Milly's illness and eventual death, James uses a technique of indirection. Milly, who first makes her appearance in the third book (the novel was published in two volumes of ten books in total), becomes more and more elusive toward the end, "a thick silence gradually burying her, silting her in place" (Schaffer 2016: 237). James takes an approach that is counter to the pattern of the Victorian novel, which would have had a deathbed scene as its climax (Schaffer 2016: 242), and counter to the sentimental tradition in general, as he "fights against sentimental demand for confessional transparency" (Artese 2006: 119). Yet, and paradoxically, as F.R. Leavis claims in his controversial *The Great Tradition* (1948), James's indirectness accompanied by "the fuss the other characters make of [Milly] as the 'Dove'" has "the effect of an irritating sentimentality" (Leavis 1993: 183). While not sharing Leavis's attitude, I agree with him that the Jamesian narrative technique indeed sentimentalizes Milly. In drifting toward a realm of non-communication and silence, Milly establishes a private and intimate relationship with death that has more potential to elicit the reader's sympathy than any conventional rhetoric does. This relationship sets her apart and creates the effect of her transcendent, ethereal presence in the novel, on the levels of both plot and narrative.

Milly's asymmetrical position in relation to other characters does not necessarily translate into moral superiority. James is not portraying a devoted philanthropist, for example. It is easy for Milly to be generous: she spends money effortlessly and even so her biggest "investment" in the novel is in the "staging" of the last act of her drama in the Leporelli palace to where she has retired. A rich American, she uses "Venice's easily purchased cultural legacy" to turn her death into an artwork (Martin 2003: 118). Milly's isolation in the Venetian palace is, if we follow Julie Rivkin in thinking of dying and death in terms of wastefulness, at once both a luxury and a waste. In her Derridean analysis, Rivkin suggests distinguishing between Kate's "restricted economy that emphasizes preservation and gain" and Milly's "general economy that produces immeasurable gains and endless losses" (Rivkin 1996: 83). While Kate is limited by her mundane calculations, Milly engages in reproducing her "fate"—a "terrible devastation" (121)—by preserving herself in artful copies. Ironically,

Rivkin herself uses (or "copies") George Bataille's original terms without acknowledging the source, which is *The Accursed Share* (1949). Bataille's terminology seeks primarily to differentiate between capitalist "restricted" economy aimed at profit and the "general" economy of life based on excess or surplus instead of scarcity. In social or religious life, the second is the economy of gift and sacrifice that aspires to pure waste as opposed to productivity and gain (Bataille, 1988).

Distinct thinkers as they are, James and Bataille converge strikingly in the idea of expenditure as "challenging the capitalist modernity" (Maynard 2005: 135), at least in relation to aesthetic experience. In "The Lesson of Balzac," James counterpoises what he calls "the consciousness of a limited capital" (James 1957: 79) against "royal intellectual spending" when speaking about Balzac's artistic method. In "Emile Zola," he develops this thought still further by stating that "it is in the *waste*... that true initiation resides" (James 1957: 75). The artist should not be afraid to waste (time, or passion, or interest) or waste oneself away, in doing so imitating the excessive creativity or plenitude of life. While it is true that the Jamesian "sublime economy" of art implies investment, preservation, and dividends as opposed to the "splendid waste" of life (James 1934: 120), the former is unthinkable without the "gratuitous expenditure" (Maynard 2005: 135) or waste, or "generosity" (that James attributes to Turgenev and denies in Flaubert).

Milly is not an artist in the literal sense. In the "Preface" to the New York edition, James refers to Minnie Temple's "great capacity for life" (James 1934: 288), while in the private letter to William James he writes: "It's the *living* ones that die; the writing ones that survive" (James and James 1997: 72). The "living one," Milly, has the consciousness of *unlimited* capital, to paraphrase James. "I've got everything," she says to Susan Stringam in the beginning of the novel. This "everything," as Reinhard observes, "not only oscillates between signifying all of life, love, happiness, the world out there, and a disease, pain, death in here, it also comes to mean them indeterminately and simultaneously" (Reinhard 1997: 123). Everything Milly owns—and she owns "everything"—bears a mark of death, or finitude, or waste. The plenitude of unlimited "capital" is constrained by a limited and tragically shrinking time; "Milly's 'boundless' freedom is finally a freedom only to die" (Reinhard 1997: 136). Living her life, she is as destined to give away as much as she is destined to die.

"If I've got everything," Milly laughed.
"Ah, *that*—like almost nobody else."
"Then for how long?". (James 1946, 1: 146)

This "destiny" structurally aligns Milly with those Jamesian characters who give or resign (such as Isabel Archer or Fleda Veltch) rather than with those who take and keep. Comparing Milly to Maggie Verver (*The Golden Bowl*, 1904)—both, in his opinion, are dark and manipulative despite their seeming innocence—Jonathan Friedman (Friedman 1993: 224) ignores the fact that Maggie succeeds in returning her "property" whereas Milly's postmortem "gain" is debatable. At the same time, and unlike Isabel and Fleda, she does not receive any gifts to either pass on (Isabel) or give up (Fleda); instead, it is as if she monopolizes the role of the giver in the novel, thus indeed creating the effect of power or manipulation.

Milly sees herself as one who gives. In the conversation with Lord Mark in Venice, she says: "I give and give and give—there you are; stick to me as close as you like, and see if I don't. Only I can't listen or receive or accept—I can't agree. I can't make a bargain" (James 1946, 2: 177). We do not have to trust Milly's words but, significantly, she describes her inclination or imperative to give in the conversation with Lord Mark not as a merit but as a peculiar condition or even a defect—just as earlier in the novel she had stressed her inferiority to a portrait by Bronzino. The excess in the structure of the sentence—"I give and give and give"—connoting expenditure echoes the repetition of the word "dead"—"dead, dead, dead"—in that same earlier episode.

In a private London gallery that Milly visits in a company of high-class English friends, Lord Mark notices the striking similarity between Milly and Bronzino's *Lucrezia Panciatichi*, a portrait that although accurately described is unnamed in the novel. Milly looks at her pictorial double and cannot hold back her tears as she detects both the signs of mortality ("a face almost livid in hue") and a "family resemblance" to herself:

> The lady in question, at all events, with her slightly Michelangelesque squareness, her eyes of other days, her full lips, her long neck, her recorded jewels, her brocaded and wasted reds, was a very great personage—only unaccompanied by a joy. And she was *dead, dead, dead*. (James 1946, 1: 242, emphasis mine—*A.U.*)

In this scene, Milly for the first time experiences an intimacy with death, seeing in the portrait her simultaneously perfect and moribund self—a remote and distant Venetian "princess" in a gilded frame. It is one of the identities "endowed on her by others" (Van Slyck 2005: 310) that she borrows and tries on later in the novel when she "frames" her own story in the Venetian setting. It is also a clear indication of the parallel between art, for all its immortality, and death. Milly, who in a later episode claims that she is unable to "agree" and "accept," nonetheless agrees with Lord Mark's opinion and accepts her resemblance to the "dead" portrait, which offers her an otherworldly vantage point.

The novel brings together death, art, waste, and giving. Milly's gradual withdrawal from contact with others as well as from the narrative serves in preparing the perfect conditions for her ultimate unilateral gift—a bequest that is, by definition, a gift mediated by death. Bequeathal is usually understood as an autonomous transaction; unlike gift exchange, it often entails intergenerational succession and involves a legal procedure. Yet in Milly's case, it has all characteristics of the gift: she leaves an inheritance to Densher who is not her relative and not an object of benevolence; her gift is spontaneous, unexpected, and comes in the Christmas season, which makes its status as gift almost too obvious.

Jean-Luc Marion conceptualizes inheritance as a gift. Considered in the phenomenological perspective, inheritance is a pure gift because the giver is empirically absent from any possible exchange (as is also the case with the anonymous giver), which makes it impossible to reciprocate. Even if one pays taxes and fees on inheriting a fortune, these are paid to the state and the lawyers to whom one owes nothing. "To the one who gave me, on the other hand, I repay nothing because I owe nothing and because the gift requires, for me to receive it, that I not attempt to repay it" (Marion 2002: 95). As a result, we encounter a paradox: "absence (nothingness, disappearance, death) gives, not like one among many possible givers, but par excellence" (96). Marion defines a gift by reference to a *givenness* that he considers pure in the case of asymmetrical or vertical exchange as it makes reciprocity impossible. If we consider *The Wings of the Dove* from this perspective, we can say that Milly epitomizes pure givenness before she dies, as she attempts to suspend the economy of exchange. She bestows her bequest on Densher from a place of her absence where it is impossible to reach her although she can still reach out to others, hence Kate's metaphor of Milly's wings that "cover them" and that can be viewed as either protection or threat, or both.

Milly's gift comes in two parts: Densher first receives a letter from her that he passes, without reading, to Kate, in return for her sacrifice (the night she agreed to spend with him), and Kate, entitled to do with the letter whatever she pleases, burns it. Then the second letter, announcing the amount of the bequest, arrives and Densher presents Kate with an excruciating choice: to take the money and renounce their plans to marry or accept him without the money. On both occasions, Densher receives Milly's gift but does not accept it; it is as if the gift transmits Milly's self-acknowledged inability to "agree" and to "accept."

Densher's sole sentimental possession becomes the memory of the destroyed and forever-lost letter:

> He kept it back like a favourite pang… he took it out of its sacred corner and its soft wrappings; he undid them one by one, handling them, handling *it*, as a father, baffled and tender, might handle a maimed child. But so it was before him—in his dread of who else might see it. Then he took to himself at such hours, in other words, that he should never, never know what had been in Milly's letter. The intention announced in it he should but too probably know; only that would have been, but for the depths of his spirit, the least part of it. The part of it missed for ever was the turn she would have given her act. This turn had possibilities that, somehow, by wondering about them, his imagination had extraordinarily filled out and refined. It had made of them a revelation the loss of which was like the sight of a priceless pearl cast before his eyes—his pledge given not to save it—into the fathomless sea, or rather even it was like the sacrifice of something sentient and throbbing, something that, for the spiritual ear, might have been audible as a faint far wail. (James 1946, 2: 429–430)

As often is the case in the work of James, memories acquire an independent, quasi-material existence: the letter is lost but Densher repeatedly "unwraps" it as his dearest treasure. James uses sentimentally charged tropes to describe Densher's attitude: the tender handling of a maimed child, the loss of a priceless pearl in the fathomless sea, the sacrifice of something sentient and throbbing. In the 1891 story "A Discovered Pearl" by Mary Wilkins Freeman, we encounter a similar pearl-trope deployed to describe the self-sacrificial love of a female character, which she bestows on her long-lost lover as a "Christmas gift, which she had been treasuring for twenty years." Shortly before, the lover had explained in metaphor why the fact that he had forgotten her for 20 years should not be an impediment to their happiness:

s'pose some day I'd come across a pearl caught into some sea-weeds, where I hadn't no idea of findin' it. Well, I guess it wouldn't have made much difference to me whether or no I'd been thinkin' about that pearl for twenty years, or whether I'd ever seen it an' forgotten it. There'd been the pearl, an' I'd been the man that had it. (Freeman 1892: 39)

He is trying to say that the "pearl" remains out there among the "sea-weeds," regardless of whether the recipient remembers or forgets it; it has an everlasting presence as a once-offered gift (present). In *The Wings of the Dove* the situation is reversed: Densher undoes imaginary wrappings each time only to discover that the pearl is lost in the sea. It is a double loss, or "*loss of her loss*" (Reinhard 1997: 134): the letter from a dead person is itself dead (unread, unreadable) but this only increases its value for the mourner. The letter presumably contains the ultimate, irrevocable "meaning" of Milly's gift; impersonal in itself, money often comes with a note or a card when given as a gift, enclosing the gift of money in an attempt to personalize it. In this sense, the letter is both the gift's "content" and its "enclosure," part of the "wrapping." The lost letter becomes Densher's fetish—"a precious objet d'art, a sentimental keepsake, or a treasured souvenir" (Martin 2003: 124)—epitomizing his romantic or sentimental cult of the deceased. At the same time, unwrapping the "wrapping" does not bring him in any way closer to the sender. When Densher fondly, and with fatherly love, handles the "maimed child" of the destroyed letter, he masochistically handles his own loss.

Critics point at the paradox of the letter: once destroyed, it becomes omnipresent in the life of Densher and Kate, "indenturing" them (Reinhard 1997: 135), putting them in debt, infecting them with self-sacrifice. Densher may pass the physical letter on to Kate as a gift given in return for another, he may give up the gift of the bequest. But there is nothing he can do about the phantom presence of the destroyed letter—Milly's last will and gift is a bare fact, "the turn she would have given her act" concealed forever. Reduced to ashes, the letter is exempt from circulation (Reinhard 1997: 135). Death proves to be ultimately "incommensurable" in the novel (Mizruchi 2008: 94), the letter becoming a symbol of this incommensurability. The only thing that Densher allows himself to own and keep is loss, absence, a void—a melancholy gift of death, as it were.

To paraphrase Leon Edel, no two American masterpieces are more dissimilar than *The Mysterious Stranger* manuscripts and *The Wings of the Dove*

(Edel 1972: 37–38). One is a fantastic narrative with elements of parable and allegory that make it accessible to a juvenile readership and the other a sophisticated modernist novel, an example of complex, obscure, and elusive writing. The analysis above has demonstrated, however, that although Twain and James take different roads they travel in the same direction. Both texts seek to establish an intimate connection between gift and death, with death understood as finitude but also as a breach in the communality or communication and that, as such, becomes a condition of pure giving by the logic of reduction. Death is a gift that does not require any payment and does not put the receiver in debt (Twain); the giver who has crossed the boundary of life into death cannot be reached and the debt can never be repaid, which does not preclude feelings of indebtedness and guilt (James). The purity of the gift is divorced from its usual moral attributes—sympathy, goodness, or generosity. Twain's boys become good, generous, and loving but this transformation is temporary and conditional rather than fundamental. Traum, the supreme donor in the story, places himself above the Moral Law. Milly's generosity is debatable because her motivation eludes us and because her gift does more harm than good to the receivers. The pure gift is ambivalent. The boys see the gift of death as evil while the satanic giver believes it to be beneficial. Milly's monopolization of "givenness" verges on manipulation and invites polar readings. At the same time, once bestowed the gift becomes independent of the giver, prompting new chains of gift-giving or new bargains; the giver—a transcendental figure—is not responsible for the gift's afterlife or effects. Omnipotent Satan cannot take his gift back. Milly—unless we think of her as a vengeful figure foreseeing the outcome of her gesture—leaves the scene to Densher and Kate who are already entrapped in a net of mutual obligations and debts.

In both texts, we are dealing with a complex revision of the ideology of disinterested giving as rooted in the sentimental tradition. The debt to this tradition can be traced on the level of expression, with both Twain and James using the sentimental language of the gift. At the same time, both texts break from conventions of sentimental mourning and religious didacticism associated with the combination of death and gift. Finally, both writers test asymmetrical structures that exclude the possibility of exchange or bargain and bring the idea of disinterestedness to its limit by radicalizing it; in seeking to exempt death from exchange and trade, they initiate a move toward the asymmetrical ethics of gift-giving of twentieth-century intellectual thought. Pure, disinterested giving, in such an interpretation, is indissociable from feelings of grief, loss, and melancholia, which makes it fundamentally ambivalent. If death, in its finitude and irreversibility, is the condition of a gift's perfection, then we are doomed to embrace the fact that the perfect gift par excellence is anything but safe or joyful.

Works Cited

Artese, Brian. 2006. Overhearing Testimony: James in the Shadow of Sentimentalism. *Henry James Review* 27 (2): 103–125.
Brodwin, Stanley. 1973. Mark Twain's Masks of Satan: The Final Phase. *American Literature* 45 (2): 206–227.
———. 2003. Mark Twain's Theology: The Gods of a Brevet Presbyterian. In *The Cambridge Companion to Mark Twain*, ed. Forrest G. Robinson, 220–248. Cambridge: Cambridge University Press.
Brooks, Van Wyck. 1920. *The Ordeal of Mark Twain*. New York: E.P. Dutton.
Brooks, Peter. 1976. *Melodramatic Imagination: Balzac, Henry James, Melodrama, and the Mode of Excess*. New York: Columbia University Press.
Bush, Harold K., Jr. 2002. 'A Moralist in Disguise': Mark Twain and American Religion. In *A Historical Guide to Mark Twain*, ed. Shelley Fisher Fishkin, 55–94. Oxford: Oxford University Press.
Camfield, Gregg. 1994. *Sentimental Twain: Samuel Clemens in the Maze of Moral Philosophy*. Philadelphia: University of Pennsylvania Press.
———. 1997. *Necessary Madness: The Humor of Domesticity in Nineteenth-Century American Literature*. New York: Oxford University Press.
Cutting, Andrew. 2005. *Death in Henry James*. Basingstoke: Palgrave Macmillan.
Derrida, Jacques. 1995. *The Gift of Death*. Trans. David Wills. Chicago: University of Chicago Press.
Edel, Leon. 1972. *Henry James: The Master: 1901–1916*. London: Hart-Davis.
Eutsey, Dwayne. 2005. God's 'Real' Message: 'No. 44, The Mysterious Stranger' and the Influence of Liberal Religion on Mark Twain. *The Mark Twain Annual* 3: 53–66.
Fisher Fishkin, Shelley, and G. Robinson Forest. 2005. Introduction: Mark Twain at the Turn-of-the-Century: 1890–1910. *Arizona Quarterly: A Journal of American Literature, Culture, and Theory*. 61 (1): 1–6.
Flatley, Jonathan. 2008. *Affective Mapping: Melancholia and the Politics of Modernism*. Cambridge, MA: Harvard University Press.
Freeman, Mary Eleanor Wilkins. 1892. A Discovered Pearl. In *A New England Nun, and Other Stories*. Vol. 2. 23–49. Leipzig: Heinemann and Balestier.
Friedman, Johanthan. 1993. *Professions of Taste. Henry James, British Aestheticism, and Commodity Culture*. Stanford: Stanford University Press.

Gibson, William M. 1969. Introduction. In *Mark Twain's Mysterious Stranger Manuscripts*, ed. William M. Gibson. Berkeley: University of California Press.
Hénaff, Marcel. 2003. Religious Ethics, Gift Exchange, and Capitalism. *European Journal of Sociology* 44 (3): 293–324.
Hoeller, Hildegard. 2012. *From Gift to Commodity: Capitalism and Sacrifice in Nineteenth-Century American Fiction*. New Hampshire: University of New Hampshire Press.
James, Henry. 1934. *The Art of the Novel: Critical Prefaces*. London; New York: Charles Scribner's Sons.
———. 1946. *The Wings of the Dove*. Vol. 1, 2. New York: The Modern Library.
———. 1957. *The House of Fiction*, ed. Leon Edel. London: Rupert Hart-Davis.
James, Henry, and James, William. 1997. *William and Henry James: Selected Letters*. Charlottesville: University of Virginia Press.
Kete, Mary Louise. 2000. *Sentimental Collaborations: Mourning and Middle-Class Identity in Nineteenth-Century America*. Durham, NC: University of North Carolina Press.
Kim, Sharon. 2003. Puritan Realism: *The Wide, Wide World* and Robinson Crusoe. *American Literature* 75 (4): 783-811.
Kiskis, Michael J. 2011. Mark Twain and the Tradition of Literary Domesticity. In *Constructing Mark Twain: New Directions in Scholarship*, ed. Laura E. Skandera Trombley and Michael J. Kiskis, 13–28. Minneapolis: University of Missouri Press.
Leavis, F.R. 1993. *The Great Tradition: George Eliot, Henry James, Joseph Conrad*. Harmondsworth, UK: Penguin.
Marion, Jean-Luc. 2002. *Being Given: Toward a Phenomenology of Givenness*. Trans. Geoffrey L. Kosky. Stanford: Stanford University Press.
Martin, Michael R. 2003. "Branding Milly Theale". The Capital Case of *The Wings of the Dove*. *The Henry James Review* 24 (2): 103–132.
Maynard, Jessica. 2005. "Revolutionist Consumers": The Application of Sacrifice in Ruskin, Bataille and Henry James. In *Metaphors of Economy*, ed. Nicole Bracker and Stefan Herbrechter, 135–146. Amsterdam: Rodopi.
Michelson, Bruce. 1980. Deus Ludens: The Shaping of Mark Twain's "Mysterious Stranger." *NOVEL: A Forum on Fiction* 14 (1): 44–56.
Mizruchi, Susan L. 2008. *The Rise of Multicultural America: Economy and Print Culture, 1865–1919*. Chapel Hill: University of North Carolina Press.
Nancy, Jean-Luc. 1991. *The Inoperative Community*. Trans. Peter Connor, Lisa Garbus, Michael Holland, and Simona Sawhney. Minneapolis: University of Minnesota Press.
Noble, Marianna. 2000. *The Masochistic Pleasures of Sentimental Literature*. Princeton: Princeton University Press.
Osteen, Mark. 2002. Gift or Commodity? In *The Question of the Gift: Essays Across Disciplines*, ed. Mark Osteen, 229–247. London: Routledge.

Phelps, Elizabeth Stuart. 2019. *The Gates Ajar*. Penguin.
Reinhard, Kenneth. 1997. The Jamesian Thing: *The Wings of the Dove* and the Ethics of Mourning. *Arizona Quarterly* 53 (4): 115–146.
Rivkin, Julie. 1996. *False Positions: The Representational Logics of Henry James's Fiction*. Stanford: Stanford University Press.
Rohman, Chad. 1999. 'Searching for the fructifying dew of truth': 'Negative Evidence' and Epistemological Uncertainty in Mark Twain's 'No. 44, The Mysterious Stranger'. *American Literary Realism, 1870–1910* 31 (2): 72–88.
Schaffer, Talia. 2016. The Silent Treatment of *The Wings of the Dove*: Ethics of Care and Late-James Style. *The Henry James Review* 37 (3): 233–245.
Schiller, Emily. 1996. Melodrama Redeemed; or, The Death of Innocence: Milly and Mortality in *The Wings of the Dove*. *Studies in American Fiction* 24 (2): 193–214.
Smith-Gordon, George. 2013. Psychological Sentimentalism: Consciousness, Affect, and the Sentimental Henry James. In *Sentimentalism in Nineteenth-Century America: Literary and Cultural Practices*, ed. Mary G. De Jong, 181–196. New Jersey: Fairleigh Dickinson University Press.
Twain, Mark. 1969. *Mark Twain's Mysterious Stranger Manuscripts*, ed. William M. Gibson. Berkeley: University of California Press.
———. 1973. *What Is Man? and Other Philosophical Writings*, ed. Paul Baender. Berkeley: University of California Press.
Van Slyck, Phyllis. 2005. Charting an Ethics of Desire in 'The Wings of the Dove'. *Criticism* 47 (3): 301–323.
Warner, Susan [pseudonym Elizabeth Wetherell]. 1851. *The Wide, Wide World*. Vol. 1, 2. New York, 1851.

CHAPTER 9

"The Season of Gifts": Christmas and Melancholia

9.1 The Melancholic Side of Christmas

In *The Wings of The Dove*, news of the postmortem gift left by Milly Theale—her bequest—comes on Christmas Eve, during "the season of gifts," and initiates a phase of melancholic mourning on the part of the receiver, Merton Densher. The novel invites us to think of Christmas in melancholic terms. Turn-of-the-century Christmas melancholia—the focus of this chapter—is not necessarily associated with death or mourning, as this Jamesian example might suggest, but encapsulates a wider range of sentiments from nostalgia to exhaustion. Seemingly innocent Christmas gift exchange harbors numerous potential dangers including shopping fever, fatigue, compulsion, bankruptcy, disappointment, or a self-deception that could give rise to unpleasant feelings. The short stories by James's contemporaries William Dean Howells, Mary Wilkins Freeman, and O. Henry (William Sydney Porter) that are analyzed below demonstrate the controversial and ambivalent character of Christmas giving, which by the late nineteenth century bordered more precipitously on consumption and commerce than had ever before been the case.

Modern Christmas, a nineteenth-century invention, was considered a particularly joyful time of the year, not least because of its association with giving and receiving gifts. Nineteenth-century texts describe the so-called spirit of Christmas as a spirit of joy, merry-making, generosity, and goodness. At the same time, Christmas-tide joy was traditionally accompanied by a pensiveness or sadness prompted by the end of a life cycle (a passing

© The Author(s), under exclusive license to Springer Nature Switzerland AG 2022
A. Urakova, *Dangerous Giving in Nineteenth-Century American Literature*, American Literature Readings in the 21st Century, https://doi.org/10.1007/978-3-030-93270-1_9

year), the darkness of December, and the reflections provoked by seasonal charity work. An anonymous writer in *Harper's Bazar* distinguishes between "Christmas past," or the Christmas of Irving, a time of family feasts and gift-giving to children, and "Christmas present," or the Christmas of Dickens, inspiring "the spirit of unselfish kindness" (Anon. "Christmas—Past and Present" 1881a: 834).[1] Both these "Christmases," no matter how joyful or rewarding they might be, are touched by melancholy: the first triggers nostalgia in the elderly, the second involves attendance at scenes of suffering and need (834). The generic nineteenth-century sentimental Christmas story draws on the Dickensian "Christmas Carol" either in its plot (a magical transformation and the conversion of a cold-hearted unbeliever) or in the general attitude and bittersweet tone.[2] As a *Godey's* contributor Rosalie Lee put it, "I have written you a Christmas story. There are tears in it, but it ends happily, as such stories should ... I forget not how sad the memories we must entwine with our garlands and berries of the whole. But oh! Hearts that suffer, we must not be too sad at this holy season" (Lee 1881: 531).

By the end of the nineteenth century, the Christmas sentiment had undergone several changes. Historians of American Christmas cultural history tend to see the 1880s as watershed years. According to William B. Waits, it was not until this period that "the modern form of Christmas emerged"; this included the shift from homemade gifts to manufactured gifts, the substitution of religious aspects with secular aspects, and the overall "mad compulsion of giving" (Waits 1994: 2–3). Penne L. Restad writes of "the national Christmas" as a "coming of age in the last quarter of the nineteenth century"; the tradition of homemade decorations disappeared while gift wrapping, unknown earlier in the century, came into

---

[1] Irving and Dickens were both considered to be "responsible" for "inventing" Christmas. The anonymous writer in *Harper's Bazar* borrowed the terms "Christmas Past" and "Christmas Present" from *A Christmas Carol* by Charles Dickens, see n2. Stephen Nissenbaum writes about the emergence of a distinction between "presents" to family and "charity" to the needy in the nineteenth century (Nissenbaum 1996: 227).

[2] *A Christmas Carol* (1843) is a novella by Charles Dickens about a parsimonious financier Scrooge who, after visits from the Spirits of Christmas Past, Present, and Future in his dream, becomes a generous benefactor to his poor relatives and employee as well as an ardent believer in the goodness of Christmas and the Christmas spirit. The story had an unprecedented impact on American Christmas literature and culture; critics speak about the "'carol philosophy' of Charles Dickens, which combined certain religious and secular attitudes towards the celebration into a humanitarian pattern" that had an enduring appeal in the US (Barnett 1954: 14).

vogue; "commerce was becoming more dependent on Christmas sales" (Restad 1996: 106, 129, 128). While manufactured gifts were common long before the 1880s and the idea of homemade gifts in the family circle was never abandoned, even after the 1880s,[3] the end of the century did indeed witness the commercialization of Christmas on an unprecedented scale. The very introduction of gift wrapping, as a means to purify the gift from the taint of the market (Restad 1996: 130; Fennell 2002), is one of the signs of this paradigm shift.

Late nineteenth-century publications, while continuously reminding the reader of the Christmas spirit, the star in the East, and the importance of good deeds, began to address the theme of Christmas shopping significantly more than had previously been the case. An 1891 Christmas poem begins with the lines: "I've been buying Christmas presents, / Roving from shop to shop"—and ends with a statement of post-Christmas bankruptcy: "I *like* to be a bankrupt for a while / After the Christmas day" (Sangster 1891: 996). By the late 1870s the words "giving" and "buying" were often being used interchangeably; cf.: "The art of giving and receiving presents is not an intuition ... there are few more charming sensations than that of buying a present and of receiving one" (Anon. 1879: 806).[4] Still more texts advised against viewing Christmas shopping as a burden in an attempt to mitigate "negative feelings about the increased quantity of gifts in circulation and a consequent loss of the sentiments once attached to presents" (Marling 2000: 304).[5] One article expresses disapproval of the numerous "sinners against the blithe spirit of Christmas" who "haunt the shops" unable to decide what they want; "with the whole head sick

---

[3] As Karal Ann Marling observes, referring to the 1870s, "despite the modern belief that Christmas used to be an affair of modest, homemade offerings, the vast majority of gifts were purchased. The exception was the handicraft item made specifically for sale at the Christmas fair or bazaar" (Marling 2000: 9). See also Chap. 1 of this book: by the 1840s, praise for handmade presents was already to be found hand in hand with the critique of Christmas consumerism. By the end of the nineteenth century, since most women now engaged in Christmas shopping, children were "the only remaining fabricators of Christmas presents" (10). However, the fancy-work sections of women's magazines continued to publish "recipes and instructions for doing fancy-work" (10) in the Christmas season; see more about this later in this chapter.

[4] Cf. a publication entitled "The Art of Christmas Shopping" (Anon. 1881c).

[5] Ellen M. Litwicki cites Edward Bok, editor of the *Ladies Home Journal* (December 1894: 16) as demanding a modification of "this senseless habit of excessive gift-making"; another author C.B. Wheeler (1904) "suggested it was time for an 'Anti-gift League'" (Litwicki 2020: 283).

and the whole heart weary, they go home empty-headed, to plunge into the vortex again next day" until they purchase "flotsam, jetsam and ligan" in "sheer desperation" (Anon. "Taking Christmas by the Forelock" 1881b: 818).[6] The author's word choice (sick head, weary heart, etc.) suggests a new type of Christmas "malady" caused by the obligation to engage in seasonal shopping. Burdensome Christmas giving and ridiculous, useless, or excessive Christmas presents were to become the subject matter of both critical and satirical texts, followed by the emergence of organized social movements against compulsory Christmas giving (such as SPUG) in the early twentieth century.[7]

Wasteful, compulsory, and unavoidable, Christmas gifts themselves begin to trigger feelings of depression. "Christmas Every Day" by William Dean Howells, a story for children discussed below, touches upon this particular aspect of modern Christmas giving in the form of a dystopian satire, in a period in which the need to find the perfect Christmas gift was becoming even more significant in the secularized context of turn-of-the-century Christmas festivities. As the examples of the stories by Mary Wilkins Freeman and O. Henry demonstrate, the ideal Christmas gift comes "wrapped up" in nostalgia or loss. I deliberately use the word "loss" and not "sacrifice" to redirect attention from the moral or religious side of Christmas giving to its melancholic aspect. Melancholia is a state or condition that, at least in the context of the nineteenth century, is closely associated with nostalgia[8] or with "dwelling on the loss" (Flatley 2008: 1). This condition, however and as Jonathan Flatley argues, does not always have to be depressive: "some melancholies are the opposite of depressing, functioning as the very mechanism through which one may be interested in the world" (1). Flatley's observation is certainly true of the Christmas-tide melancholia that often accompanies the consolation or redemption that is to be found within the conventions of a traditional or generic Christmas story. The stories I discuss in this chapter first appeared in

[6] In another *Harper's Bazar* publication, the author condemns "self-appointed censors who see none of the joy and only the burden of Christmas. They dwell on the 'obligations' of the day, and the burden of making gifts." Further on, the author says that "a gift must always be free" (Anon. 1891: 1026).

[7] SPUG was the Society for the Prevention of Useless Giving, an early twentieth-century organization opposing the custom among retail and factory workers of giving gifts to supervisors. See Litwicki (forthcoming).

[8] "By the early nineteenth century ... nostalgia had to come to be more consistently viewed as a form of melancholia" (Jackson 1986: 378).

Christmas-related magazine issues. Therefore, some positive outcome—be it redeeming humor, or harmony achieved, or the triumph of selfless love—was expected. At the same time, the dangers or ambiguities of Christmas gift-giving that these texts describe were symptomatic of a "modern form of Christmas" (Waits 1994: 2) that presented new challenges to the almost century-old sentimental customs.

9.2 "Hollowdays," or the Christmas Dystopia of William Dean Howells

The title of "Christmas Every Day," a famous children's story by American realist writer William Dean Howells, is likely a pun on the widespread sentimental attitude to Christmas. Less than a decade later, another author would use a similar title—"Every Day is Christmas"—to convey the message that "a desire to do something for someone" in the Christmas season should not be confined to "the twelfth month of the year" (Colver 1904: 238). In Howells's fantasy, however, "Christmas Every Day" anticipates twentieth-century time-loop plots by quite simply describing a Christmas that reoccurs every day of the year. Moreover, the story shows that having Christmas every day inevitably leads to hatred instead of kindness and to depression instead of joy; Christmas giving becomes truly dangerous once it becomes excessive.[9]

This story, first published in *St. Nicholas; an Illustrated Magazine for Young Folks* (January 1886), is the opening story in a collection entitled *Christmas Every Day and Other Stories Told for Children* (1893), which contains a number of stories told by a father, the alter ego of Howells, to his little daughter and son during the Christmas season. All of these stories have some link to either Christmas, New Year, or Thanksgiving but "Christmas Every Day" is the only story about Christmas. In the frame narrative, a little girl asks her papa for a Christmas story, he consents and comes up with a fantasy about "a little girl who liked Christmas so much that she wanted it to be Christmas every day in the year" (Howells 1893: 2). The Christmas Fairy fulfills her wish on the condition that after a year, the girl should decide if she wants to keep the gift or return it.

---

[9] Ironically, the modern remake of the story, a 1996 American comedy film, has a different message: the selfish teenager learns the true meaning of Christmas through reliving the same Christmas day over and over again. Like *A Christmas Carol* and unlike Howells' fantasy, it is a narrative of conversion.

Predictably, the "year of Christmases" (Howells 1893: 9) turns out to be a nightmare. After a splendid Christmas day—albeit one that ends for the girl in stomachache, caused by eating too many candies, as well as in some family tension—another Christmas day begins. The girl's merry siblings wave their stockings in front of her and the same abundance of presents—books, portfolios, boxes of stationery breastpins, and so on[10]—awaits her on the library table. "I'm sure I don't see how I'm to dispose of all these things," says her mother, "ready to cry" (10). By the next day everybody is already getting "crosser" (11); people, forced to celebrate Christmas and exchange gifts again and again, start losing their tempers. The Fairy's gift turns out to be a harmful one but the girl thinks it would be "ungrateful and ill-bred" to give it back straight away (11).

Using a time-loop device, the story ironically portrays a grim dystopian society whose members spend more than they produce. Ruled by a grotesque post-capitalist version of the gift economy, this society faces economic and ecological catastrophe: excessive gift-giving results in the depletion of financial and natural resources. "Turkeys got to be about a thousand dollars apiece ... And they [people] got to passing off almost anything for turkeys—half-grown humming-birds, and even rocs out of the *Arabian Nights*—the real turkeys were so scarce" (12). The same happens to cranberries ("they asked a diamond apiece for cranberries") and Christmas trees since "all the woods and orchards were cut down ... After a while they had to make Christmas-trees out of rags, and stuff them with bran, like old-fashioned dolls" (12). All the people grow poor, "buying presents for one another" (13). Instead of idealizing gift-giving as a manifestation of goodness and as an alternative to market exchange, Howells portrays capitalism at its worse: gifts are consumer goods that eventually consume the givers. The only members of society who prosper—confectioners, fancy-store keepers, picture-book sellers, and expressmen—are engaged in selling and delivering candy and gimcracks, tokens of sheer waste.

"Christmas Every Day" anticipates the twentieth-century concept of American Christmas as a type of "gigantic potlatch," as suggested by Claude Lévi-Strauss: "Through the uselessness of the gifts, and their frequent duplication because of the limited range of objects suitable as presents, these exchanges also take the form of a vast and collective destruction of wealth" (1969: 56). In showing how gift exchange may spiral out of

---

[10] The story provides us with a catalogue of late-nineteenth-century commodified gifts.

control, Howells's story perfectly illustrates this observation. There are so many gifts that everyone has to build "barns to hold their presents, but pretty soon the barns overflowed, and then they used to let them lie out in the rain, or anywhere" (Howells 1893: 15). The economy of expenditure and waste that dominates in Howells's dystopia draws upon the compulsion to give and receive that the modern custom of Christmas giving purportedly has in common with the rituals of North American tribes.

Yet, there is also a significant difference. When commenting on Lévi-Strauss's parallel between modern Christmas festivities and the ritual of potlatch, Restad cautiously observes that "the presence of a market economy and the fairly static condition of the middle class endowed gift-giving with a related but essentially different purpose." For example, "by using the gifts bought and given through the medium of shops and stores, Americans engaged in a 'potlatch' of magnification, not reallocation, of personal goods" (70). In Howells's story, the magnification of goods (piles and piles of presents stocked in barns and elsewhere) is the main cause of everyone's bankruptcy. It has little to do with "the solemn destruction of riches" in the structure of North American potlatch as poeticized by Georges Bataille (1988: 67). The liberating Bataillesque destruction of riches takes place only at the end of the story when children dump "candy and raisins and nuts" in the river and burn "their gift-books and presents of all kinds" (Howells 1893: 20). The joyful blaze of bonfires ("They had the greatest *time!*" [20]) is the polar opposite of the image of the heaps of undesired and useless gifts lying out in the rain, a dark and deeply melancholic symbol of Christmas giving.

Even more importantly, the story misses another essential element of the potlatch ceremony—challenge or competition. The consumerist potlatch described by Howells is meaningless and hollow; it is a true "hollowday," as his youngest daughter Winny called "holidays" (Goodman, Dawson 2005: 130). The repetitive Christmases are days of waste, scarcity, and ruin, hollowed out of any of the meaning that holds together even the most bizarre traditional rituals. The story is an early example of absurdist satire: Christmas makes other holidays "hollowdays" as well. For example, "the Fourth of July orations all turned into Christmas carols, and when anybody tried to read the Declaration, instead of saying, 'When in the course of human events it becomes necessary,' he was sure to sing, 'God rest you, merry gentlemen'" (17).

Mutual hatred (people sign their gifts: "Take it, you horrid old thing!" (14), frustration, and gloom are the predictable outcomes of this forced, never-ending, and hollow Christmas. The little girl's own depression passes through different stages. After three or four months, discovering "ugly, lumpy stockings dangling at the fire-place, and the disgusting presents around everywhere," she bursts out crying (13). After six months, she is exhausted and cannot cry anymore. By October, she has taken to sitting on dolls wherever she finds them: "French dolls, or any kind—she hated the sight of them" (14). By Thanksgiving, she is slamming presents across the room. The first published version of the story contained images illustrating the different states of the girl's depression: hopeless (Fig. 9.1), exhausted, mad, and furious. Harmony is restored only after the girl strikes a bargain with the Fairy that there should be just one Christmas a year: the story not only shows the anti-sentimental side of Christmas but also turns the generic model upside down: happiness and joy come when Christmas ends.

Fig. 9.1 Illustration to the story. Howells, William Dean. "Christmas Everyday." *St. Nickolas; an illustrated Magazine for Young Folks* (1873–1907); New York. (Jan. 1886). PDF Page 3. (Courtesy of ProQuest's *American Periodical Series*)

9 "THE SEASON OF GIFTS": CHRISTMAS AND MELANCHOLIA

For Howells, the problem with Christmas lies in its coercive character: you must celebrate and exchange presents no matter how absurd and unnecessary this might seem to you. The motif of coercion playfully replicates itself in the frame narrative and in the description of the storytelling scene.

The little girl came into her papa's study, as she always did Saturday morning before breakfast, and asked for a story. He tried to beg off that morning, for he was very busy, but she would not let him. So he began:
"Well, once there was a little pig—"
She put her hand over his mouth and stopped him at the word. She said she had heard little pig-stories till she was perfectly sick of them. (3)

The father fails in his attempt "to beg off that morning." We also learn that he is called upon to tell stories every Saturday and that his storytelling resources are depleted. He has only "little pig-stories" in stock but the girl is "perfectly sick" of these, just as the little girl in the embedded story becomes sick of having too many candies and dolls. The little girl also demands a Christmas story because "it's getting to be the season. It's past Thanksgiving already" (3). As a result, he tells her about the dangers of coercive giving, hinting, tongue-in-cheek, that enough is enough.[11]

The metafictional framework engages with the fictional narrative and introduces a spirit of playfulness that, together with the overall humorous, witty, and teasing tone, reminds us that we should not take the story's subject matter too seriously. The girl, a despotic and demanding listener, rewards her papa's efforts by nestling "into comfortable shape" in his lap and calling his story "first class" (4). Ironically, she draws a "deep sigh of satisfaction" listening to the troubles of her fictional counterpart (18). The framework thus offers a remedy of a sort against the Christmas melancholia as described in the story—a modern disease caused by onerous gift exchange, overconsumption, and the feeling of waste; the image of the

---

[11] "Christmas Every Day" echoes a series of allegorical and satirical Christmas sketches Howells wrote for an adult audience in the 1890s exploring "longstanding personal problems for Howells: how can an artist publicly committed to realism write sketches in a hackneyed romantic tradition, the 'Christmas sketch'"? (Carrington 1977: 257). In these sketches, the author's editor obliges him to write a Christmas piece and the author calls upon the Christmas Muse to help him. For Howells, Christmas coercion infiltrates different spheres, including the professional.

happily nestled child is a sentimental note in the decidedly anti-sentimental Christmas-related fantasy.

Howells was most likely using the format of a humorous story with a moral for children as a means to sublimate some of his personal anxieties. In a letter to his father dated December 26, 1869, he writes of "rather a merry Christmas" in his family, describing in much detail the doll's house they bought for their daughter Winny. His feelings, however, are mixed:

> Then we filled a pair of stockings for each of the little ones, and by the time I'd thought of so many Christmases at home that my heart was aching; and anniversaries in this way are always painful to me. I thought what scanty feasts and presents used to make us happy, and then looked sadly around on Winny's splendor and abundance, and felt that the world was somehow going the wrong way. (Howells 1979: 347)

The sentiment the writer experienced in 1869—a combination of nostalgia and alienation—was likely to have increased in the decade that followed, as Christmas festivities came to be organized on an even larger scale. Yet in "Christmas Every Day" negative emotions associated with Christmas become the source of an amusing story, justified by the child's presence, attention, and satisfaction. After all, Howells manages to market his dystopia—a witty piece of social criticism and satire—as a Christmas story appropriate for children or for reading in the family circle.

A similar approach is taken in *The Night before Christmas*, a play that Howells wrote much later (in 1916) than "Christmas Every Day" and that expresses his continued exasperation with all-consuming nature of Christmas shopping. The autobiographical character Mr. Fountain, exhausted from sorting presents after a long day of shopping, is a Christmas anarchist: he declares that the modern Christmas is a pagan holiday and threatens to send the presents back. Some of his rejoinders are reminiscent of "Christmas Every Day": "We ought to have put on our cards, 'With the season's bitterest grudges,' 'In hopes of a return,' 'With a hopeless sense of the folly,' 'To pay a hateful debt,' 'With impotent rage and despair'" (Howells 1916). Yet his attitude alters when his youngest child comes into the room in the middle of the night, worried that his father will follow through on his threat to send the gifts back. This immediately restores Fountain's Christmas spirit; he changes his mind about the holiday and enters into an agreement with his wife that they will do their shopping for the following Christmas the day right after that Christmas Day. Ironically, the play follows the conventional "Christmas Carol" pattern that a realist such as Howells might be expected to sneer at: the conversion of the Christmas anarchist or negativist into its champion, whose fatherly love is stronger than all the "morbid" (Howells 1916) feelings that Christmas preparations may evoke. As parenthood reconciles the character with the dangers of and fatigue associated with Christmas giving, the "hollowday" acquires a sentimental meaning and, at least for the moment, becomes wholesome. "…I hope that my son will be writing, Dec. 26, 1899, to his father with love I now feel for you, and then I sha'n't care much how the world has gone" (Howells 1979: 349–350).

9.3 Melancholy Gifts and Givers in Mary Wilkins Freeman's Christmas Stories

This section will discuss three Christmas stories from a volume by Mary Wilkins Freeman tellingly entitled *The Givers. Short Stories* (1904), with a special focus on "The Reign of the Doll." Christmas gift-giving is a subject of research interest in Jana Tigchelaar's article on gifts, community, and regionalism in the Christmas stories of Sarah Orne Jewett and Mary Wilkins Freeman. Both of these authors are representative of the regionalist women's writing that Tigchelaar, following Judith Fetterley (1994), views in terms of "resistance to both national narrative and generic forms" (Tigchelaar 2014: 237). When considering three Christmas stories from Freeman's *A New England Nun and Other Stories* (1891), she compellingly argues that the author "uses Christmas stories to explore the damaging effects of self-interested gifts" (247–48) and promotes "the neighborly Christmas" as an alternative to the national narrative of "domestic Christmas" (247–52). Unlike Tigchelaar, I will not focus on the social, moral, or regional aspects of Freeman's stories. Placing the New English regional author within a broader national context of popular Christmas writing,[12] I will instead explore her contribution to the turn-of-the-century idea of a Christmas melancholy associated with the perils of

---

[12] Like Howells, Freeman contributed to editions including Harpers and Brothers. (On Freeman's collaboration with Harper's Bazar and her subversive critique of capitalism, see Elbert 1993). While the regional context sheds light on certain themes and attitudes in the work of Freeman or Jewett, it also, to some extent, autonomizes and isolates both of these authors—one of the reasons I prefer to read Freeman in the broader, national and not regional, framework.

Christmas shopping and consumption; I will also show how a commodified Christmas gift may become the object of melancholic longing.

The Givers. Short Stories includes six previously published Christmas stories that feature character types, either givers or receivers (or both) already familiar to Freeman's readers: thoughtless, or self-interested givers ("The Givers"); generous and self-sacrificial givers ("Joy," "The Chance of Amarinta," "The Last Gift"); Christmas "impostors" and "thieves" ("Lucy," "The Reign of the Doll," "The Last Gift").[13] For example, "The Givers" (first published in *Harper's Monthly Magazine* in December 1903) is an attack on thoughtless gift-giving—for example, gift-giving that does not consider the needs of the receiver, in this case Flora Bell who, in exchange for beautifully-knit mittens, gets a chess-set though she does not play, a card-set though she does not go calling, and a fire-set although there is no open fireplace in the house. Her aunt Sophia Lane is later set in rage by another bout of useless gift-giving; this time the gifts are wedding presents for Flora brought by the *givers* who are a mother—Sophia's cousin—and her two daughters. Three in number like the biblical magi, they bring ridiculous and absurd finger-bowls for a couple who cannot afford to receive visitors. Sophia recounts how the previous Christmas she had returned similarly inconsiderate gifts and encouraged relatives, friends, and neighbors to provide Flora with useful household items or to invest in her marriage. This longish narrative has the desired effect on the visiting ladies, who ultimately feel ashamed of their presents. "The Givers" is one of Freeman's stories that illuminate "the primacy of building community" through generosity and self-help (Tigchelaar 2014: 249): Sophia Lane succeeds in making the communal gift economy function effectively as her niece, a girl of scarce means, eventually gets what she needs in form of gifts. All the givers described in the story are fundamentally generous and kind but they have become thoughtless due to the habits of fashionable Christmas shopping: they focus on the items they choose rather than on the needs of the receiver and ultimately give to please no one but themselves.

One minor detail in the story casts a slight shadow over Sophia Lane's New English severity, practicality and straightforwardness, and

---

[13] These types appear in other stories by Freeman: for example, the self-sacrifice and self-denial of a Christmas giver is a theme of "A Discovered Pearl" (1887); a Christmas thief features in "A Stolen Christmas" (1887). The motif of self-interested gifts would later recur in "A Friend of My Heart" (1913).

undermines the triumph over self-interested gift-giving that had been brought about by her devotion to her niece: it is the description of what she considers a perfect or a model gift. "'Sit down in that chair and see how easy it is,' said Sophia, imperatively, to Mrs. Cutting, who obeyed meekly, although the crushed plush was so icy cold from its sojourn in the parlor that it seemed to embrace her with deadly arms and made her have visions of pneumonia" (Freeman 1904: 14–15). Accusing the givers of being thoughtless, Sophia is thoughtless herself by inviting a cousin who had suffered with pneumonia the previous winter to sit in an icy cold chair. The "deadly arms" make the chair—a perfect gift that Sophia displays in her poorly heated house—a symbol of the failed empathetic connection that is restored at the end of the story when the givers send new, practical, *and* thoughtful gifts but do so remotely, without exposing themselves to the risks of Miss Lane's hospitality.

In the closing story of *The Givers*, "The Last Gift" (first published in *Harper's Monthly Magazine* in February 1903), we encounter the polar opposite to this type of giver. Robinson Carnes, a poor, pulpit-less clergyman, suffers from excesses of "unselfish love" and "involuntary generosity" that compel him to give away everything he has (Freeman 1904: 268). On Christmas Eve, he comes across a desperate homeless family in the street and commits a crime—appropriating a sum of money he finds in the pocket of a coat he has taken by mistake—to help them out: "He had given the last gift which he had to give—his own honesty" (296). A true Christian and a selfless giver in the supreme sense, Carnes transcends the moral norms of a society that values and respects private property in order to save a poor family marginalized by community. Carnes himself is a marginal and marginalized figure, standing out from the joyful Irvinesque Christmas crowd in the story. Yet his selflessness that is presented almost as a sentimental cliché has a hint of ambiguity about it: it is described as "mania" or a form of neurosis akin to intemperance (268). Paradoxically, the all-giving Carnes is an altruistic counterpart of the compulsive Christmas shopper. The vision of Christmas parcels alone gives him "a feeling of melancholy so intense" that it amounts "to pain" (268). For the same reason, his joy at the end of the story is not only laden with remorse but is also transient: he will never have sufficient means to satisfy his generosity. His pathological generosity is simultaneously a Christian value and a type of dangerous, self-destructive giving.

Carnes is both a selfless giver and a "Christmas thief." In him, two character-types overlap: he steals to give away. In another story in the collection, there is an example of a different type of "Christmas thief," in this case a pair of "thieves" who take possession of a gift that apparently does not belong to them. "The Reign of the Doll" (first published in *Harper's Monthly Magazine* in January 1904) is a sentimental, bittersweet story about two old maids who achieve peace and harmony after they "steal" a present they think belongs to a child. It stands out in the volume, as it centers not so much on the figure of the giver but on the gift that gives more than expected.

"The Reign of the Doll" tells the story of two sisters, old maids Fidelia and Diantha, who live close by one another but who, after a quarrel over their mother's inheritance, are not on speaking terms. On a particularly stormy Christmas Eve, the mail express delivers a mysterious parcel to Fidelia, with a large doll inside; Diantha comes over, curious to know what has happened, and stays overnight at her sister's house engaged in making clothes for the doll. The sisters are confident that the doll was delivered by mistake and that the owner of the gift is a child living next door. Before returning the parcel, as they plan to do, they decide that it would be thoughtful to enhance the present by sewing dresses for the doll. "'It seems,' said Diantha, still in an indignant tone, 'a pity to give away a doll to any child, not dressed'" (170). However, the more the sisters invest their time and energy in the doll, the less they are willing to return it: "I am not stealing her, anyway. My conscience is clear. All I am doing is keeping her a little while, until the little Merrill girl is old enough to play with her and not destroy her" (185). The sisters are described as "children themselves who ... could not spare [the doll] to another child" (188).[14]

When a remorseful Fidelia finally forces herself to return the doll, it turns out that the parcel was in fact intended for her all along: the doll is a "prank present" (Elbert 2002: 196) from one Salome May. While the giver who sent a leftover doll to Fidelia did so simply to amuse herself, the doll unexpectedly brings reconciliation, harmony, and affection to the sisters. Delivered during an "awful," "furious," and "frightful" storm, and accompanied by the "angry" shout of the delivery man (156–164), this mysterious box is an anti-Pandora's box of a kind: anger and fury are outside, inside is a doll with "a smile of everlasting amiability and peace" (174). The sisters must become children again so that they can forget such boring "adult" business as the inheritance that sowed discord between

---

[14] Cf. also: they feel "like greedy and dishonest children stealing another child's doll on Christmas-eve" (185).

them. "The Reign of the Doll" is a Christmas story with a happy ending that follows the popular pattern: Christmas is a magical time at which one eventually achieves harmony with oneself and others.

Nonetheless, there is much ambiguity surrounding this gift. The attachment of two elderly women to the doll is ridiculous; "The Reign of the Doll" is one of Freeman's stories about "a false sense of longing for 'missing' or 'absent' or non-existent children in a sentimental and mawkish description of childhood bric-a-brac and bibelots" (Elbert 2002: 196). The meaning of this attachment, however, is not reduced to a fetishized displacement of the unrealized maternal desire. Now dressed in "the funniest old-fashioned things" (188), the doll is a miniature replica of the young Fidelia and Diantha. In her doll-like stillness and serenity, she seems to immortalize the irrecoverable time that both sisters have long lost. Only when the neighbors with their ironic smiles and comments enter the scene, do we realize how fragile, self-centered, and alien is the world of the two old maids where the doll has begun to reign. "The Reign of the Doll," however, provides a positive example within the conventional framework of a Dickensian magic-Christmas-transformation pattern of dealing with melancholia: the old women who decide not to grow up learn to live at peace with themselves and with their loss(es). The gift appears to be at once timely (it brings harmony to the sisters) and untimely (they are too old to play with dolls) but this latter aspect only adds value to the gift: unlike a child who might destroy the doll, the sisters appreciate her presence in their lives.

"The Reign of the Doll" is also a story about the magical transformation of a Christmas gift. The doll that the sisters discover "in a nest of tissue-paper" (167) is a sophisticated product of the turn-of-the-century toy industry: "Golden ringlets clustered around her pink-and-white countenance, her little kid arms and hands lay supine at her side, her little kid toes stuck up meekly side by side" (168). Wilkins describes the popular "three-dimensional doll— the real, huggable doll-child which in the early nineteenth century became an infant for the first time, teaching the little girls who changed their babies' clothes and took them for walks" (Marling 2000: 300). Although a mass-produced commodity, the doll fascinates and delights the sisters not least because Christmas presents are not within their "present environments" (Freeman 1904: 159). The very fact that the doll was given to Fidelia and not to little Abby Merrill makes the present singular and unique.

We know that the gift of the doll is a direct result of excessive shopping: "Salome May had a doll left over" (188). The girl's mother informs Fidelia that "Salome sent a doll for Abby two days ago" and that "Abby has five dolls this Christmas" (187). A child of the period of Fidelia and Diantha's youth could not have hoped to receive five dolls for Christmas; common presents up until the mid-century were candies and nuts, and presents depended on a child's good behavior.[15] In Howells's fantasy of daily Christmases, the little girl has so many French dolls that she cannot bear to look at them any longer and sits on them instead of playing with them. While a grotesque exaggeration, this hints at the satiety of turn-of-the-century children with Christmas toys and especially with dolls. Toy catalogues in the 1880s and 1890s contain "an astonishing variety of dolls … most of them richly dressed in the hats and coats and muffs and lace dresses worn by the very nicest little girls" (Marling 2000: 300).

The fact that the doll is (to Diantha's indignation) undressed when it is delivered makes it "a "halfway" gift (Restad 1996: 129). By the 1880s, it had become fashionable "to purchase partially assembled goods to which givers applied their personal, finishing touches," for example "handkerchiefs that needed hemming, furniture that needed assembling, and patterns still to be colored with embroidery stitches" (Restad 1996: 129). The handmade clothes that Fidelia and Diantha sew, ostensibly for the sake of the little Merrill girl, convert the doll from a magical commodity to their own personal belonging.[16] Adding a personal touch to the commodified gift was part of the routine of Christmas-related industry. Yet in this particular case, it may be seen as a nostalgic escape to a time of scarce and handmade presents—the time of Fidelia's and Diantha's childhood. Without realizing it, Fidelia and Diantha, first the "thieves" and then the rightful owners of the doll, become melancholic givers who bestow the doll on each other as a token of their newly acquired sisterhood.

The perfect gift that Freeman imagines in this story is, ironically, the very opposite of the concept of the useful and thoughtful present in "The Givers." The doll is a present intended to amuse a child, to teach a girl to be a future mother, to sew, and to develop a taste for fashion. Giving a doll

---

[15] In early nineteenth century, Santa Claus bringing a rod instead of presents to naughty children and the change of custom see, for example, Restad (1996: 55–56).

[16] The clothes that the sisters sew lead them to construct an argument for keeping the doll rather than giving it to the child: "'She would spoil the clothes in no time.' Yes; she would let her wear that pink silk and her best gar every day'" (178).

to old maids who will never become mothers and who are too old to play with toys is as absurd as giving finger-bowls to the newly wed couple whose means are too modest to allow them to receive visitors. In this case, however, the inappropriate, thoughtless present—a gift with a "defect," as it were—becomes the "true" gift indeed. Unlike the Merrill girl, the owner of five dolls, Fidelia and Diantha are in need of affection. While they are capable of giving such affection to each other, they can do so only indirectly, "through the mediation of the universal plaything of childhood, which had come to them out of a mystery" (Freeman 1904: 190).

Christmas giving in Freeman's stories borders on risky or dangerous—the danger is of inconsiderate giving, or of a hazardous practice of giving away more than one can afford, or of giving a potentially inappropriate present. However, redemption from these dangers is easily achieved: thoughtless givers learn their lesson and improve; a Christmas thief finds consolation in saving a family with the money stolen; the gift of a doll inappropriately sent as a prank or joke to the old maids turns out to be a pleasant surprise. Freeman's Christmas stories which pay homage to sentimental tradition and respond to the challenges of the time invite us to see melancholy as a resource rather than as an obstacle. Even the Christmas market, largely responsible for useless gifts, is seen as a resource: do Christmas shopping thoughtfully, use any means to help the poor, or employ a commodity to make peace. The doll who comes out of the Pandora-like Christmas box on a dark stormy night to please and to console is true symbol of such resourceful and redeeming melancholia.

9.4 The Dangers of Perfect Giving in O. Henry

O. Henry's "The Gift of the Magi" (1905), perhaps the most well-known Christmas story after *A Christmas Carol*, not only in the United States but also worldwide, is a secular "rewriting" of the sacred Christmas plot. The gifts given to each other by the modern "magi" of the story, Jim and Della Young, are manifestations of the same spirit of selflessness, devotion, and veneration symbolized by the offerings of the Biblical magi to the newborn Christ. Both Jim and Della sacrifice their most valuable possessions so that each can afford to buy a present for the other: Della sells her beautiful hair to buy Jim a chain for his pocket watch; Jim sells his watch to purchase a set of combs for Della. As with many of O. Henry's short stories, "The Gift of the Magi" (first published in *The New York Sunday World* under the title the "Gifts of the Magi") is a "sentimental story with a surprise ending" (Eckley 1994), with this combination of sentiment and surprise one of the commonest devices in O. Henry's work and the "keynote of his technique" (Current-Garcia 1965: 137). Disregarded by critics (as O. Henry's fiction in general has tended to be), it holds a firm position in the popular imagination, as testified to by numerous adaptations and media publications.

Due to its popularity, "Gift of the Magi" has served as an example of a perfect, pure, and gratuitous gift in several works on gift theory, including in seminal studies by James Carrier (1995) and Russell Belk (1996). Defining the perfect gift as "priceless, unconstraining, and immaterial" (Belk 1996: 59), Belk uses "The Gift of the Magi" as its primary example. In what follows, I will ask whether this threefold definition of the perfect gift—priceless, unconstraining, and immaterial—indeed applies to the story.

No matter how symbolically priceless Jim's and Della's gifts may be, they do have actual price tags. In fact, the story opens with the mention of the exact sum of money that Della has to spend on a present for Jim: "One dollar and eighty-seven cents" (O. Henry 2014: 10). She sells her hair for 20 dollars and buys the gift for 21 dollars, leaving her with the 87 cents. The inclusion of exact figures and calculations in the story is symptomatic: in the early 1900s, when Christmas giving and Christmas shopping had become synonymous, even the priceless gift had a price. Della and Jim, however, believe that a true gift should be expensive. "Something just a little bit near to being worthy of the honor of being owned by Jim," as Della puts it (11).

The gifts Jim and Della exchange are unconstraining in the sense that both givers refuse to accept the fact that their financial means are insufficient and both sacrifice their most precious possessions with the sole intention of pleasing the receiver. At the same time, it is hard to call their gifts unconstraining if this is to be understood in terms of being truly free. Like Belk, James Carrier idealizes the gift exchange in the story and yet he admits, "in the face of the purity of Jim's watch and Della's hair," that even "the perfect present" involves a tension: "how can the giver freely give in a relationship of mutual obligation?" (Carrier 1995: 149). The commercialization of Christmas imposed the obligation of shopping for luxurious and expensive gifts on even poor families. Late nineteenth-century *Harper's Bazar* issues included a number of articles that overtly criticized such hazardous practice. "When it shall be made a general custom to give only inexpensive gifts at Christmas-time, a great and needed reform will have been wrought, and one that will bring more comfort to many people than a wilderness of gifts can ever do" (Anon. "Christmas Giving" 1887: 886). Jim and Della are constrained by a widespread belief that a Christmas gift should not be a gimcrack and that it should not be too practical either—and this is despite the fact that Jim "needed a new overcoat and ... was without gloves" (13). The type of gifts Della and Jim are looking for are so-called consumption items, expensive and having little practical value (Waits 1994: 62)—the perfect Christmas present, as many of their contemporaries believed.

Finally, it is problematic to call Jim's and Della's gifts immaterial. The story emphasizes rather than shuns or suppresses the materiality of the gifts, which were perfect commodities as might be displayed in a shop window. Della "ransack[ed]" the stores for Jim's present, a "platinum fob chain simple and chaste in design, properly proclaiming its value by substance alone and not by meretricious ornamentation—as all good things should do" (11). Pocket watches were common turn-of-the-century gifts and contributed to a man's prestige and appearance (Waits 1994: 89): with a nice watch-chain, Jim would not be ashamed to take his watch out in public. Della first sees the combs that Jim brings her in the shop window. "The Combs—the set of combs, side and back, that Della had worshipped long in a Broadway window. Beautiful combs, pure tortoise shell, with jewelled rims—just the shade to wear in the beautiful vanished hair" (O. Henry 2014: 15). She discovers that her gift from Jim is indeed the much longed-for combs only after tearing through the paper wrapping that was tied with a string. "Although the author doesn't say so, the chances are good that Della's beautiful combs rested in an ornate box with a plush lining made by an underpaid woman who never quite managed to get the glue off her fingers" (Marling 2000: 15). Wrapping presents caused "terrible nervous tension" for working-class women (Marling 2000: 16); we know that Della does not work and that Jim provides for the family. Her subsequent nervous collapse is a result not of weary, repetitive work but of the disappointment of a consumer, as the combs are useless now that her hair has been cut off: "And then an ecstatic scream of joy; and then, alas! a quick feminine change to hysterical tears and wails, necessitating the immediate employment of all the comforting powers of the lord of the flat" (O. Henry 2014: 15). In "The Gift of the Magi," we encounter not only a sexist stereotype of female hysteria but also a "non-productive consumer" type, a term coined by Charlotte Perkins Gilman in her proto-feminist treatise *Women and Economics* (1898) (Gilman 1997: 59).

Nonetheless, to call Della's and Jim's gifts "immaterial," as Belk does, is not wrong or counterintuitive. First, these gifts are more than things; for example, the combs are the object of veneration and pure love. Della's "heart had simply craved and yearned over [the combs] without the least hope of possession" (O. Henry 2014: 15). It is not surprising that "Combs" is written with a capital C, just as the Watch, as the most valuable family possession, is capitalized: the worshipped and unattainable commodities become almost abstract entities, like concepts or ideas. Second, the uselessness or futility of both presents is an important tool in their de-commodification, as both Carrier and Belk discuss. "The very futility ... points out the foolishness of thinking of these presents as commodities or even as material objects to be judged by their utility" (Carrier 1995: 148). "The very uselessness ... ensures and reinforces the emphasis on the symbolic character of the gifts" (Belk 1996: 59). The Christmas presents that Jim and Della bestow on each other become pure symbols the moment they cease to be commodified objects of desire. O. Henry's changing of the title—from "Gifts of the Magi" in *The Sunday World* to "The Gift of the Magi" when included in *The Four Million: The Gift of the Magi and Other Short Stories* (1906)—is telling. The shift from the plural to the singular stresses the idea of love as a divine spiritual gift.

What becomes of an object that is both material and immaterial, present and absent? It becomes a phantom. Although symbols of love, the presents that Jim and Della exchange do not cease to be the symbols of loss: the combs recall the hair that was sold and that represented beauty, the chain—the watch that was sold and that represented social prestige. In this regard, the objects are "phantom" inasmuch as they are "immaterial." They ensure the phantom presence of the lost family treasures—just as an empty sleeve serves as a constant reminder of an amputated limb. The combs for the hair and the chain for the watch are inextricably linked with the missing belongings and carry a ghostly touch of their absence—which is why Jim suggests putting them away.

The story focuses mainly on Della's plotline while the revelation of Jim's unfortunate gift comes as a final twist. Ironically, Della has to sell herself, or at least her best "part," in order to buy a gift. An anonymous writer in *Harper's Bazar* considers woman's asymmetrical position as an "advantage": "she has her *hands*, while men must transact all their present-giving in hard cash" (Anon. 1879: 806). Della does not even consider a handmade gift as an option even though the *Harper's* and *Godey's* of the time continued to publish suggestions for handmade Christmas presents and instructions on how to make ornaments in their fancy-work sections. Using her hair instead of her hands, she transacts her present-giving in hard cash. In the hair shop, a Frenchwoman Madame Sofronie orders Della to take her hat off and lifts the mass of hair "with a practiced hand." The conversation between the two—"'Twenty dollars', said Madame … 'Give it to me quick,' said Della" (12)—emphasizes the soulless business-like character of the deal; selling a woman's "natural" possession suggests prostitution. Della's self-sacrifice is also a distant echo of more violent sacrifices. Madame Sofronie mercilessly weighing and cutting Della's hair is an ironic urban counterpart of a Comanche warrior scalping the enemy in a frontier novel; we should not forget that, brought up in the Southwestern storytelling tradition, O. Henry "never outgrew" frontier humor (Lense 1994: 651).

In the first half of the nineteenth century, a lock of hair was an ideal sentimental gift—a love souvenir, a parting gift, or a memento mori. While such tradition had become an anachronism by the turn of the century, it was still part of the cultural memory. Nobody would think of giving a lock of hair as a Christmas gift, yet an 1879 *Harper's Bazar* article suggests using hair as part of a Christmas present: "in order to give [handkerchiefs] intrinsic value … she can embroider the name or monogram with her own hair. If the hair is dark, it has a very pretty, graceful effect … Such gifts are made precious by love, time, and talent" (Anon. 1879: 806). By making Della *sell* her hair to buy a present for Jim, O. Henry de-sentimentalizes the model sentimental gift and emancipates his female character who now has the right to convert a part of her body into cash. Della's gift is equal to Jim's even if she has to sell her natural beauty to gain this equality.

Selling one's own hair is not prostitution, the cutting of tresses is not scalping but these faint, remote associations are indications of the fragile and endangered position of a female character with limited means in the "stone" jungles or prairies of New York. The beautiful, self-ruinous gesture of the "silly children" (O. Henry 2014: 16) exposes them to the risks of a cruel world where everyone is struggling to survive. Commodities, dazzling and dangerous and tangibly present in the story, continue to haunt the characters who were ready to spend all they had for the sake of love that can only be expressed via costly, luxurious items. As phantom reminders of the watch and the hair, the chain and the comb that Jim and Della no longer possess hint that the couple are standing on the shaky ground, their solid family and romantic values notwithstanding. Behind the story's bittersweet happy ending, which brings harmony and consolation just as a generic and sellable Christmas story should, lurks the melancholic trope of ruin. O. Henry's story is about the dangers of imprudent giving in a capitalist society as much as it is about the perfect gift of love but the latter motif comes to the fore and overshadows the former.

O. Henry's perfect sentimental gift is, paradoxically, not the antipode but the "product" of consumerism; the givers cannot imagine the gift as existing outside of the market, without a market value or a price tag, while the story possibly inspires real-life Jims and Dellas to do luxury Christmas shopping. At the same time, not unlike Caroline Kirkland's keepsake (see Chap. 2), it is a flawed commodity, albeit in this case because of its futility. O. Henry stresses even more markedly than his predecessors that the perfect gift is one that is not to be consumed, at least for the time being. Practical, down-to-earth presents such as those championed by Sophia Lane, presents that suggest a critique of meaningless consumerism, would not touch the heart of the reader in the same way the perfect failure of the gift-giving did in "The Gift of the Magi," gaining lasting popularity for O. Henry's story as a result.

Looking back at the three stories mainly discussed in this chapter—"Christmas Every Day," "The Reign of the Doll," and "The Gift of the Magi"—we can identify both similarities and differences between their respective versions of the Christmas melancholia. In "Christmas Every Day," excessive and compulsory Christmas gifts directly provoke depression while the humor of the storyteller and the genuine interest of the child offer a remedy. In both "The Reign of the Doll" and "The Gift of the Magi," the connection between Christmas consumerism and melancholic sentiment is less direct but is nonetheless important. The mysterious doll that brings about the reconciliation of the sisters is a leftover, a surplus present; pure gifts of love are exchanged between Jim and Della because society compels them to shop and to spend at Christmas time for the sake of love. The perfect gift is part of the Christmas-related commodity culture, yet the condition of its perfection is a de-commodification that occurs as the result of a flawed or failed exchange. The "wrong" receivers of the doll become her rightful owners in the supreme, symbolic sense. The combs and the watch are "symbolically useful" (Belk, 1996: 59) only after they lose their practical functionality.

In these three stories, melancholia has a different temporality associated with the time of the gift, as it were. In "Christmas Every Day," the everlasting present tense—the depressive sameness of "hollowdays"—is particularly haunting. "The Reign of the Doll" dwells on a nostalgic past;

after all, the sisters' present, "a universal plaything" is itself lost in time. Della and Jim put the gifts of the combs and the chain aside in the hope of using them in the future. While Della's hair will certainly grow out, it is less likely that Jim will be able to restore the family's financial situation, especially considering the couple's thoughtlessness, fascination with commodities, and sacrificial love for each other. The present, in both its meanings, contains a spectral shadow of a fragile, financially insecure future, destabilizing the perfect symmetry of the gift exchange.

The time that gets out of control, moves backward, or is fraught with instability is counterpoised to the so-called timeless, universal values such as fatherly, sisterly, and marital affection, which makes the stories sellable Christmas products. All three stories exploit the sentimental trope of childhood associated with Christmas. The active presence of the child in Howells's story justifies the burdensome business of Christmas for the loving papa. Fidelia and Diantha are big children just as Jim and Della are "silly children." Childhood allows us to enjoy the illusion that there is an easy and natural way of redeeming or at least mitigating the melancholic sentiment that comes, as "strings attached," with the modern Christmas. Ultimately, we are invited to enjoy the singularity of the present moment—the moment of storytelling, playing, or romance—and to forget about the dangers that even the perfect and well-intended gift box may contain.

WORKS CITED

Anon. 1879. Christmas Presents. *Harper's Bazar* XII (51): 806–807.

———. 1881a. Christmas—Past and Present. *Harper's Bazar* XIV (53): 834.

———. 1881b. Taking Christmas by the Forelock. *Harper's Bazar* XIV (52): 818–819.

———. 1881c. The Art of Christmas Shopping. *Harper's Bazar* XIV (51): 802-803.

———. 1887. Christmas Giving. *Harper's Bazar* XX (52): 886.

———. 1891. The Gift of Christmas. *Harper's Bazar* XXV (52): 1026.

Barnett, James H. 1954. *The American Christmas*. New York: The Macmillan Company.

Bataille, Georges. 1988. *The Accursed Share: Essays on General Economy*. Trans. Robert Hurley. New York: Zone Books.

Belk, Russell. 1996. Perfect Gift. In *Gift Giving: A Research Anthology*, ed. Cele Otnes and Richard Betramini, 59–84. Bowling Green: Bowling Green State University Popular Press.

Carrier, James G. 1995. *Gifts and Commodities: Exchange and Western Capitalism Since 1700*. London: Routledge.

Carrington, George, Jr. 1977. Howells' Christmas Sketches: The Uses of Allegory. *American Literary Realism, 1870–1910* 10 (3): 242–253.
Colver, Frederick L. 1904. Everyday Is Christmas. *Lesley's Monthly Magazine* 59: 238.
Eckley, Wilton. 1994. The Gift of the Magi: Overview. In *Reference Guide to Short Fiction*, ed. Noelle Watson. St. James Press. Gale Literature Resource Center. Accessed 19 Feb. 2021. link.gale.com/apps/doc/H1420006523/LitRC?u=uppsala&sid=LitRC&xid=b7c97d19.
Elbert, Monica. 1993. Mary Wilkins Freeman's Devious Women, 'Harper's Bazar,' and the Rhetoric of Advertising. *Essays in Literature* 20 (2): 251–272.
———. 2002. The Displacement of Desire: Consumerism and Fetishism in Mary Wilkins Freeman's Fiction. *Legacy: A Journal of American Women Writers* 19 (2): 192–215.
Fennell, Lee Anne. 2002. Unpacking the Gift: Illiquid Goods and Emphatic Dialogue. In *The Question of the Gift: Essays across Disciplines*, ed. Mark Osteen, 85–102. London: Routledge.
Fetterley, Judith. 1994. 'Not in the Least American': Nineteenth-Century Literary Regionalism. *College English* 56.8: 877–9.
Flatley, Jonathan. 2008. *Affective Mapping: Melancholia and the Politics of Modernism*. Cambridge, MA: Harvard University Press.
Freeman, Mary E. Wilkins. 1904. *The Givers. Short Stories*. New York: Harper & Brothers.
Gilman, Charlotte Perkins. 1997. *Women and Economics*. New York: Dover Publications.
Goodman, Susan, and Carl Dawson. 2005. *William Dean Howells: A Writer's Life*. Berkley: University of California Press.
Howells, William Dean. 1893. *Christmas Every Day and Other Stories Told for Children*. New York: Harper and Brothers.
———. 1916. *The Night Before Christmas*. https://americanliterature.com/author/william-dean-howells/short-story/the-night-before-christmas-a-morality.
———. 1979. *Selected Letters*, Vol. 1: 1852–1872. Boston: Twayne Publishers.
Jackson, Stanley W. 1986. *Melancholia and Depression: From Hippocratic Times to Modern Times*. New Haven: Yale University Press.
Lee, Rosalie. 1881. Bachelor Rogers' Christmas Party. *Godey's Lady's Book* (103): 525–531.
Lense, Edward. 1994. O. Henry and His Fiction (*O. Henry: A Biography of William Sydney Porter*, by David Stuart; *O. Henry: A Study of the Short Fiction*, by Eugene Current-Garcia). *Mississippi Quarterly* 47(4): 651–660.
Lévi-Strauss, Claude. 1969. *The Elementary Structures of Kinship*. Trans. John Richard von Sturmer, James Harle Bell, and Rodney Needham. Boston: Beacon Press.

Litwicki, Ellen M. 2020. Gifts and Charity. In *The Oxford Handbook of Christmas*, ed. Timothy Larsen. Oxford: Oxford University Press.

———. 2022 (forthcoming). Taking Aim at 'Exchange Gifts' and the 'Christmas Tax': Dangerous Gifts in the Progressive Era and the Society for the Prevention of Useless Giving. In *The Dangers of Gifts from Antiquity to the Digital Age*, ed. Alexandra Urakova, Tracey Sowerby, and Tudor Sala. New York and London: Routledge.

Marling, Karal Ann. 2000. *Merry Christmas! Celebrating America's Greatest Holiday*. Cambridge, MA: Harvard University Press.

Nissenbaum, Stephen. 1996. *The Battle for Christmas: A Cultural History of America's Most Cherished Holiday*. New York: Alfred A. Knopf.

O. Henry. 2014. *Short Stories*. New York: Maple Press.

Restad, Penne L. 1996. *Christmas in America: A History*. Oxford: Oxford University Press.

Sangster, Margaret E. 1891. Christmas Presents. *Harper's Bazar* 24 (51): 996.

Tigchelaar, Jana. 2014. The Neighborly Christmas: Gifts, Community, and Regionalism in the Christmas Stories of Sarah Orne Jewett and Mary Wilkins Freeman. *Legacy: A Journal of American Women Writers* 31 (2): 236–257.

Waits, William B. 1994. *The Modern Christmas in America: A Cultural History of Gift Giving*. New York: NIY Press.

CHAPTER 10

Conclusion

This study has highlighted the importance of gift-giving and the prominent role of dangerous giving in nineteenth-century American culture. It has been argued that to view nineteenth-century discourse of the gift exclusively in terms of the conventionally understood ideology of disinterested giving is to miss the point and oversimplify its complex and controversial legacy. Nonetheless, this discourse provided an important standpoint for the consideration of dangerous giving, whether in the corpus of texts traditionally attributed to sentimental tradition or in the other texts that, in seeking to transform, deny, or mock it, relate to this tradition. Summing up the findings of my research, I would like to highlight several patterns of dangerous giving that recur in the texts I have examined. These patterns fall into the two broad categories of (1) dangers associated with the structure and nature of gift exchange and (2) those associated with the gift as an object.

Both symmetrical (bilateral) or asymmetrical (unilateral) structures of gift exchange are dangerous in their own way. Symmetrical exchange usually involves danger when there is an element of competition and rivalry involved; exaggerated competition may lead to excessive giving, material destruction of riches, and self-destruction. Asymmetrical exchange, by contrast, threatens to place the recipient in a position of unrepayable debt. This book has discussed both cases.

An example of excessive and unbalanced gift exchange is that of sentimental potlatch in Child's *Hobomok*. Sentimental potlatch, a term introduced in this study, is different from unilateral self-sacrifice—a conventional motivation attributed to the so-called noble or "selfless" "savage" character in frontier fiction—due to its bilateral structure that engages both parties and imposes a counter-action on the rival. Using this model, Child chooses an alternative, non-conventional way of capturing the dynamics of early colonial history and allegorizing the origins of American nation. If potlatch is a continuation of warfare through gift-giving, blood feud resembles gift exchange in form. The replacement of the generic gift book formula—a heteronormative exchange of tokens—with a symmetrical exchange of "evil turns" in Poe's "The Purloined Letter" resonates with *Hobomok* where homosocial competition in generosity and selflessness seeks to replace violence and bloodshed. Excessive reciprocal exchange may be ruinous or self-ruinous even in the absence of antagonism or competition. An example of the former is found in O. Henry's "The Gift of the Magi," a story where the true gifts of love are simultaneously outlets of consumerist culture that exhaust the financial resources of the family. An example of the latter is Howells's "Christmas Every Day," which demonstrates through irony how a modern consumerist "potlatch" may deplete the resources of the entire nation.

Asymmetrical or unilateral exchange as explored here functions primarily as a form of power relations. The racial aspect of asymmetrical giving is especially telling as it imperils the receiver by initiating a symbolic bondage to the donor. The analysis of the abolitionist discourse of *The Liberty Bell* revealed the controversial rhetoric and narrative of the gift in the context of emancipation; giving a gift of freedom is not quite the same as restoring a right to freedom as the racial hierarchy is already inscribed in this structure of unilateral giving. Paradoxically, the inverted model—a Black person becomes a donor to a white person—risks disempowering rather than empowering the donor due to the shifting boundary between giving and servitude and between voluntary help and gratuitous slave labor in the cultural memory of the nation. While Emerson warns us that asymmetrical giving is dangerous for both parties—one loses autonomy while the other may face not only rejection but also violence and aggression from the former—Frederick Douglass radicalizes the form in applying it to the condition of slavery. If a gift other than liberty is given to a slave, the gift annuls itself. Asymmetrical giving may endanger women who, especially within the codes of Victorian culture, often figure as passive receivers unable to reciprocate. In O. Henry's story, written in the early 1900s, Della in buying an equal gift for her husband with her own money is an emancipatory figure of the new era. At the same time, unilateral and unreciprocated giving renders a woman particularly vulnerable—as with

Beatrice Rappaccini, Elsie Venner, or, perhaps less obviously, Milly Theale whose role of an unreciprocated giver is both an inevitability and an ethical choice.

Symmetrical and asymmetrical exchanges can challenge one another. An obligation of reciprocal exchange—a gift as a "munus" as opposed to the unilateral "donum"—is redeeming for the contributors to Cassey's album as they search for their communal identity. Unilateral giving, in its turn, becomes one of the means to escape the *do ut des* principle inherent in a bilateral structure. Both Twain in *The Chronicle of Young Satan* and James in *The Wings of the Dove* emphasize the asymmetry of giving as a way of purifying the gift from the taint of the bargain.

Regardless of its structure, gift-giving can be compulsive and coercive. By the end of the nineteenth century, when the tradition of Christmas celebration had expanded and its commercialization reached new levels and scale, reciprocal Christmas giving had become associated with obligatory seasonal shopping. We encounter coercive giving in, for example, *Hobomok* and in *Elsie Venner*: Brown regards Hobomok's generous offering as burdensome; Elsie imposes her gifts on characters who detest, fear, reject, and even destroy them. In the Introduction I mentioned that since a gift must be free by default (as we have also learned, from Emerson and Kirkland, among others), a constrained gift ceases to be a gift in the eyes of its nineteenth-century ideologists. However, in the examples listed above, including that of Jim and Della's Christmas exchange, the true, pure gift and the obligation to give are not necessarily mutually exclusive.

The gift as a dangerous object figures in a number of texts examined in this book, in several cases as a seemingly innocent object that eventually causes harm and damage. The Bible becomes a mockery of a gift when given to a slave; the "boons" of life including love and wealth turn out to be deceptive and mean in Twain's parable; the gift of Christmas every day sows discord and destruction, and so on. A famous mythological example of a deceptive gift is Pandora's box, which is applied ironically to gift books in Sedgwick's "Cacoethes Scribendi." Whereas in Sedgwick's story the trope of Pandora's box engages with a humorous narrative about the transgression of gender boundaries and irrational fears of eternal spinsterhood, in "The Reign of the Doll," the story about two old maids by Wilkins Freeman, we encounter a playful archetypal pattern of the *anti-Pandora's box*. What first appears to be a dangerous surprise turns out to be a pleasant gift that brings peace to the feuding sisters.

Another recurring pattern—the poisonous gift—also has Ancient Greek roots; a legend about a poisonous maiden sent as a present to Alexander the Great is recalled in both "Rappaccini's Daughter" and *Elsie Venner*. In their fascination with the "poisonous" female body and its emanations, both texts interpret poison rather broadly: gifts might seem poisonous but be harmless or redeeming while gifts that are intended to heal or please ultimately poison and kill. Ironically, in both texts we are dealing with the inversion of the original myth: female "poisoners" become victims, unintentionally poisoned by male characters. The significance of female poison in the stories is not least in the otherness that it marks out in the female character and that presents a serious challenge to the male recipient of her gift/s. Similarly, the metaphor of the repellent gift of a spider in *Uncle Tom's Cabin* has much to do with the racial otherness that the novel seeks to tame and repress but also, as my analysis has shown, has a subversive effect by undermining the structure of "sentimental ownership." In contrast to the narratives where the "vice" is associated with a female character, "Brother Dunstan and the Crabs" by turn-of-the-century author Caroline Wilder Paradise teases out a connection between gifts "poisoned" with sins and male sexuality.

Related to this is the pattern that can be seen across texts of evoking the gift-pharmakon in its narrow sense (the antidote that turns out to be deadly poison in "Rappaccini's Daughter") and understood broadly—for example, a gift that may heal or kill, save or harm. An example of the latter is the veil that Parson Hooper wears in Hawthorne's "The Minister's Black Veil." Not a gift in the strict sense, the veil is, however, a blessing for sinners. The veil isolates and unites, frightens and consoles, disturbs and delights.

The last pattern that I would like to highlight is the anti-gift, as it were—that is, the gift that subverts or overturns the wholesome and benign gift. One example is the purloined letter in Poe's story that functions, in the contextual framework of where it was published, as a gift book inverted. Another is Topsy as a "topsy-turvy" gift, her surplus energy and vitality turning the conventional goodness advertised in the novel upside down.

The patterns listed above demonstrate a degree of consistency; they reappear in various combinations and across texts from different genres and trends. One might argue that it is possible to detect these same patterns in other literatures and cultures, yet the configuration, meaning, and significance would be different in each of these cases.

The patterns I outlined capture the convolutions of the thinking about, and through, gifts representative of modernity. For example, in the context of the dominant ideology of disinterested and free giving, it should not surprise us that compulsion or repression tops the list of actual or imaginary dangers. At the same time, the ambivalence of giving, present in several of the patterns highlighted, is itself partially responsible for the poetization of the dark and dangerous side of the gift. That such giving could be rebellious and redeeming while challenging either the pragmatics of commercial exchange or the conventional formulas and normative schemes associated with moralist attitudes to the gift had a deep connection with, as well as a lasting effect on, modern sensibility. Valentin Groebner writes about the utopianism of twentieth-century gift theory, which expresses itself in the "yearning for salvation from the contemporary profit economy by means of the archaic, voluntary gift" (Groebner 2002: 8). A fascination with the dangers and risks of gift-giving is an intrinsic part of this "utopianism," with a belief in salvation as represented by the superiority of the "archaic" gift economy over capitalist relations dating back to the nineteenth century.

Finally, the patterns described in this study have a distinctly American accent and contributed to the building of an American national identity throughout the nineteenth century—a fluid and dynamic rather than fixed identity that developed under an overseas influence as well as under the influence of drastic challenges and changes at home. Without being overly deterministic, it is possible to suggest that both a resistance to any form of coercion, either within the asymmetrical or symmetrical exchange of gifts, and a pathological fear of being indebted are especially relevant in the context of the renowned cult of American self-reliance and enterprise that is rooted in the Puritan past. The same spirit of self-reliance may partially explain the recurrence of competitive, potlatch-type of exchanges in nineteenth-century fiction while the ambivalence attributed to gifts may be seen as a means of sabotaging the efforts of Europe-imported sentimentalism to mitigate and smooth over nation-specific controversies related to gift exchange. Finally, as has been shown throughout this book, social, economic, and political phenomena including slavery and racism, the forcible removal of Native American population, and the rapid expansion of industry and market relations had a lasting impact on the way Americans thought about gifts and giving.

I wish to conclude this study with the discussion of a text that while partially stemming from the Anglo-American tradition I have been describing differs from others in its attitude to giving. "The Coffee-Making" (1900) by Sioux Dakota writer and activist Zitkála-Ša (Gertrude Simmons Bonnin) is the work of a mixed-race Native American author, a marginalized voice in the nineteenth-century literary canon. Zitkála-Ša's canonization in the early twentieth century "ironically began with the popular fascination with the 'exotic Indian'" (Okker 1994: 89)—a fascination that also fostered the development of gift theory within classical anthropology. "The Coffee-Making" forms part of the autobiographical collection "Impressions of an Indian Childhood," originally published in *Atlantic Monthly* in 1900[1] and usually discussed in the context of sentimental tradition (e.g., Bernardin 1997; Kelsey 2008; Zink 2018, etc.).[2] "Deploy[ing] the twinned rhetoric of sentimentality and domesticity" (Zink 2018: 247), Zitkála-Ša demonstrates an awareness of the literary and cultural conventions familiar to the readers of *Atlantic Monthly* as "she struggled to present an alternative reality within the constraints imposed by the mainstream press" (Chiarello 2005: 10).

"The Coffee-Making" is a short essay about hospitality—a subject that I have not specifically addressed in the book but that has a direct relationship to giving and gifts. The essay falls into two parts. A little girl, who is both narrator and an autobiographical version of the author, is in a wigwam alone. She is afraid of "a tall, broad-shouldered crazy man, some forty years old, who walked loose among the hills" (Zitkála-Ša 2012: 9) who, she thinks, might come to their tepee in her mother's absence. The narrator adds that this man, Wiyaka-Napbina, "was harmless, and whenever he came into a wigwam he was driven there by extreme hunger" (9). The girl's mother teaches the daughter to pity the man who once was a good warrior but she prefers to pity him "at distance" (10). In a turning point in the narrative, a hand lifts "the canvas covering of the entrance; the shadow of a man fell within the wigwam, and a large roughly moccasined foot was planted inside" (10). The girl "did not dare to breathe or stir," thinking that the visitor was Wiyaka-Napbina. "The next instant I sighed aloud in relief. It was an old grandfather who had often told me Iktomi legends" (10).

---

[1] Together with "Impressions of an Indian Childhood," "School Days of an Indian Girl," and "An Indian Teacher among Indians."
[2] Another familiar framework of reading Zitkála-Ša is regionalist literature, as represented in this book by Mary Wilkins Freeman's Christmas stories; on the complex and uneasy relation of Zitkála-Ša's work to American regionalism, see, for example, Totten (2005).

10 CONCLUSION

The fragment cited is toward the end of the narrative section that is about a potentially dangerous and unwelcome guest—a story that never develops—and signals the beginning of the second section describing the grandfather's visit and the girl's attempt to "play the part of a generous hostess" (10). The second section which confounds the reader's expectations, relates to the first, albeit loosely, through the figure of the visitor. The shadow of the man crossing the threshold belongs to another former warrior: a loving grandfather rather than a crazy man—Wiyaka-Napbina's good and safe counterpart, at least in the child's imagination. It is therefore no surprise that Wiyaka-Napbina leaves the narrative as the grandfather enters the wigwam.

The threshold is a liminal space where familiar codes are suspended. While in many cultures the threshold plays an important ceremonial and symbolic function, it is also a place of the unknown: you do not always know who will enter, friend or foe, kin or stranger.[3] Crossing the threshold might be equally hazardous for the guest unsure of how she or he will be received or what will be offered.

As soon as the grandfather seats himself upon the mat to wait for his daughter, the girl follows custom by starting to make coffee for her guest, in an imitation of her mother. She "boils" the empty coffeepot on the dead fire, pours out "a cup of worse than muddy warm water," and offers it to "the old warrior" "with the air of bestowing generous hospitality" (10). Having been watched during the performance of coffee-making, she now watches her grandfather nibble at the bread and sip from the cup, feeling "proud to have succeeded so well in serving refreshments to a guest" all by herself (10–11). The cup of muddy water bestowed by the girl on her grandfather instead of coffee is not fit for drinking but it would not be accurate to call it a poisonous drink: it causes no harm and the girl offers it with good intentions, observing the rules of hospitality as best as she can.

The episode recalls the make-believe game that children often play when they offer adults pretend food and drink and the adults in turn pretend to enjoy the treat. In another essay in the collection, the narrator describes how she and other little girls "used to exchange [their] necklaces, beaded belts, and sometimes even [their] moccasins." "We pretended to offer them as gifts to one another. We delighted in impersonating our own mothers." Imitation and impersonation are part of the learning

---

[3] Derrida's (2000) famous notion of hospitality revolves around this idea.

process and this is one of the reasons why the adults, grandfather and mother, say nothing about the coffee. They treat the child "with [the] utmost respect" (11) that is part of an indigenous upbringing, as opposed to the oppressive Indian boarding school system that Zitkála-Ša resisted (Enoch 2002; Kelsey 2008: 72–73); "even though she is young and has much to learn, Zitkála-Ša is respected for her contribution to the kinship network" (Suhr-Sytsma 2014: 150). At the same time, the narrator remarks that it was "the law of our custom" that had "compelled" the grandfather, the old warrior, "to partake of [her] insipid hospitality" (11). The law of custom compels the visitor to accept whatever is offered, just as it compels the host to greet whoever enters the wigwam, whether Wiyaka-Napbina or grandfather.[4]

On the one hand, we encounter a familiar sentimental theme. As in "The Gift of the Magi," in Zitkála-Ša's story, it is the thought that counts: whether the gift is a useless luxury item or a cup of mud, it is valuable and "pure" as a token of affection bought or prepared with love. On the other hand, there is a difference in attitude, reinforced by the structure of the story. The little girl was expected to perform the role of a host in the event of any guest visiting the wigwam; the grandfather is described as the double of an unwelcome guest, Wiyaka-Napbina. We do not know whether the girl would have served coffee to Wiyaka-Napbina but the motif of doubling and replacement in the story implies she might have or, at least, and following the basic rules of hospitality, should have. In contrast to most of the gifts discussed in this study, the offering of coffee is, to use Marcel Hénaff's term, *a ceremonial gift* (Hénaff 2010).[5]

The ceremony serves to mitigate the dangers that a visit may incur. Coffee-making as a form of initiation rite helps the girl overcome her fear of the uncanny, the foreign, and the strange that manifest at the border or at the threshold. At the same time, the ritual does not exclude or deny the possibility of danger or ambivalence, albeit here neutralized by the narrator's humor and irony as well as by the motif of childhood and play. The child is too small to tell the good treat from the bad, coffee from mud; it is only much later that she realizes that her hospitality was "ridiculous." Ultimately, however, even such a worthless object as a cup of muddy water has its place in the ceremony of exchange sanctified by custom: "Answering

---

[4] There is also an important gender aspect to this ritual, as highlighted by Kelsey (2008: 72).

[5] I discussed ceremonial gifts in *Hobomok*; however, there is a huge difference between Child's ethnographic description and Zitkála-Ša "insider" perspective.

the question in my mother's eyes, the warrior remarked, 'My granddaughter made me coffee on a heap of dead ashes, and served me the moment I came'" (11). At the end, it is not so much the thought or the feeling as the respect for custom by both parties that matters.

While conforming to the conventions of the literary culture she seeks to enter as an author, Zitkála-Ša speaks on behalf of a tradition that has its own and very different culture of hospitality, gifts, and giving—as well as of education and narrative—and that resists the otherwise inevitable Westernization of indigenous tribes described throughout the same collection. The vestige of this tradition remains in the text and "The Coffee-Making," an essay on the margins of the nineteenth-century literary canon, offers a glimpse of an alternative, non-Euro-American vision and attitude.

The history of dangerous giving in American literature does not end in the 1900s, where this study concludes. My goal was to cover, however partially, one lengthy and important period that I believe was, due to its transitory character, which bridged pre-modern and modern mentalities and sensibilities, formative for the literary and intellectual tradition that was to follow. As I hope to have shown, for nineteenth-century American authors, whatever their gender, cultural and ethnic background, giving—and dangerous giving in particular—was one of the prisms through which they could reflect upon this transition.

Works Cited

Bernardin, Susan. 1997. The Lessons of a Sentimental Education: Zitkála-Ša's Autobiographical Narratives. *Western American Literature* 32 (3): 212–238.

Chiarello, Barbara. 2005. Deflected Missives: Zitkála-Ša's Resistance and Its (Un)Containment. *Studies in American Indian Literatures* 17 (3): 1–26.

Derrida, Jacques. 2000. *Of Hospitality (Cultural Memory in the Present): Anne Dofourmantelle Invites Jacques Derrida to Respond*. Trans. Rachel Bowlby. Stanford: Stanford University Press.

Enoch, Jessica. 2002. Resisting the Script of Indian Education: Zitkála-Ša and the Carlisle Indian School. *College English* 11 (2): 117–141.

Groebner, Valentin. 2002. *Liquid Assets, Dangerous Gifts: Presents and Politics at the End of the Middle Ages*. Trans. Pamela E. Selwyn. Philadelphia: University of Pennsylvania Press.

Hénaff, Marcel. 2010. *The Price of Truth: Gift, Money and Philosophy*. Trans. Jean-Louis Morhange with the collaboration of Anne-Marie Feenberg-Dibon. Stanford: Stanford University Press.

Kelsey, Penelope Myrtle. 2008. *Tribal Theory in Native American Literature: Dakota and Haudenosaunee Writing and Indigenous Worldview*. Wisconsin: University of Nebraska Press.

Okker, Patricia. 1994. Native American Literatures and the Canon: The Case of Zitkála-Ša. In *Realism and the Canon*, ed. Tom Quirk and Gary Scharnhorst, 87–101. Newark: University Press of Delaware.

Suhr-Sytsma, Mandy. 2014. Spirits from Another Realm, Activists in Their Own Right: The Figure of the Yankton/Romantic Child in Zitkála-Ša's Work. *Children's Literature* 42: 136–168.

Totten, Gary. 2005. Zitkála-Ša and the Problem of Regionalism: Nations, Narratives, and Critical Tradition. *The American Indian Quarterly* 29: 1–2 (Electronic Resource).

Zink, Amanda J. 2018. *Fictions of Western American Domesticity: Indian, Mexican, and Anglo Women in Print Culture, 1850–1950*. Albuquerque: University of New Mexico Press.

Zitkála-Ša. 2012. *American Indian Stories*. New York: Dover Publishers.

Index[1]

A

Abolitionism, 12, 14, 99–115, 101n5, 119, 120, 124–125, 128, 132, 140, 218
Africa, 29n7, 54, 138
African American
  abolitionists, 103, 108–110, 114–115
  authors, 103, 108, 109, 116–120
Album, 90–92, 102, 114–120
  culture, 102, 116
  flower, 26, 90–92
  friendship, 14, 17, 114, 115, 120, 219
  as a gift, 90
  and a gift book, 91, 92, 114–115, 116n22, 119, 120
  See also Florilegium
Alexander the Great, 63, 64, 145, 146, 148, 153, 220
  See also Poisonous maiden
Allegory, 17, 50, 149n7, 150n11, 151, 152, 165, 187, 199, 199n11, 218
Alms, 4, 35, 106, 106n13, 108, 110, 112
  See also Benevolence; Pauperism; Philanthropy
Altruism, 9, 12, 34, 38, 42, 48, 59, 61, 112, 203
American Anti-Slavery Society, 103
American Bible Society, 108
American South, 109, 109n15, 113, 117, 125, 125n3, 128, 131, 131n8, 134, 139
Ancient Greece, 12, 127, 145, 146, 220
Androgyny, 81, 82, 93, 147
Antagonism, 29, 47–49, 51, 57, 218
  interracial, 48, 49, 57, 58, 66

---

[1] Note: Page numbers followed by 'n' refer to notes.

Anthology, 25, 72, 115, 119
Anthropology, 11, 51, 52, 61, 62, 137, 137n11, 139, 145, 161, 163
  classical, 2, 10, 48, 49, 222
Antidote, 128, 132–140, 144, 146–148, 150, 153, 154, 159, 220
  See also Gift, poisonous; Poison
Antiquity, 169
  See also Ancient Greece
Appadurai, Arjun, 3
Armstrong, Erica R., 115
Artese, Brian, 181
Asclepius, 159
Ashtor, Glia, 87
The Atlantic Monthly, 153, 222
The Atlantic Souvenir, 71, 72, 76
  See also Gift book; Sedgwick, Catharine Maria
Atreus and Thyestes, 93
Autographs for Freedom, 102, 103n9
  See also Gift book, anti-slavery; Griffith, Julia

B
Baldwin, James, 132
  Everybody's Protest Novel, 132
Balzac, Honoré de, 182
Bargain, 15, 16, 28n5, 33, 62, 95, 104, 129, 148n6, 162, 169, 177, 179, 180, 180n13, 183, 187, 198, 219
  vs. gift-giving, 43, 148n6, 187
Bataille, George, 10, 11, 13, 127, 134, 182, 197
  The Accursed Share, 182
  See also Economy, general; Economy, restricted
Baym, Nina, 47n3, 50, 55, 150n10
Belk, Russell D., 11, 208, 210, 212

Benevolence, 3, 4, 29n7, 35, 42, 111, 120, 129, 133, 184
  white, 15, 62, 103, 105–115, 129, 130, 132–135, 139
  See also Alms; Giving, charitable; Philanthropist; Philanthropy
Benevolence literature, 110
  See also Bergman, Jill; Bernardi, Debra
Benjamin, Park, 81
Bensick, Carol Marie, 146, 154
Benveniste, Emile, 25
Bequest, 5, 16, 179, 180, 184–186, 191
  as a gift, 5, 16, 179, 180, 184, 186, 191
  See also Marion, Jean-Luc
Bergland, Renée L., 50, 63
Bergman, Jill, 5, 110
  See also Bernardi, Debra
Berkhofer, Robert Jr., 47n2
Berkovitch, Sacvan, 51n7
  See also Ritual of consensus
Bernardi, Debra, 5, 110
  See also Bergman, Jill
Bernardin, Susan, 222
Best, Stephen M., 124, 133
Bible, 16, 108–110, 120, 129, 130, 130n7, 134, 170, 219
  as a gift, 16, 108, 109, 120, 129, 134
Bluestocking, 79, 80
Body
  polluted, 14, 143, 144, 162
  venomous, 143–160
Bonnin, Gertrude Simmons, 222
  See also Zitkála-Ša
Boone, N.S., 83
Boston, 65, 76, 103
Bourdieu, Pierre, 10, 25
Brahmin, 154, 158, 159
  See also Holmes, Oliver Wendell

Brenzo, Richard, 145n3, 146, 148, 150n11
Bribe, 33, 37, 125
Brickhouse, Amy, 150n11, 153n14, 154
Brodwin, Stanley, 173n7, 174, 174n9
Bronzino, Agnolo di Cosimo, 183
 Lucrezia Panciatichi, 183
Brooks, Peter, 171n6
Brooks, Van Wyck, 173
Brown, Gillian, 123, 124
Brown, Harry, 48
Brown, William Hill, 29n6
 The Power of Sympathy, 29n6
Bunyan, John, 172
 The Pilgrim's Process, 172

C

Caillé, Allen, 14
Calvinism, 3, 50, 85, 136, 158, 171–174
 anti-, 172, 174
 and gift-giving, 2, 172
 sentimental, 172
Camfield, Gregg, 171, 174
Capitalism, 8n3, 125, 125n3, 133, 180, 182, 196, 201n12
 anti-, 9
 critique of, 9, 38, 201n12
 and gift-giving, 2, 9
Carrier, James G., 2, 8, 49n6, 126, 137n12, 208, 210
Cassey, Amy Matilda, 14, 114–117
 Cassey's album, 12, 14, 114–120, 114n19, 219
Cassey, Joseph, 115
 See also Cassey, Amy Matilda
Catholicism, 160
 and anti-catholicism, 160
Cellini, Benvenuto, 146
Cenci, Beatrice, 150n9

Chambers-Shiller, Lee, 101, 103
Channing, William N., 99
Chapman, Maria Weston, 100, 102–104, 102n8, 108
 See also Gift book, anti-slavery; *The Liberty Bell*
Charles III, King of England, 53
Cheal, David, 10, 14
Chiarello, Barbara, 222
Child, Lydia Maria, 6, 12, 14, 16, 48–67, 72, 100, 100n2, 105, 105n12, 106, 106n13, 217, 218, 224n5
 Hobomok: A Tale of Early Times, 12, 14, 48–62, 64–66, 217, 224n5
 "Jan and Zaida," 105
Childhood, 146, 205–207, 213, 224
 gift-giving and, 66, 67, 169, 192
Christmas, 77n10
 American, 192, 192n2, 196
 consumption, 27, 172, 191, 193, 196–203, 206, 209, 212
 of Dickens, 192, 192n1
 fatigue, 14, 178, 191, 198, 201
 festivities, 172, 194, 197, 200
 gift wrapping, 192, 193
 of Irving, 192, 192n1
 malady, 15, 194
 and melancholia, 15, 191–213
 and potlatch, 196, 197, 218
 season, 3, 71, 184, 191–213
 shopping, 14, 15, 191, 193, 193n3, 194, 196, 197, 200, 202, 206–209, 211, 212, 219
 spirit, 191, 192n2, 193, 199, 200, 207
 story, 13, 15, 27, 191, 192, 192n2, 194, 195, 197, 199, 201, 205, 207, 212, 222n2
 See also Gift, Christmas; New Year
"A Christmas Hymn," 109
Civil War, 71n2, 115, 124, 140, 159

Clark, William, 48n5
  See also Meriwether, Lewis
Clemens, Jean, 14, 178
  See also Clemens, Samuel; Twain, Mark
Clemens, Samuel, 175n11, 178
  See also Twain, Mark
Coale, Samuel, 82
Cobb, Jasmine Nichole, 115, 116, 116n22
Colesworthy, Rebecca, 6
Colonial history, 2, 12, 47, 218
Colver, Frederick L., 195
  "Every Day is Christmas," 195
  See also Howells, William Dean
Commodification, 9, 15, 34, 38, 76, 89, 177, 196n10, 202, 210
  de-commodification, 34, 73, 129, 130, 210, 212
Commodity
  and anti-commodity, 37
  culture, 23, 212
  as a gift, 5, 8–10, 15, 23, 33, 34, 125, 132, 135, 137, 137n11, 137n12, 139, 172, 180, 205–207, 209, 210, 212
  as object of desire, 149, 211, 213
  vs. the gift, 5, 9, 10, 15, 37, 131, 134, 135, 137n11, 164
Communitas, 12, 117, 118
  See also Community; Esposito, Roberto; Munus
Community
  and death, 177, 178
  of the free Black people in Philadelphia, 15, 114–120
  and gift exchange, 114–120, 162, 177–178
  inoperative, 177
  of monks, 160, 163, 164
  See also Communitas

Competition, 12, 16, 48, 49, 54, 59–62, 64, 66, 125, 197, 217, 218, 221
  See also Potlatch
Conduct literature, 23, 24, 27, 28, 32, 34, 41
Conformism, 66, 75n7, 138, 139, 225
Conspiracy, 179
Consumerism
  critique of, 27, 28, 152, 193n3, 196–200, 209, 212
  spiritual, 130, 173
  See also Sentimentalism and sentimentality, and consumerism
Consumption (disease), 179
Contagion, 8, 14, 29n7, 77, 79
  "generous contagion," 124, 135
Contract
  and gift exchange, 51, 60–62, 104, 162, 179, 180
Convention
  gift book, 14, 75, 86, 93–95, 115
  heteronormative, 13, 14, 28, 75, 77, 78, 81, 93–95, 150n11, 164
  sentimental, 27, 110, 115, 116, 119, 120, 152, 181, 187, 217, 221, 222
Cooper, James Fenimore, 16, 48n4, 52, 62–67
  The Deeslayer, 52
  The Pioneers, 63
  The Spy, 64
  The Wept of Wish-ton-Wish, 66
Courtship, 11, 40, 51, 72–75, 88, 90, 103, 146
Cromphout, Gustaaf von, 26
Crosby, Sarah L., 145, 146, 150n10, 154
Current-Garcia, Eugene, 208
Cutting, Andrew, 179

D

Daineka, Frederick A., 178
  See also Payne, Albert Bigelow; Twain, Mark
Davis, Clark, 86
Davis, Cynthia L., 154
Davis, Natalie Zemon, 4
Dawson, Carl, 197
  See also Goodman, Susan
Death, 4, 5, 10, 11, 13–16, 42, 64, 66, 82, 85, 111, 123, 126, 127n5, 137, 151, 153, 154, 157, 158, 161, 162, 169–188, 173n8, 175n11, 177n12, 191
  See also Donner la mort; Gift, of death
Debt, 6, 29, 31, 41, 61, 63, 65, 67, 99, 105, 105n12, 120, 126–128, 153, 175, 186, 187, 217
Deming, Richard, 26
Democratic Review, 144
Depression, 39, 194, 195, 198, 212
Derrida, Jacques, 9–11, 13, 25, 31, 43, 127, 128, 135, 170, 170n2, 177n12, 181, 223n3
Diadem, 1
  See also Emerson, Ralph Waldo; Furness, William Henry
Dickens, Charles, 192, 192n1, 192n2, 205
  A Christmas Carol, 192n1, 192n2, 195n9, 207
Dickinson, Cindy, 28, 71n1, 72, 73
Didacticism, 12, 25, 32, 39, 43, 75, 88, 90, 91, 109, 144, 151, 154, 160, 162, 163, 176, 178, 187
Diller, Christopher, 126, 136
Disinterested giving/gift, ideology of, 4, 7–9, 12, 13, 23–43, 129, 132, 139, 165, 187, 217, 221

Doll
  as a gift, 198–200, 204–207, 206n16, 212
Domesticity, 80, 172, 222
Donner la mort
  See also Gift, of death
Donum, 12, 117, 118, 120, 219
  See also Esposito, Roberto; Munus
Douglas, Ann, 75n7
Douglass, Frederick, 6, 14, 16, 103n9, 108, 109, 109n16, 113, 116, 119, 218
  "Bibles for the Slaves," 108, 109, 113
Douglass, Sarah Mapps, 116
  See also Cassey, Amy Matilda
Do ut des, 176, 219
Dystopia, 195–201

E

Eastburn, James Wallis, 63, 64
  Yamoyden, A Tale of the Wars of King Philip, in Six Cantos, 63
  See also Sands, Robert
Easton, Alison, 145n2, 146, 150n10
Eckley, Wilton, 208
Economy
  of expenditure, 197
  general, 134, 181, 182
  gift, 2, 10, 51, 100, 103, 124, 196, 202, 221
  libidinal, 76, 103
  moral, 128
  political, 5, 107
  restricted, 181, 182
  speculation, 125, 125n2
  sublime, 182
Edel, Leon, 171n4, 186, 187
Elbert, Monica, 150n10, 201n12, 204, 205

Elmer, Jonathan, 29, 29n6
Emerson, Ralph Waldo, 1, 5, 6,
    12, 17, 17n5, 23–35, 24n1,
    25n2, 26n4, 29n7, 32n8, 37,
    39, 41, 43, 102, 113, 146,
    218, 219
  "Gifts," 1, 12, 23, 24n1, 25–31, 33
  "Love," 30
  "Nature," 25n2, 31
  "Self-Reliance," 25, 25n2, 29
Endorsement, 39, 42
England, 3, 50, 52, 53, 55, 57, 58,
    60, 62, 100, 101n5, 105,
    179, 183
Enoch, Jessica, 224
Esposito, Roberto, 12, 117, 118
  See also Communitas;
    Donum; Munus
Estlin, Mary A., 103
Ethics
  asymmetrical, 39, 187
  sentimental, 28
Eucharist, 16, 127, 127n5
Eve, 135, 140, 158
Exchange
  asymmetrical, 172, 174, 184, 187,
    217–219, 221
  calculated, 7, 8, 40, 41
  equivalent, 33, 40, 48, 59, 170n2
  excessive, 30, 195–197, 218
  market, 3, 125, 196
  object of, 8, 15, 34, 36, 59,
    128, 132
  reciprocal, 2, 4, 6, 29, 41, 43, 48,
    51, 52, 114, 117, 137n11,
    139, 207, 208, 218, 219
  self-destructive, 2, 49,
    58–60, 62, 217
  sentimental, 128–132, 139, 173
  symbolic, 127
  symmetrical, 217–219, 221
  violent, 29, 47, 48, 58
Exchange value, 60

F
Fee, Frank E., 102–104
  See also Fritz, Meaghan M.
Feldman, Paula D., 73
Felski, Rita, 73n6
Female Anti-Slavery Society, 107
Femininity
  as a danger, 81, 81n15, 82, 128,
    130, 164, 166
  endangered, 75, 80
Femme fatale, 153
Fennell, Lee Ann, 5, 116n21, 193
Fetishism, 123, 186, 205
Fetterley, Judith, 76, 77, 201
Fichtelberg, Joseph, 3
Fiedler, Leslie, 47n2
Flatley, Jonathan, 171n6, 194
Flaubert, Gustave, 182
Florence, 27, 148n6
Florilegium, 26
Flower
  as a gift, 17, 25, 27, 30, 31, 37, 43,
    73, 83, 90, 91, 116, 117,
    143–148, 150
Floyd, Janet, 32
Follen, Eliza Lee, 110, 111n17, 112,
    114, 120
  "A Morning Walk," 110, 112, 114
  See also The Liberty Bell
Forten, Margaretta, 117, 118
  "The Forget Me Not," 117
  See also Cassey, Amy Matilda;
    Forten, Mary
Forten, Mary, 117n24, 118
  See also Forten, Margaretta
Forten, Sarah Louisa, 119
Foster, Hannah, 7
France, 36, 53, 104, 108n14, 144,
    160, 177, 198, 206
Freedom, 4, 7, 38, 42, 64, 99, 100,
    104–109, 112, 120, 124–127,
    182, 218
  See also Gift, of freedom

Freedom's Gift, 100n4, 102
  See also Gift book, anti-slavery
Freeman, Mary Eleanor Wilkins, 6, 13, 15, 17, 185, 186, 191, 194, 201–207, 222n2
  "The Chance of Amarintha," 202
  "A Discovered Pearl," 185, 202n13
  "The Givers," 202, 206
  The Givers and Other Stories, 201, 202
  "The Last Gift," 15, 202, 203
  "Lucy," 202
  A New England Nun and Other Stories, 201
  "The Reign of the Doll," 15, 201, 202, 204–207, 212, 219
Freud, Sigmund, 86, 147
Friedman, Jonathan, 180, 183
Fritz, Meaghan M., 102–104
  See also Fee, Frank E.
Frontier fiction, 47n3, 48, 50, 57, 62, 64, 218
  domestic frontier romance, 50
  frontier novel, 12, 16, 47, 66, 211
Fuller, Margaret, 81, 158n16
Furness, William Henry, 1
  See also Diadem; Emerson, Ralph Waldo

G

Gallagher, Kathleen, 152, 153
Garrison, William Lloyd, 103, 104, 114, 115
  "The Abolition Cause," 114
Garrisonians, 100n3, 103n9, 104, 104n11
Gender
  fluidity of, 94
  in gift theory, 150n10
  roles, inversion or transgression of, 75, 80, 82, 85, 86, 92–94

  See also Convention, heterosexual; Homosexual panic; Homosocial rivalry; Sentimentalism and sentimentality, gender normativity in
Generosity, 47, 106, 125, 126, 130, 131, 137, 175, 180, 181, 187, 192n2, 202, 219, 223, 6, 14, 17, 48, 49, 59, 59, 62, 62, 79, 99, 111, 124, 125, 125, 127, 128, 129, 129, 162, 162, 163, 163, 175, 179, 180, 180, 182, 187, 187, 191, 202, 203, 203, 218
Gentility, 14, 28, 49, 115, 119
Gérando, Joseph-Marie de, 108, 108n14
Gibson, William, 175n11
The Gift, A Christmas and New Year's Present, 5, 72, 87–95, 103
"The Gift" (a poem), 83
Gift
  anonymous, 41, 43, 184
  anti-gift, 128, 135, 220
  birthday, 33, 92
  as a bribe, 33, 125
  bridal, 33, 202
  as a burden, 14, 55–62, 118, 162, 180, 193, 194, 194n6
  ceremonial, 51, 53, 54, 224, 224n5
  chains of, 66, 119, 187
  Christmas, 1, 2, 16, 23, 34, 71, 71n2, 77n10, 100, 102, 102n8, 109, 111, 130n7, 172, 178, 179, 184, 185, 191–213
  of a compliment, 39, 42
  deadly, 127, 147, 148, 156–158
  of death, 4, 10, 11, 15, 16, 42, 169–188
  with a defect, 207, 212, 223–225
  diplomatic, 52, 149
  of freedom, 4, 7, 12, 100, 109, 112, 125, 218

Gift (*cont.*)
  gratuitous, 27, 87, 100, 125, 128, 137, 208
  handmade, 15, 27, 28, 28n5, 43, 210
  impossible, 7, 14, 43, 127, 135, 170n2
  insulting, 30–32, 34, 35, 120
  of love, 4, 15, 146, 150, 152, 212
  as manipulation, 146, 180, 183, 187
  modern, 10, 11, 72, 137n12
  of money, 4, 102n8, 105, 113, 125, 126, 179–181, 185, 186
  parting, 125, 126, 158, 159, 170, 211
  perfect, 9, 13, 15, 16, 23, 36, 37, 43, 137n12, 159, 170–178, 184, 188, 194, 203, 206–213
  of the poem, 29
  poisonous, 13, 123–140, 143–145, 148, 151, 153, 164, 165, 220
  pure, 5, 9, 11, 23, 26, 27, 30, 35, 37, 38, 41, 43, 95, 127, 128, 134, 137n12, 143–145, 148, 151, 157, 159, 164, 170, 178, 179, 184, 187, 208, 209, 212, 219, 224
  of shit, 127
  spiritual, 4, 35, 36, 135, 210
  of time, 175, 176
  topsy-turvy, 135, 220
  transient, 26, 30, 37
  useful, 35, 194, 206
  useless, 27, 107, 108, 194, 196, 197, 202, 207, 209, 210, 224
  of words, 4, 8, 10, 136, 136n10, 139, 143
  See also Gift book; Giving; Present; Token; Keepsake
Gift book
  about, 71–76
  and anti-gift book, 102, 111
  anti-slavery, 14, 72n3, 99–114, 100n4, 102n8, 114n19
  See also Courtship; Print culture; Token
Giftness, 34
Gift theory, 2, 5–7, 10–12, 24, 25, 48, 49, 116, 170, 208, 221, 222
  in utero, 23–43
Gilded Age, 9, 38, 38n14
Gilman, Charlotte Perkins, 209
  Women and Economics, 209
Gilmore, Michael T., 151, 152
Ginzberg, Lori D., 5
Givenness, 5, 12, 184, 187
  See also Marion, Jean-Luc
Giving
  altruistic, 9, 10, 12, 30, 48, 49, 59–61, 105, 110–112, 176, 177, 203
  American attitude to, 3, 4, 221
  ambivalence/ambiguity of, 2, 3, 10, 12, 24n1, 38, 43, 48, 53, 62, 80, 82, 113, 123, 126, 129, 144, 149, 151, 175, 187, 188, 191, 221
  and modern history of, 8, 10
  as bordering on the enslavement, 99, 100, 105, 106, 218
  as impossible under slavery, 108, 109
  as putting someone in debt, 29, 40–42, 99, 105, 120, 127, 128, 136–138, 186, 187, 217, 221
  as suppressed warfare, 49, 62, 66, 218
  charitable, 4, 5, 17n9, 29, 36, 36n10, 105–114, 123, 192, 192n1
  coercive, 39, 62, 108, 109, 175, 180, 194, 196–199, 208, 219
  dangers of, 1, 4, 13, 15, 29, 33, 54, 63, 77, 144, 148, 151, 195, 199, 212, 217, 218, 221

enslaved persons as gifts, 4,
    128–139, 149
excessive, 15, 30, 39, 49, 193n5,
    194–196, 212, 217, 218
gender stereotypes of, 13, 14, 28,
    72–81, 83, 94, 145, 150,
    164, 210–212
indigenous rituals of, 11, 50, 51,
    51n6, 53, 54, 56,
    197, 222–225
in nineteenth-century intellectual
    thought, 5–7
luxury of, 110, 112
meaning and significance for
    nineteenth-century American
    literature, 4
pathological, 203
philosophy of, 24, 32, 34
as putting someone in debt, 29,
    40–42, 99, 105, 120, 127, 128,
    136–138, 186, 187, 217, 221
racialist stereotypes of, 49, 50,
    101–107, 112
redeeming, 4, 10, 14, 180,
    219, 221
romantic, motif of, 89, 91–93, 148,
    157, 209–214
self-interested, 33, 39–41, 111, 127,
    151, 152, 163, 164, 182, 203,
    204, 204n13
as suppressed warfare, 49,
    62, 66, 218
thoughtless, 202
unilateral, 41, 42, 48, 101, 170,
    172, 184, 187, 217–219 (see
    also Exchange, asymmetrical)
See also Gift; Disinterested giving/
    gift, ideology of
God, 2, 4, 7, 16, 30, 35, 84, 105,
    112, 129, 133, 137, 138,
    170, 172–174
Calvinist, 173, 174
and the gift of death, 170, 172, 173
as a sentimental giver, 172, 173
Godbout, Jacques, 14
See also Caillé, Allen
Goddu, Teresa A., 100
Godey's Lady's Book, 4, 31, 160,
    192, 210
Goodman, Susan, 197
See also Dawson, Carl
Gothic tradition, 79, 86, 95, 125
Grace, 172
See also Calvinism
Gratitude
the dark side of, 63
as a debt, 14, 63, 101, 107, 115
as a duty, 174
expectation of, 35
as reward, 115, 117
as symbolic weapon, 68
token of, 164, 165
Greenberg, Kenneth S., 12, 99,
    100, 109
Gregory, Chris, 137n11
Greven, David, 147, 150n10
Griffith, Julia, 102
Griffith, Maria, 89–91, 89n23
    "The Old Valentine," 89–91
Griswold, Samuel Goodrich, 71, 81
See also Gift book; *The Token*, or
    Atlantic Souvenir
Groebner, Valentin D., 11, 221
Gruzin, Richard A., 25

H
Habbeger, Alfred, 179
Hale, Sarah Josepha, 24n1, 34
Hallissy, Margaret, 146, 150n11,
    153, 158
Halpern, Faye, 126n4
Harper's Bazar, 192, 192n1, 194n6,
    201n12, 208, 210, 211

Harper's Monthly Magazine, 202–204
Harris, Katherine D., 73
Haskell, Thomas L., 8n3
Hau, 36, 36n11
  See also Mauss, Marcel
Hawthorne, Nathaniel, 12–14, 16, 17, 17n5, 72, 81–86, 81n15, 94, 95, 144–154, 148n6, 149n8, 150n9, 150n10, 151n12, 153n14, 159, 163, 164, 220
  American Notebooks, 86, 148n6
  "The Gentle Boy," 81
  "The Minister's Black Veil," 14, 72, 81–86, 94, 151n12, 220
  The Mosses of the Old Manse, 144
  "Rappaccini's Daughter," 14, 15, 17, 144–153, 151n12, 153n14, 220
  "Sights from the Steeple," 85
Hayes, Kevin J., 91
Hénaff, Marcel, 2, 51, 172, 224
Hobbes, Thomas, 39
Hoeller, Hildegard, 2n2, 7, 9, 51, 52, 56, 62, 172
Holden's Dollar Magazine, 93n24
Holland, Nancy J., 128
Holmes, George Frederick, 139, 140
Holmes, Oliver Wendell, 13, 14, 17n5, 145, 152–159, 163, 164
  Elsie Venner, 14, 145, 152–159, 219, 220
  See also Brahmin; Medicated novel
Homo economicus, 127
Homosexual panic, 57, 94
Homosocial rivalry, 60, 75, 92–94, 218
Hopper, Isaak T., 104
  See also Abolitionism; *The Liberty Bell*
Hospitality, 32, 203, 221n3
  as act of disinterestedness, 112, 125
  failed, 205
  and indigenous rituals and traditions, 52, 222–225
Howells, William Dean, 13, 17, 191, 194–197, 199–201, 199n11, 201n12, 206, 213, 218
  "Christmas Every Day," 15, 194–200, 199n11, 212, 218
  Christmas Every Day and Other Stories Told for Children, 195
  The Night before Christmas, 200
Hutchinson, Thomas, 48n5
Hyde, Lewis, 8, 9, 11, 163

I
Identity
  communal, 219
  national, 221
  racial, 61, 99–120, 138
Inalienable property, 30, 61, 82, 104, 106, 124n1, 125, 131, 133, 137
  See also Weiner, Annette
India, 10, 146, 148, 149, 162
Indian giver, 48, 48n5
  See also Racism
Indigenous ritual, 11, 49n6, 223–224
  See also Hospitality; Potlatch
Intellectual history, 2, 5, 6, 180
Intemperance, 79, 203
Irving, Washington, 192, 192n1, 203
Italy, 117, 146, 147, 154

J
Jackson, Leon, 7–9, 11, 16, 72, 93n24, 114, 120n27
Jacobs, Harriet, 100
  Incidents in the Life of a Slave Girl, 100
James, Henry, 13, 16, 17, 170, 171, 171n4, 179–187, 219
  "Emile Zola," 182

The Golden Bowl, 183
The Portrait of a Lady, 183
The Spoils of Poynton, 183
The Wings of the Dove, 5, 16, 170, 179–187, 191, 219
James, William, 182
Jewelry, 27, 73, 87, 93, 149, 183
   as a gift, 27, 87, 88, 158, 159
   as a metaphor, 27, 73, 79, 185
Jewett, Sarah Orne, 201, 201n12
Jim Crow, 132
Johnson, Samuel, 108
Jordan, Cynthia, 93n25, 94
Joy, Morny, 11, 150n10

K

Kant, Immanuel, 25, 26, 26n4
   The Critique of Judgment, 26n4
Karcher, Carolyn L., 56, 57, 64, 65
Keats, John, 153
   Lamia, 153
Keeping-while-giving, 61
   See also Weiner, Annette
Keepsake, 3, 15, 36, 37, 43, 53, 123, 135, 159, 172, 173, 186, 212
   See also Gift; Gift book; Token
Kelley, Mary, 116
Kelsey, Penelope Myrtle, 222, 224, 224n4
Kete, Mary Louise, 6, 7, 25n2, 28, 114, 123, 171
Kim, Sharon, 172
Kirkland, Caroline, 6, 12, 15, 17, 24, 24n1, 25, 31–39, 36n12, 41, 43, 87n21, 109n16, 212, 219
   "About Presents," 24, 24n1, 25, 31–38
   A Book for Home Circle, 32
   "Hints for an Essay on Presents," 25, 31
   A New Home: Who'll Follow?, 32

Kiskis, Michael J., 170n3, 171
Kloeckner, Alfred J., 146
Kopytoff, Igor, 34, 129, 137

L

La belle dame sans merci, 180
Lacan, Jacques, 92, 94, 127
Lamia, 152
Laocoon, 156, 156n15
Lawson, Andrew, 38
Leavis, F.R., 181
   The Great Tradition, 181
LeCarner, Thomas, 25, 30, 31
Ledbetter, Kathryn, 79
Lee, Rosalie, 192
Lehuu, Isabelle, 72, 78n11, 79n13, 129
Leslie, Charles R., 87
   "The Toilette," 87
Leslie, Eliza [Miss Leslie], 17, 27, 28, 28n5, 33, 34, 75, 85
   Behaviour Book, 28, 33
   "Constance Allerton, or The Mourning Suits," 85
Letter
   as a gift, 39, 41, 43, 89, 92, 95, 159, 172, 184, 186–188
   love, 88, 89
Leverenz, David, 32
Levinas, Emanuel, 31
Liberal theology, 173, 174
Liberia, 138
Liebersohn, Harry, 5, 6, 47n1
The Liberty Bell, 12, 14, 99–112, 100n3, 103n9, 111n18, 114, 114n19, 115, 218
   See also Abolitionism; Chapman, Maria Weston; Gift book, anti-slavery
Lincoln, Abraham, 140
Literary market, 41, 64, 71, 124

Litwicki, Ellen, 2, 25n2, 32, 193n5
Louisiana, 131
Lunt, Joanna Skelton Fosdick, 143, 144, 152
Forget-me-Not, or the Philipena, 143
Luxury
and waste, 181
flower as, 27, 37
of giving, 110, 112
as a product of slavery, 115
gift, 73, 87, 130, 208, 211, 212, 220
Lynch, Anne C., 87, 89
"The Necklace," 87
See also Leslie, Charles R.; Plate article/poem
Lyons, Deborah, 11, 12, 145n1
Lyotard, Jean-François, 49n6

M

Marion, Jean-Luc, 5, 12, 184
Marling, Karal Ann, 193, 193n3, 205, 206, 209
Martin, Judith, 25n3
See also Miss Manners
Martin, Michael R., 186, 187
Martineau, Harriet, 103
Maruo-Schröder, Nicole, 32
Masturbation, 164
and anti-masturbation policies, 164
Materiality
and the afterlife, 173
of the gift, 4, 30, 37, 173, 201, 209
of the gift book, 72, 73, 76, 82, 86–88, 93, 94, 100
and immateriality, 4, 144, 145, 149, 173, 185, 208–210
Mauss, Marcel, 5, 7, 10, 11, 13, 25, 29, 31, 36, 36n12, 49, 49n6, 127
The Gift, 5, 127

May, Samuel, 104
See also The Liberty Bell
Maynard, Jessica, 182
McGill, Meredith, 72, 73, 81, 81n15, 86
Medicated novel, 153, 159
See also Holmes, Oliver Werner
Melancholia, 15, 178, 188, 191–213
and Christmas gifts, 191–213
associated with mourning and death, 180, 187, 188, 190
as a resource, 209
See also Depression; Nostalgia
Memento mori, 211
Meriam, Eliza F., 100
Meriwether, Lewis, 48n5
See also Clark, William
Metafiction, 16, 199
and self-referential devices in gift books, 74, 78, 89, 91–93, 97, 113
Metanarrative, 9, 101, 110, 111, 114
Michelson, Bruce, 174
Miller, J. Hillis, 82, 83
Miscegenation, 50
Mise en abyme, 76, 89, 91, 95, 148
Misogynous, 130, 149
Misreading, 95, 151, 156
Miss Manners, 25, 25n3
See also Martin, Judith
Mizruchi, Susan L., 186
Modernism, 6
Modernity
and dangerous giving, 16, 221
and the emergence of sentimentalism, 8
See also Gift, modern
Mohawk, 93
"literary Mohawk," 93
See also Poe, Edgar Allan
Moore, Gerald, 127, 128
Morgan, Jo-Ann, 130n7
Mott, Frank Luther, 77n10

Mott, Lucretia, 107, 108
  "What is Anti-Slavery Work?," 107, 108
Munus, 12, 117, 118, 219
  See also Donum; Esposito, Roberto

N

Nancy, Jean-Luc, 11, 177, 177n12, 178
Neoliberalism, 8
New Criticism, 145
New England, 50, 63, 154, 201, 202
New Orleans, 131
New Year, 1, 25, 26, 29, 33, 71n2, 77n10, 102, 102n8, 111, 195
  See also Christmas
New York, 65, 79, 182, 211
The New York Sunday World, 207
Nissenbaum, Stephen, 71, 109, 192n1
Noble, Marianne, 172
Noble savage, 47, 48n5, 55, 58, 60, 61, 66
  See also Selfless savage
Norris, Frank, 7, 9
  McTeague, 9
North American Review, 63, 65
Nostalgia, 15, 38, 191, 192, 194, 194n8, 200, 206, 213
  See also Melancholia
Nyong'o, Tavia, 134

O

The Oasis, 102
  See also Gift book
Object of desire, 5, 60, 92
Obligation
  related to gift-giving, 6–8, 23, 32n8, 38, 41, 42, 49, 52, 56, 99, 112, 137, 194, 196n6, 208, 219

Offer, Avner, 94, 99n1
O. Henry, 9, 12–15, 17, 191, 194, 207–213, 218
  The Four Million: The Gift of the Magi and Other Short Stories, 210
  "The Gift of the Magi," 9, 12, 14, 15, 207–210, 212, 218
  See also Porter, William Sydney
Okker, Patricia, 222
The Opal, a Pure Gift for the Holy Day, 130n7
  See also Gift book
Opfermann, Susanne, 51n7, 65
Osteen, Mark, 2n2, 9, 11, 25, 29, 31, 180

P

Palfrey, John Gorham, 63, 64
Pandora, box, 16, 75, 77, 80, 94, 140, 207, 219
  and anti-Pandora, box, 204, 219
Paradise, Caroline Wilder Fellowes, 13, 14, 145, 160–164, 220
  "Brother Dunstan and the Crabs," 145, 160–164, 220
  See also Godey's Lady's Book
Parker, Gail T., 154
Parker, Theodore, 109
Parody, 17, 75, 77, 171
Patronage, 24, 29, 42
Patterns
  of dangerous giving, 13, 144, 217–221
  of gift-giving, 77, 94, 109
Paul, the Apostle, 172
Pauperism, 108
  See also Alms
Payne, Albert Bigelow, 178
  See also Daineka, Frederick A.; Twain, Mark

Person, Leland S., 94n26
Pharmakon, 127, 127n5, 140, 144, 151n12, 220
Phelps, Elizabeth Stuart, 16, 172, 173, 178
The Gates Ajar, 16, 172
Phenomenology, 128, 184
Philadelphia, 15, 76, 107, 114, 114n19, 115, 117n24
Philanthropist
 Black, 110–114, 120
 pseudo-, 35, 108, 109
Philanthropy, 5, 23, 42, 108, 111
 See also Alms; Benevolence; Giving, charitable
Picanniny, 136
Plate article/poem, 8, 76, 77, 77n9
 See also Gift book
Poe, Edgar Allan, 12, 14, 17, 17n5, 72, 87–95, 87n20, 93n23, 94n26, 218, 220
 "The Murders of the Rue Morgue," 93, 93n24
 "The Purloined Letter," 14, 72, 82, 87–95, 218
Poirier, Richard, 26
Poison
 as a metaphor, 13–17, 24n1, 135, 138–140, 143–146, 145n1, 150–165
 See also Antidote; Gift, poisonous
Poisonous maiden, 145, 146, 220
Porter, William Sydney, 191
 See also O.Henry
Postcolonial criticism, 49n6
Potlatch, 10–12, 16, 47–67, 197, 217, 218, 221
 sentimental, 47–67, 217
 See also Mauss, Marcel
Present, 31, 32, 37, 213
 See also Gift
Print culture, 3, 71, 115

Prostitution, 211
Protestantism
 Episcopal church, 50
 Evangelicalism, 136, 138
 Unitarianism, 99
 See also Calvinism; Puritanism
Puritanism, 3, 50, 53, 54, 57, 221
Pyyhtinen, Olli, 34, 36

Q
Quincy, Edmund, 14, 111, 111n17, 111n18, 113, 114, 120, 128, 129
 "Dinah Rollins," 14, 111, 128
 See also Abolitionism; *The Liberty Bell*

R
Race, 2, 12–14, 38, 48, 50, 54, 61, 99, 110, 116, 123–140
Racism, 49n6, 115, 120, 124, 133, 134, 221
Rappoport, Jill, 2n2, 73–75
Reciprocity
 negative, 10, 48
Reinhard, Kenneth, 180–182, 186
Restad, Penne L., 4, 192, 193, 197, 206, 206n15
Reynolds, David S., 125n3
Richards, Eliza, 80
Richardson, Robert D., 25
Richardson, Samuel
 Clarissa: Or the History of a Young Lady, 29n6
 Pamela, or, Virtue Rewarded, 29n6
Riss, Arthur, 125n3
Ritual of consensus, 52
 See also Berkovitch, Sacvan
Rivkin, Julie, 181, 182
Roger, Patricia M., 57, 146, 147
Romanticism, 24n1, 57, 119, 151

Rorty, Richard, 26, 33
Rousseau, Jean-Jacques, 47
Russian Formalists, 86
Ryan, Susan M., 5, 17n4, 29, 100, 100n2, 138

S

Sacrifice, 35, 47, 51, 52, 54–56, 58–60, 62, 66, 82, 84, 86, 95, 123, 145, 170, 182, 184, 185, 194, 207, 208, 211
  See also Self-sacrifice
Sahlins, Marshall, 10, 49
Saint Valentine Day
  Valentine card, 23, 89–91
  Valentine story, 89–91
Sala, Tudor, 11, 127n5
Samuels, Shirley, 54, 75n7
Sanchez-Eppler, Karen, 107
Sands, Robert, 63, 64
  Yamoyden, A Tale of the Wars of King Philip, in Six Cantos, 64
  See also Eastburn, James Wallis
Sangster, Margaret E., 193
Satan, 174–177, 174n9, 187
  See also Twain, Mark
Sawaya, Francesca, 5–7, 42
Schaffer, Talia, 181
Schiller, Emily, 180
Schmidt, Leigh Eric, 1n1, 24–25n1, 32, 34, 36n12
Schrift, Alan, 25
Schwartz, Barry, 10, 11
Scott, Walter, 63
Second Great Awakening, 171
Secularization, 13, 192, 194, 207
Sedgwick, Catharine Maria, 6, 12, 14, 16, 17, 66, 72, 76–81, 81n14, 89–92, 94, 219
  "Cacoethes Scribendi," 14, 16, 72, 76–82, 90, 94, 95, 219

Hope Leslie, 66
  "A Sketch of a Blue Stocking," 79
  "The Unpresuming Mr. Hudson," 90, 92
Sedgwick Kosofsky, Eve, 83n18
Selfless savage, 12
  See also Noble savage
Self-reliance, 2, 25, 29, 221
Self-sacrifice, 9, 12, 17, 29, 48, 49, 59, 62, 150, 158, 170, 179, 180, 186, 202, 202n13, 211, 217
Sentimental
  and anti-sentimental, 29, 198, 200
  discourse, 8, 17, 29, 48, 59
  education, 58, 116, 133, 136, 159
  gift, 12, 27–30, 36, 38, 51, 52, 72, 116, 136, 211
  identity, 61, 156
  ideology, 3, 13, 124, 135, 138, 165
  language, 17, 25–31, 58, 66, 102, 116, 120, 155, 173, 177, 178, 187
  language of the gift, 9–10, 25–31, 66, 102, 177, 178, 187
  property, 124, 124n1, 131
  subject, 58, 59, 105
  and unsentimental, 3, 39, 109, 120, 124, 174
  value, 37, 43, 53, 130, 134
  See also Sentimentalism and sentimentality
Sentimentalism and sentimentality
  in American literary and cultural history, 3, 17, 17n5, 75n7
  and anti-slavery discourse, 99–114, 123–140
  in Black friendship album, uses of, 114–120
  and Calvinism, 3, 136, 171–173
  and commercial culture, resistance to, 27, 33, 37, 38, 41, 102, 103, 111, 179, 180, 212

Sentimentalism and
  sentimentality (*cont.*)
  commercial of, 11, 23, 72, 87, 89,
    95, 114, 124, 146, 192, 193,
    208, 212
  conformism of, 75n7, 136–139, 225
  and consumerism, 100, 212
  gender normativity in, 12, 28, 34,
    71–76, 79, 80, 83, 85–89, 93,
    101, 150, 155, 158, 159, 164,
    165, 211
  gift-giving idealized in, 3, 23, 27–29,
    31, 35–38, 40, 41, 48, 56, 71,
    83, 87, 91, 99, 105, 106,
    110–112, 123, 124, 136, 137,
    143, 158, 159, 172, 173, 176,
    177, 179, 180, 208, 211, 224
  in gift theory, 8, 9
  indigenous people idealized in,
    47–48, 55, 62
  and masculinity, 50, 81, 154
  masochism in, 62, 158, 186
  mid-nineteenth century
    crisis of, 159
  parody of, 17, 171, 217
  religion and religiosity idealized in,
    4, 35, 54, 55, 109, 110, 112,
    123, 130, 131, 136–138,
    171–173, 178
  repressive mechanisms of, 138, 158,
    159, 172, 220
  in the work by male American
    authors, 17, 17n5, 26, 27, 82,
    152, 164, 171, 181, 201,
    207, 208
  See also Sentimental
Sexuality
  female, 147, 150n11, 163, 164
  male, 145, 164, 165, 220
  repressed, 149
Shakespeare, William
  Macbeth, 155–156
Shapiro, Gary, 25, 26n4, 31

Showalter, Elaine, 75n7
Sigourney, Lydia, 80, 85, 171
  "The Bride," 85
Simmel, Georg, 5
Simms, William Gilmore, 117
Simulacrum, 133
Sin, 10, 14, 84, 159–164, 220
  original sin, 154
Sioux Dakota, 222
Siren, 140
Slavery, 2, 12, 14, 15, 99, 100, 104,
    105, 107–109, 113, 115,
    116n23, 117, 119, 120, 124,
    128–132, 149, 149n8, 150,
    218, 221
  See also Abolitionism; Racism
Slotkin, Richard, 47n2
Smith-Gordon, George, 171
Sollors, Werner, 100
The Southern Literary Messenger, 140
Souvestre, Emile M., 104
  See also Abolitionism; *The
    Liberty Bell*
Sowerby, Tracey, 3, 10, 11, 13,
    33n9, 93
Spinner, Cheryl, 158
Spiritism, 54
The Star of Emancipation, 102
  See also Gift book, anti-slavery
Stewart, Susan, 3
Stowe, Harriet Beecher, 6, 13, 15, 16,
    27, 54, 123–140, 124n1, 125n2,
    125n3, 170, 220
  "Christmas Story or, The Good
    Fairy," 27
  *Dred: A Tale of the Great Dismal
    Swamp*, 126
  A Key to Uncle Tom's Cabin, 124,
    128, 133, 135
  "The Tea Rose," 27
  Uncle Tom's Cabin, 13, 15, 16, 54,
    123–140, 124n1, 126n4,
    130n7, 170, 220

Strathern, Marilyn, 123
Subversion, 64, 75n7, 135, 149, 201n12, 220
Suhr-Sytsma, Mandy, 224
The Sunday World, 210
Sweet, Nancy, 55
Sympathy, 3, 29, 53, 83, 84, 86, 101, 104, 104n11, 105, 107, 108, 133, 134, 151, 155, 157, 163, 174, 181, 187
　See also Sentimentalism and sentimentality
Synecdoche
　and the gift, 28, 72
　See also Kete, Mary Louise

T

Tambling, Jeremy, 147
Tawil, Ezra F., 50, 61
Temple, Minnie, 179, 182
Tennyson, Alfred, 79
Thanksgiving Day, 111, 195, 198, 199
Thing
　person as a, 15, 124, 126, 129, 132, 157
　sentiment of the, 24, 31–38
　See also Materiality; Thingness
Thingness, 30, 38, 131, 133
　See also Materiality; Thing
Thompson, Ralph, 73, 77, 91, 100, 103
　See also Gift book
Tigchelaar, Jana, 201, 202
Time-loop plot, 195
Token
　sentimental, 29, 52, 118, 126
　of affection, 81, 84, 95, 224
　See also Gift; Present; Keepsake
The Token, or Atlantic Souvenir, 76, 81–86
　See also Gift book; Griswold, Samuel Goodrich; Hawthrone, Nathaniel
Tompkins, Jane, 75n7
Traister, Bruce, 154, 159
Transaction
　commercial, 15
　sentimental, 53
　spiritual, 128, 130
Transcendentalism, 25, 39, 151
Transgression, 13, 29, 75, 80, 95, 219
　See also Bataille, George
Trollope, Frances Milton, 3
Turgenev, Ivan, 182
Turgenev, Nikolai, 103
Twain, Mark, 6, 11–17, 17n5, 24, 38–43, 38n13, 39n14, 169–171, 170n3, 171n4, 173–179, 173n7, 173n8, 187, 219
The Adventures of Tom Sawyer, 176
Autobiography, 41, 178
The Chronicle of Young Satan, 16, 171–178, 219
"The Death of Jean," 178
"The Five Boons of Life," 169, 175
The Mysterious Stranger, 175n11, 178
The Mysterious Stranger manuscripts, 170, 174, 175, 186
[Reflections on a Letter and a Book], 24, 38, 42
"What is Man?," 42
　See also Clemens, Samuel

U

Ullén, Magnus, 152
Urakova, Alexandra, 3, 10, 11, 13, 16, 26, 33n9, 75, 76, 82n16, 93

V

Vanderbilt, Amy, 25, 25n3
Victorian tradition, 72, 74, 75, 78n11, 181, 218
Virgil, 155, 156
  Aeneid, 155, 156
Virus, 29n7, 77, 81, 136, 139, 153

W

Waits, William B., 192, 195, 209
Walker, Amasa, 105, 106
  "Pater Noster," 105, 106
  See also The Liberty Bell; Gift book, anti-slavery
Wardley, Lynn, 54, 123
Warner, Susan, 16, 172, 173, 178
  The Wide, Wide World, 16, 172
Waste, 134, 181, 182, 184, 196, 197, 199
  See also Economy, of expenditure; Economy, general; Luxury
Wedgwood, Josiah, 101, 101n5, 105, 106
Weiner, Annette, 61

Wells, Samuel Roberts, 28
  How to Behave: A Pocket Manual for Republican Etiquette, and Guide to Correct Personal Habits, 28
Willis, Nathaniel Parker, 72n4, 87n21
Wood, Marcus, 32, 100, 136
World War I, 6
Worthy poor, 110
Write, Susan C., 119

Y

Young, Elizabeth, 133n9, 139

Z

Zagarell, Sandra, 32
Zink, Amanda, 222
Zitkála-Ša, 13, 222–225, 222n2, 224n5
  "The Coffee-Making," 13, 222–225
  Impressions of an Indian Childhood, 222
  See also Bonnin, Gertrude Simmons